FINANCIAL TURNAROUNDS: PRESERVING VALUE

Henry A. Davis
Henry A. Davis & Co.

William W. Sihler
Darden Graduate School of Business Administration
University of Virginia

Prentice Hall PTR
One Lake Street
Upper Saddle River, NJ 07458
www.phptr.com

Editorial/Production Supervision: KATHLEEN M. CAREN
Executive Editor: JIM BOYD
Marketing Manager: BRYAN GAMBREL
Manufacturing Manager: MAURA ZALDIVAR
Cover Design: NINA SCUDERI

fei. ©2002 Financial Executives Research Foundation, Inc.

FINANCIAL TIMES
Prentice Hall
Published by Financial Times/Prentice Hall PTR
Pearson Education, Inc.
Upper Saddle River, NJ 07458

Prentice Hall books are widely used by corporations and government
agencies for training, marketing, and resale.

The publisher offers discounts on this book when ordered in bulk quantities.
For more information, contact: Corporate Sales Department, Phone: 800-382-3419; Fax:
201-236-7141; E-mail: corpsales@prenhall.com; or write: Prentice Hall PTR, Corp. Sales
Dept., One Lake Street, Upper Saddle River, NJ 07458.

Printed in the United States of America

10   9   8   7   6   5   4   3   2   1

ISBN 0-13-008757-2

Pearson Education LTD.
Pearson Education Australia PTY, Limited
Pearson Education Singapore, Pte. Ltd.
Pearson Education North Asia Ltd.
Pearson Education Canada, Ltd.
Pearson Educación de Mexico, S.A. de C.V.
Pearson Education—Japan
Pearson Education Malaysia, Pte. Ltd.
Pearson Education, Upper Saddle River, New Jersey

ADVISORY COMMITTEE

FINANCIAL TIMES PRENTICE HALL BOOKS

For more information, please go to www.ft-ph.com

Thomas L. Barton, William G. Shenkir, and Paul L. Walker
  Making Enterprise Risk Management Pay Off:
  How Leading Companies Implement Risk Management

Deirdre Breakenridge
  Cyberbranding: Brand Building in the Digital Economy

William C. Byham, Audrey B. Smith, and Matthew J. Paese
  Grow Your Own Leaders: How to Identify, Develop, and Retain
  Leadership Talent

Jonathan Cagan and Craig M. Vogel
  Creating Breakthrough Products: Innovation from Product Planning
  to Program Approval

Subir Chowdhury
  The Talent Era: Achieving a High Return on Talent

Sherry Cooper
  Ride the Wave: Taking Control in a Turbulent Financial Age

James W. Cortada
  21st Century Business: Managing and Working
  in the New Digital Economy

James W. Cortada
  Making the Information Society: Experience, Consequences,
  and Possibilities

Aswath Damodaran
  The Dark Side of Valuation: Valuing Old Tech, New Tech,
  and New Economy Companies

Henry A. Davis and William W. Sihler
  Financial Turnarounds: Preserving Enterprise Value

Sarvanan Devaraj and Rajiv Kohli
  The IT Payoff: Measuring the Business Value
  of Information Technology Investments

Jaime Ellertson and Charles W. Ogilvie
  Frontiers of Financial Services: Turning Customer Interactions
  Into Profits

Nicholas D. Evans
Business Agility: Strategies for Gaining Competitive Advantage through Mobile Business Solutions

Kenneth R. Ferris and Barbara S. Pécherot Petitt
Valuation: Avoiding the Winner's Curse

David Gladstone and Laura Gladstone
Venture Capital Handbook: An Entrepreneur's Guide to Raising Venture Capital, Revised and Updated

David R. Henderson
The Joy of Freedom: An Economist's Odyssey

Philip Jenks and Stephen Eckett, Editors
The Global-Investor Book of Investing Rules: Invaluable Advice from 150 Master Investors

Thomas Kern, Mary Cecelia Lacity, and Leslie P. Willcocks
Netsourcing: Renting Business Applications and Services Over a Network

Frederick C. Militello, Jr., and Michael D. Schwalberg
Leverage Competencies: What Financial Executives Need to Lead

Dale Neef
E-procurement: From Strategy to Implementation

John R. Nofsinger
Investment Madness: How Psychology Affects Your Investing… And What to Do About It

Tom Osenton
Customer Share Marketing: How the World's Great Marketers Unlock Profits from Customer Loyalty

Stephen P. Robbins
The Truth About Managing People…And Nothing but the Truth

Jonathan Wight
Saving Adam Smith: A Tale of Wealth, Transformation, and Virtue

Yoram J. Wind and Vijay Mahajan, with Robert Gunther
Convergence Marketing: Strategies for Reaching the New Hybrid Consumer

FINANCIAL TIMES
Prentice Hall

In an increasingly competitive world, it is quality
of thinking that gives an edge—an idea that opens new
doors, a technique that solves a problem, or an insight
that simply helps make sense of it all.

We work with leading authors in the various arenas
of business and finance to bring cutting-edge thinking
and best learning practice to a global market.

It is our goal to create world-class print publications
and electronic products that give readers
knowledge and understanding which can then be
applied, whether studying or at work.

To find out more about our business
products, you can visit us at www.ft-ph.com

Pearson
Education

C O N T E N T S

Turnarounds are not for the faint of heart. The hardest aspect of a financial turnaround to convey on paper is the emotional strain on everyone involved. Family breadwinners lose their jobs and worry about their mortgage payments. Financial officers, lawyers, line managers, and others directly involved in the turnaround work 18 hours a day, seven days a week and live from deadline to deadline. Their adrenaline wanes. The company has violated its loan covenants. The bank has given it only until the next meeting—about two weeks—to stop the bleeding, reposition the business, motivate the staff, and develop a plan to deleverage the balance sheet. The company's bankers will not simply agree to relax some of the covenants; they will concede only under pressure in a room full of lawyers with everyone screaming.

When a turnaround team comes into a company and makes changes, it may create resentment, skepticism, and suspicion among employees who feel their stewardship of the business is being condemned. But once the bleeding has stopped and the business has been "fixed," many of those same skeptical employees will have to stay on to ensure the turnaround's success. Companies must therefore convince employees to look at members of a turnaround team as essential elements in a new business direction, not as outsiders.

In short, turnarounds are not simply a matter of tinkering with the company's product development, marketing, or financial strategy. A turnaround is an emotional roller coaster representing a fundamental upheaval. The turnaround team has the fate of the company *and its employees* in its hands. The knowledge that hundreds, if not thousands, of people's livelihoods depend on its decisions and actions, combined with that most visceral of emotions—the fear of public failure—makes a turnaround one of the most stressful business endeavors imaginable. Although some managers thrive on the pressure and even consider it a career opportunity, others become paralyzed with indecision.

That's why this guide to the turnaround process is so important. It analyzes 20 case-study companies in various industries, explaining how they ran into financial difficulty and how they turned themselves around through financial restructuring, strategic redirection, new marketing strategies, better controls, and other measures. If you're a senior financial executive—and especially if you're the CFO of your company—this is the book to have in your hand when you talk strategy with your CEO—whether the news is good or bad.

Robert Sartor
President, Business Support and Chief Financial Officer
The Forzani Group, Ltd.

Introduction

Every business has its ups and downs. Whether the pressures stem from external or internal forces, management must monitor the company's financial pulse rate and bring the necessary resources to bear on troubled areas. If management stops paying attention, the company's very survival may soon be at stake.

This study details how CFOs in particular helped steer their companies back to profitability when they ran aground financially. It explains how the finance function can learn to identify early warning signs and prevent financial trouble. Being a visionary CFO means knowing that things are changing, why they are changing, what you can do about it, and how you can accomplish the necessary changes. Therefore, to help financial officers understand when and where problems crop up and which turnaround methods work best, we examined 20 companies of varying sizes, industries, and levels of financial difficulty. We focused on the causes of their financial woes as well as their turnaround strategies.

The story that emerges is not new, but as a cautionary tale it bears repeating. Every successful business has a model that assumes the company can profitably deliver a product or service. This assumption, in turn, is based on certain projections about the economy, customer behavior, product volume, revenues, and costs. With that model in mind, the CFO and the finance function work in partnership with the CEO and line management. The CFO must develop and gain consensus for a realistic plan to run the business profitably and the performance measures to track whether the company is meeting its targets. To put it simply, management must understand how the numbers work and know how to spot when they are off track. Although this seems elementary, we found case after case in which that did not happen, for many different reasons.

Here's a quick glance at the companies we studied. The case studies listed in table 1.1 show the broad range of industries they span—manufacturing, retailing, high technology, real estate, and service.

Table 1.1
Case-Study Companies by Industry Sector

Manufacturing

Asset-Heavy	Asset-Light
Maytag—appliances	Forstmann—garment fabrics
Navistar—trucks	Pepsi-Cola Bottling, Charlotte, N.C.—beverages
USG—building products	Sampson Paint—coatings

Retailing

Ames—discount general merchandise	Forzani—sporting goods
Jos. A. Bank—menswear	Musicland—recorded music and accessories
Edison Brothers—apparel and footwear	Red Rooster—auto parts

High Technology

Computervision/Parametric Technology Corporation—imaging systems

GenRad—test equipment and software

Kollmorgen—periscopes, weapon-positioning systems

Real Estate

Cadillac Fairview—office buildings and shopping malls

Service

Asset-Heavy	Asset-Light
Burlington Motor Carriers—transportation	Microserv—computer maintenance and repair
Fairmont Hotel Management—hospitality	
St. Luke's Hospital—health care	

How This Book Is Organized

After this introduction there is an executive summary covering the principal themes of the book, the main points in each case study, and a discussion of our principal findings. Then we offer an analysis of the early warning signs, followed by a comparison of the case studies by causes of financial difficulty and turnaround methods. The section concludes with implications for financial officers of healthy companies. The remainder of the book contains the 20 case studies grouped by industry, an annotated bibliography, a glossary, plus a listing of turn-around experts we interviewed.

Executive Summary

Most sick businesses were once healthy. As you might expect, financial executives of healthy businesses want to help keep them that way. Know what can kill you, because otherwise it will—is the operative message.

This is not always as simple as it seems in hindsight. One reason for this study is to identify the causes of companies' financial woes more precisely than past studies have done. The financial executive of a healthy organization who recognizes the symptoms of trouble early enough to effect a cure is much less likely to end up with a sick company.

To avoid findings relevant to only one industry, we looked at 20 companies in five major industry sectors. We also wanted to identify effective strategies for reversing a troubled situation. That's why we sought to include only companies whose management succeeded in turning them around. In two instances, however, case-study companies encountered a second set of problems that led them to liquidate.

Causes and Remedies

Our study shows that incompetent management was seldom the sole cause of corporate problems. Only in the smallest businesses did we find managers whose abilities were not equal to the task. What we did find was that acquired companies sometimes had weaker management teams than the acquirer anticipated, distracting the purchaser's executives from the company's core business and exacerbating existing problems. Also we found that takeover threats might have encouraged management to take riskier actions in the short run than it normally would—and sometimes the short-term solution metastasized into a serious, long-term problem.

We also found a few instances of financial problems caused by major external shifts, although often some economic event was a contributing factor. For example, style shifts created problems for

Jos. A. Bank, the clothing retailer, and Forstmann, the garment-fabric manufacturer.

In any case, the majority of problems stem from broader strategic misjudgments in three areas, often in combination:

- Ill-advised strategic decisions—too big and too rapid expansion, overdiversification, and the failure to invest profitably and sufficiently

- Marketing failures—lack of customer and product focus, poor product quality, poor matches between sourcing and selling, and ineffective pricing structures

- Inadequate financial management—excessive leverage; lack of proper performance measures; accounting, information, and control systems that don't supply important data quickly and effectively; and poor management of daily cash flows

We found that companies used both short-term and long-term measures to reverse their ailing fortunes.

Short-term remedy

- Move from negative to neutral or positive cash flow

Long-term remedies

- Refocus on core strengths

- Redeploy assets to support this position

- Develop control systems to monitor the progress of the strategy

- Install incentive and compensation systems that reinforce strategic direction

Short-term crisis management is necessary if the business is bleeding to death. Management must staunch the cash outflow immediately and direct available cash flow toward maintaining essential operations. The situation, the responses, and their effects must be explained to the creditors, who usually have forced the crisis by calling a loan or refusing to extend additional credit. The sick company must be stabilized, at least to a cash-neutral position. If possible, management should aim for a cash-positive situation because at this point it can at least make token payments to suppliers. This helps persuade suppliers that the situation is under control and that they will benefit more by supporting management's efforts to revive the business than by attempting to enforce their creditor rights.

Once the emergency is over, long-term remedial action can begin. This phase involves a careful but quick assessment of what caused the problems. In which of the three categories, or, more typically, in which combination of categories, did the trouble originate?

There are many potential responses to this question. All troubled companies, however, should concentrate on their core business or businesses, where they have the greatest competitive strength. They should restructure and deploy their assets to support those strengths. Then they must reinforce that strategy by setting up control systems that will provide sound information, which will accurately measure the company's successes and alert management to problems. Finally, they should design incentive and compensation systems that will motivate employees to achieve the company's goals.

Even if all the remedial actions succeed, management sometimes cannot avoid seeking bankruptcy-court protection. Despite the favorable press this remedy has received, our study suggests this route should be a last resort, to be considered only after efforts to solve the problem by negotiation fail. A Chapter 11 proceeding is expensive and time consuming. It is distracting for management, and, worse, it can be devastating if customers flee because they lack confidence in the company's ability to survive and stand by its product. In the long run, bankruptcy probably means that the common equity will be wiped out. Nevertheless, in some circumstances, we found that bankruptcy may be the only way for the business to restructure for survival.

Summary and Implications for CFOs

Overall, we found strong similarities in both causes and remedies across all industry types and company sizes. This fact may not be comforting to those who have spent their careers in one industry and believe "It can't happen that way in my business." Likewise, turnaround specialists—

company doctors—sometimes think the same way if they specialize in a particular industry. The good news here is that we can learn some universal lessons about pulling a company out of a financial nosedive even when we factor in industry and size variations.

On a more human note, CFOs of troubled companies often face similar personal and professional quandaries. Of the three major causes of fiscal woes—ill-advised strategic decisions, marketing failures, and poor fiscal management—the CFO is directly responsible only for the third. However, he must alert the CEO and other executives to the financial implications of their actions, such as an aggressive credit policy, a change in inventory policy, or a rapid expansion of fixed assets.

Ultimately, however, the CEO makes the final decisions, and his strategic objectives can preempt the CFO's efforts to maintain fiscal responsibility. CEOs who are top-line driven, for example, are often impatient with any actions that would slow sales growth. They may override the CFO's recommendations or neglect to invest in adequate systems or personnel.

A CFO whose concerns have been overruled faces a serious dilemma: to seek a new employer or to remain at the post to maintain some continuity if the situation unravels. Without the CEO's cooperation and support, however, it is impossible for the CFO to function effectively. By the same token, the absence of a competent and supportive CFO will endanger the company, regardless of the CEO's abilities.

If you're the CFO of a company with financial problems, you should consider whether the satisfaction you might gain from contributing to the company's survival is worth the personal stress. This is especially true if the problems developed because management did not heed your advice. Managing a turnaround is not easy, particularly for those who were there as the problems arose. First, there is often friction between existing management and new management. The existing management naturally has an emotional commitment to the failed policies, plus, it is saddled with blame by subordinates and outside stakeholders. By contrast, the new management arrives unconcerned about who did what in the past.

Effecting the turnaround requires painful decisions about marshalling the company's cash, decisions that often result in layoffs or asset sales. Again, those decisions may be emotionally easier for new management team members, who lack personal ties with laid-off employees and closed or sold facilities.

In addition, a turnaround requires a completely different managerial focus, at least temporarily. Rather than thinking of customers, products, and production, management must concentrate on cash flow and placating financial sources to keep the necessary resources available. This change in focus is so distracting that troubled companies often choose to have two teams at the top—one to run the business and one to negotiate the turnaround. Otherwise, neither job is done well.

In any case, whether your company is troubled or sound, you can learn a great deal from the cautionary tales that follow. Although these companies all faltered, in some instances more than once, their stories—however varied—demonstrate that strong leadership, a clear focus on the company's core products and markets, and sound fiscal management are still the bedrock of success.

Case-Study Summaries, Key Findings, and Early Warning Signs

Manufacturing Sector (Asset-Heavy)

Maytag Corporation

In 1980, Maytag was a high-end, niche manufacturer of clothes washers, dryers, and dishwashers. The company grew by acquisition through the mid-1980s, becoming a full-line manufacturer of major appliances. Late in the decade, Maytag added overseas acquisitions for international growth. While that strategy helped diversify the corporation's product lines, the overseas businesses did not meet its internal profitability standards. Maytag subsequently sold off its poorly performing European and Australian operations. Maytag used the proceeds to pay down debt and strengthen its balance sheet, reinvest in its core North American business, and initiate a share repurchase program. Maytag once again performed as a high-margin producer with strong synergies among its laundry, dishwashing, cooking, and refrigeration lines.

Navistar International Corporation

In the 1960s and 1970s, International Harvester was in the farm equipment, construction equipment, truck, and gas and solar turbine businesses. It paid a high percentage of profits in dividends and earned less than its cost of capital in most years. In the early 1980s, the combination of a strike, high interest rates, and a recession nearly bankrupted the company. After a five-year, multistage restructuring of bank and insurance-company debt, the company closed a dozen plants and sold its farm equipment, construction equipment, and solar turbine businesses. Renamed Navistar, it now focuses on becoming a world-class competitor in trucks and diesel engines.

USG Corporation

In 1988, USG had a conservative balance sheet and an established market leadership position selling essential building materials. It used excess cash to diversify into other building-related products. A hostile takeover attempt put the company in play, and management responded with a leveraged recapitalization. The combination of high leverage and a poor housing market in the early 1990s forced USG to default on several loans and to undergo a complex financial restructuring that eventually led to a prepackaged bankruptcy. Fortunately, despite its balance-sheet problems, the company had an underlying business worth saving. It has regained an investment-grade credit rating and developed a less hierarchical corporate culture that is entrepreneurial and team oriented.

Manufacturing Sector (Asset-Light)

Forstmann & Company

Forstmann, a manufacturer of high-quality woolen fabrics for the garment industry, filed for Chapter 11 protection in September 1995 and emerged from bankruptcy in July 1997. At the time, its major problems were an unfocused sales strategy and capital-expenditure program, compounded by a lack of product-profitability analysis and cost controls, poor inventory management, and high leverage. A new CEO and his team turned Forstmann around by communicating with all the stakeholders, reorganizing management, developing a more focused business strategy, rationalizing products, reducing overhead, and setting up systems for cash-flow management, cost analysis, quality control, and customer service. However, after failing to react quickly enough to a sharp decline in market demand, the company filed for Chapter 11 protection again in July 1999. A Canadian competitor purchased its assets under bankruptcy court proceedings in November 1999.

Pepsi-Cola Bottling Company of Charlotte, N.C.

By the time a new CEO assumed control of this family-owned company in 1981, it was nearly bankrupt. Production facilities and trucks were in poor shape. Customers were undersupplied, morale was low, and employee turnover was high. There were few internal controls. The company was in real danger of losing its Pepsi-Cola franchise, the foundation of its value. The new CEO and chief operating officer (COO) built a solid management team and restored production, sales, distribution, financial management, and data processing. As a result, case volume has increased two and a half times and profitability has quadrupled.

Sampson Paint Company

The net worth of the family-owned Sampson Paint Company eroded from about $6 million in 1970 to near zero in 1980. The big culprits were inappropriate pricing, poor marketing, inadequate financial controls, high overhead and manufacturing costs, and a lack of product and customer profitability analysis. Sampson Paint needed a new owner with management experience and fresh insight. With financing from an asset-based lender and the previous owners, turnaround specialist Frank Genovese restored the company to profitability by reducing overhead; rationalizing and repricing the product line; and establishing a marketing strategy, operating procedures, and financial reporting and controls.

Retailing Sector

Ames Department Stores, Inc.

Ames Department Stores, Inc., is the fourth-largest discounter and the largest regional discounter in the United States. The company was forced to declare bankruptcy after it sustained heavy financial losses from an ill-advised acquisition. Ames also lost sight of its core customer, a major strategic mistake. A new CEO and his team turned the company around by reconnecting with Ames' core customer base and establishing a market niche that allows Ames stores to coexist with the larger Wal-Mart and K-Mart stores.

Jos. A. Bank Clothiers, Inc.

When turnaround specialist Timothy Finley became CEO of this upscale men's clothier in 1990, he discovered that heavy debt from a leveraged buyout (LBO) was the company's biggest problem. But there were also other operating and marketing problems. To avoid bankruptcy, Finley persuaded the bondholders to accept equity. Ensuring Jos. A. Bank's profitability over the longer term required reinforcing its commitment to its target customer and redefining the company's merchandising, sourcing, selling, store-design, and store-location strategies.

Edison Brothers

Edison Brothers was a low-end, private-brand operator of mall-based stores with a retailing strategy based on price points. It overexpanded and suffered from a glut of stores and a shift in consumer tastes toward more expensive, name-brand merchandise. The company filed for Chapter 11 protection in 1995 and reemerged in 1997, making creditors whole. Despite efforts to improve merchandising and systems, the company faced heavy competition from better-known stores after emerging from bankruptcy and filed for Chapter 11 protection again in March 1999. This case study charts the course of a failing retailing strategy and the role of intercreditor issues. It also demonstrates that building the company's value, even during a bankruptcy, ultimately helps creditors receive a high percentage of their claims.

The Forzani Group, Ltd.

Forzani, the largest retailer of sporting goods in Canada, had an opportunistic development strategy. As a result, it had too many retailing concepts under too many trade names. The company stumbled when it simultaneously tried to expand nationwide and improve its information systems and business processes. With the help of a new CFO and head of retailing, the Forzani Group stemmed the tide of failure. The new management astutely managed cash flow, negotiated with suppliers, landlords, and other key constituents, consolidated store trade names, and reengineered the merchandise mix and store design. It also introduced incentive compensation for salespeople, improved information systems, reduced overhead, and increased the company's focus on key performance indicators.

Musicland Stores Corporation

Musicland is the largest specialty retailer of prerecorded music in the United States. Between 1993 and 1996, after paying down debt from an LBO, the company substantially increased its leverage to finance the continuing expansion of its store network. In 1994, cash flow available to service debt obligations began to decline because of competition from discount stores and flat industry sales. By closing stores and negotiating with vendors, landlords, and lenders, the company narrowly avoided bankruptcy. Its financial performance rebounded sharply in 1997 with a pickup in overall music sales. In 2000 Musicland was acquired by Best Buy Co.

Red Rooster Auto Stores

After decades of steady growth, this privately-owned auto parts wholesaler and retailer demonstrated an overconfidence that mushroomed into financial problems. Red Rooster did not pay enough attention to profit margins, and its financial controls were weak. Plus, its employee compensation was well above industry standards. Management turned the company around by basing performance measures and employee compensation on gross profit rather than sales and reducing headcount through attrition and job redesign. The company has also improved information and inventory management systems, and it has begun sharing a great deal more information among employees.

High Technology

Computervision and Parametric Technology Corporation

Computervision, a market leader in CAD/CAM (computer-aided design/computer-aided manufacturing) products in the early 1980s, ran into financial difficulty for two reasons: Its competition overtook it technologically, and it was overleveraged after a hostile takeover and LBO.

Parametric Technology Corporation, a younger, more nimble competitor that purchased Computervision, turned out to be its savior.

GenRad, Inc.

GenRad, a Boston-area high-technology company, was handicapped by having an engineering culture rather than a business culture. Therefore, it diversified away from its strengths and lost its leadership position in test equipment. After a period of losses, a new CEO was hired. He simplified management, listened to the customer, and defined core businesses. The CEO also sold unproductive assets and shifted the business from test equipment to diagnostic services.

Kollmorgen Corporation

Kollmorgen, a producer of motion-control and electro-optical equipment for industrial and military applications, lost money for several years. It depleted much of its equity through overdiversification. A decline in government defense spending and the expense of fending off a hostile takeover attempt were also major factors. A new management team turned the company around by selling off businesses that did not fit within its core competencies. The team used the proceeds to rebuild the company's balance sheet, and it began investing in new businesses to strengthen Kollmorgen's core business segments. The company was acquired by Danaher Corporation in 2000.

Real Estate

Cadillac Fairview

Cadillac Fairview, based in Toronto, is one of North America's largest fully integrated commercial real-estate operating companies. It was taken private through an LBO in 1987. To succeed, the LBO required continued growth in cash flow and property values. That didn't happen because the Canadian real-estate market was depressed between 1989 and 1995. Since reorganization under the Canadian Companies' Creditors Arrangement Act (CCAA) in 1995, Cadillac Fairview has pursued a strategy that limits growth to what can be financed through internally generated funds and debt financing allowable under its capital-structure policies.

Service Sector (Asset-Heavy)

Burlington Motor Carriers, Inc.

Burlington Motor Carriers filed for Chapter 11 protection six years after its LBO because of poor operating margins and overexpansion. New owners with experience in the trucking business purchased the company from bankruptcy and reduced its overhead, invested in state-of-the-art information systems, and strengthened relationships with high-volume customers.

Fairmont Hotels & Resorts

Before its turnaround between 1991 and 1994, the Fairmont Hotel Management Company was reluctant to offer discounts from its top-tier prices for fear of compromising its market image. Recognizing the need to increase occupancy, a new management team allowed average daily rates for hotel rooms to drop while increasing occupancy and revenue per available room, restoring profitability. This case study illustrates the importance of customer- and product-profitability analysis as well as understanding a business' key performance indicators.

St. Luke's Hospital–San Francisco

The staff of this independent, not-for-profit hospital will do whatever it takes to help the institution survive and fulfill its mission of serving the needy in a low-income neighborhood. The hospital has had to make continuous cost reductions during the past decade—a volatile time in the health care industry—while maintaining its quality of service. It also has had to increase its income by developing new products and services. Essentially, this means that St. Luke's is continually turning itself around, reinventing its strategies to survive in a highly competitive health-care environment while staying true to its mission.

Service Sector (Asset-Light)

Microserv Technology Services

Microserv was started in 1985 to provide computer equipment repair services to corporate clients. Since then, the information technology business has evolved considerably. Not surprisingly, the competitive requirements for service providers have also become much more daunting. The founder and the original management team were computer repair experts with few financial, marketing, and general management skills. After sorting out cash-flow, capital-spending, and borrowing problems, a new management team redirected Microserv's marketing strategy. Instead of focusing on direct selling to corporate customers, the company began to build partnerships with large original equipment manufacturers (OEMs), independent service organizations, value-added resellers, and other information-technology organizations. To spur the company's growth and to prepare for the future, the CEO hired a management team capable of running a much larger organization.

Key Findings

In all the companies we studied, the CFO played a vital role in turning the company around by contributing to strategic development, not to mention its financing and controls. Working with the CEO and line management, the CFO needs to develop an understanding of and consensus on the company's business model by which the company delivers a product and earns a profit. The CFO and CEO must also develop a "balanced scorecard" of financial and nonfinancial key performance indicators (KPIs) that take the company's pulse on a regular basis.

In this and many other respects, the CFO performs a vital function in keeping the company healthy. But as the corporate scorekeeper and an important member of the strategic planning team, the CFO is also in a position to spot early warning signs of possible financial difficulty. These include a change in corporate strategy, rapid growth, an increase in leverage, loss of market share, and deterioration in key performance indicators. When the company runs into problems, despite the CFO's best efforts, the CFO must sound the alarm. And, if the CFO is up to the challenge and can work with new management, the CFO will be one of the key players spearheading the turnaround.

The CEO of Microserv has worked with several CFOs with varying abilities. This has led him to conclude that a CFO cannot function well without understanding the business thoroughly. The CFO also must demonstrate a detailed knowledge of costs in order to manage margins effectively. In Microserv's business, that translates to an understanding of all the direct and indirect costs of the complex computer-parts business so that he can create profitable pricing proposals.

CFOs and CEOs also need to anticipate market shifts, which should seldom come as a surprise. In reality, however, companies often fail to spot a market change. For example, Computervision rejected a proposal to develop three-dimensional modeling capabilities. This short-sightedness was one of the factors that nearly drove the company into bankruptcy.

Although we identified very few cases of outright inept management—and those were in small, privately held companies—most financial problems were still caused, at least in part, by management error. Furthermore, the study uncovered similarities in both the causes of and remedies for financial difficulty that extended across all industry groups. Companies that got into trouble had poor business plans, lost focus, overdiversified, took on too much debt, tried to grow too fast, or had problems with acquisitions. Examples include Burlington Motors and Musicland, both of which allowed growth to leapfrog profitability, and Maytag and Kollmorgen, whose acquisitions were derailed, in part, by corporate culture issues and by poorly performing acquired companies.

If you're the CFO of a thriving company, you may think your company would never make these mistakes. But no company can afford to be smug because all of the case-study companies started out as sound, profitable, dynamic organizations. Every sound company should be aware of its potential Achilles' heels and understand the warning signs.

For example, Edison Brothers' strategy to sell off-brand, low-price-point apparel to a fashion-conscious young market was a good one for a number of years. But it stopped working as customers moved up to name-brand merchandise, and the company was too slow to react. Similarly, Ames Department Stores lost sight of its core customer base.

Other companies had a slightly different problem with their market strategy—the inability to focus in areas of competitive advantage. For example, Kollmorgen, which makes electro-optical equipment and weapons-positioning systems, made the mistake of overdiversifying, and it then had to reestablish its focus on its core businesses. The company concluded that companies without a strong focus on their customers and competitive advantage risk being knocked out of the market by competitors that do. To underscore this point, when USG pursued its building-materials conglomerate strategy, even the appearance of being unfocused subjected the company to takeover threats from investors, who saw an opportunity to profit from breaking it up.

Overleveraging was another major stumbling block in our study group. More specifically, none of the companies that became overleveraged performed stress tests to determine how much debt they could handle in adverse conditions. Cadillac-Fairview, Jos. A. Bank, Musicland, and USG, among others, survived the turnaround process largely because their underlying businesses were fundamentally strong, despite their balance-sheet problems.

During the crisis period in a turnaround situation, the finance function often must run the business, negotiating with creditors, collecting receivables, trimming inventories, controlling capital expenditures, and monitoring cash. Musicland is an excellent example of a proactive finance function. Its strong accounting and reporting system was critical in helping management determine what actions to take during the turnaround. Before deciding to reduce costs in a particular category, management could "drill down" to analyze subcomponents and distinguish necessary from unnecessary costs. This exercise helped management estimate whether cutting certain costs would hurt the business or incur additional risks.

Of course, finance's role does not end once the company is out of immediate danger. For the CFO and other members of management who are directly involved, saving the company means conflict, stress, and long hours. Turnarounds demand perseverance and difficult decisions, such as eliminating jobs and operations. Plus, management usually does not have the luxury of time. It must act decisively to cut staff and close stores or facilities, as Ames Department Stores, Computervision, and Edison Brothers all clearly demonstrate. Because a turnaround is more than a full-time job, some companies, such as Jos. A. Bank and USG, divided their management staffs, assigning some to handle turnaround issues and others to dispatch day-to-day business matters.

After a company emerges from restructuring, it needs to reestablish its financial and management credibility. The finance function takes the lead in gaining access to the capital markets. CFOs have a major hand in telling the company's story to shareholders, institutional investors and analysts, and particularly in explaining why a similar situation will not develop again.

Companies that are restructuring also need to rebuild management credibility, and one way to do that is to supplement management expertise with specialized advisers. Cadillac Fairview and Musicland both retained lawyers, investment bankers, and financial advisers with restructuring experience. In addition to providing advice, these professionals also bolstered management credibility. Credibility is vital to a company in crisis; in fact, many of the case-study companies, notably Forzani and Musicland, found that good long-term working relationships with bankers, vendors, and landlords helped their turnaround efforts. This was especially important when company management needed to negotiate immediate solutions with its creditors.

Despite the best efforts of senior management, however, there are bound to be changes in the management team during a turnaround. Typically, either a consultant specializing in turnarounds or a seasoned manager with turnaround experience helps the company make the changes necessary for its survival. These changes are understandable given leadership and management requirements that must evolve along with the company. One of the reasons companies get into trouble is that they do not recognize this requirement early enough. Many entrepreneurs are not capable of managing the companies they started once the business reaches a new stage of development.

This is yet another powerful argument for the CFO's stewardship role. The onus is on the CFO to warn the CEO of any strategic or leadership blind spots. It is perhaps the CFO's most important responsibility.

Early Warning Signs

Companies that are headed for trouble exhibit a number of early warning signs that every CFO needs to recognize, and, if necessary, to compel his CEO to recognize. Denis Hickey, in a 1991 article in the *Commercial Lending Review,* observed that troubled companies often begin their decline before their financial statements reveal problems. One of the most important indicators is the presence of imbalances—that is, an undue emphasis on one functional area, such as sales. High lifestyles among managers are another sign, and, along with that, a lack of values, such as a get-rich-quick rather than a long-term-building philosophy.

"Follower" attitudes can lead to insufficient creativity in product development and in other areas that affect margins, and this is often accompanied by an entrenched management that lacks the energy and adaptability to face new challenges. Two other signs are a lack of strategic plans and product-profitability reporting and harmful relationships, such as bad hiring decisions or acquisitions/mergers that distract management.

As for the more tangible indicators, one common signal of impending problems is a combination of a decline in sales profitability and a decrease in asset efficiency (receivable or inventory turnover). For example, Forzani, the Canadian sporting-goods retailer in our study, experienced increased inventory and decreased margins at the same time. Eight other companies saw declining margins or sustained cash drains.

Wes Treleaven, a partner with Deloitte & Touche in Toronto, highlights six common attributes of underperformers:

- Weak management

- Poor board governance processes

- Badly planned or executed expansion

- Lack of accurate and timely management information

- Inadequate interdepartmental communication

- Inability to effect change

Treleaven believes a decline in a company's cash position is the most important early warning sign. He recalls a large company that did a 45-day rolling cash-flow forecast—but failed to realize that it would run out of cash in four months. This example demonstrates the need to understand where the company's cash comes from and how it is used. Management must have a reliable system to forecast receipts and disbursements—day by day and over the next year—and know how to react if the cash position starts to deviate from the forecast.

Gerald Ryles, the CEO of Microserv, couldn't agree more. Essentially, he says, "Operating cash flow determines whether the company survives." The income statement, balance sheet, and statement of cash flows in a company's annual report are accounting based, but the bills are paid from operating cash flow. Therefore, a company that does not consistently generate enough cash to operate effectively is headed for a fall.

On a different front, a change in a previously reliable business strategy, while not necessarily bad, is still a potential trouble sign. For example, among our case-study companies, GenRad and Kollmorgen strayed from their primary businesses, and Ames Department Stores drifted similarly from its core customer base. Maytag decided it needed critical mass to avoid a hostile takeover and made international acquisitions that it was not equipped to absorb.

Market shifts, such as the change in the health care service environment that affected St. Luke's Hospital, are also early warning signs, but they are not always easy to identify. Finally, high leverage is *always* an early warning sign of financial difficulty, even though highly leveraged companies sometimes succeed.

David Steadman, president of Atlantic Management Associates, Inc., a company that specializes in turnarounds, points out two other early warning signs: loss of market share and difficulty in signing up new customers. Of course, continued and expanding business from existing customers is important, but, he notes, longstanding customers sometimes have a remarkable tolerance for suffering, so they should not be the only barometer of success.

Seymour Jones, a former Coopers & Lybrand partner now on the faculty of the Stern School, New York University, finds that nearly every troubled company has some degree of inventory mismanagement. Most companies hold on to inventory far too long, he observes. Commercial finance companies lend 80 to 85 percent on receivables but only 50 percent on inventory, he reports, because that might be all they can get in liquidation. Even without accounting for obsolescence, Jones estimates that it costs a company 20 to 30 cents on the dollar to hold seasonal inventory until the same time next year. Instead, companies are better off selling at a discount and getting the cash.

In a similar vein, Jeff Goodman, president of Best Practices, Inc. a turnaround consulting firm, reports that one company he worked with had not paid enough attention to the balance sheet and was running out of cash. It had 96 days of accounts receivable, and its inventory turnover was two and a half times per year, compared with an industry average of between eight and nine. Reducing inventory and receivables to a normal industry level fixed the cash shortage and eliminated the need for external financing. These situations crop up, he believes, because developing companies often get addicted to revenue growth that masks underlying weaknesses—until that growth starts to plateau.

Both experts believe that many failing companies exhibit some early evidence of poor controls and fraud. One important clue is the use of profit-driven bonuses as a form of management compensation. Fraud is often behind awarding high management bonuses after the business starts to go bad, when underlying problems may be masked through methods like misvaluation of inventory. Other factors include the presence of only a few decision makers at the top, weak controls, a poor relationship with auditors, and one-person accounting departments.

Goodman adds that troubled companies often lack financial metrics tied to the company's financial objectives. A company needs to have a full range of key performance indicators in place so it can judge whether it is operating profitably and building shareholder value. In a healthy company, such metrics are used regularly to monitor performance in every area. For example, Navistar, a case-study company, went through the important process of establishing new capital budgeting disciplines as part of its turnaround efforts. Before then, the company had not recognized the importance of earning more than the cost of capital and of slowing down growth so that it could be properly financed.

Other case-study companies also discovered through the turnaround process that they had kept their eye on the wrong ball in terms of financial metrics. For example, Fairmont Hotel Management found that in a high-fixed-cost business, generating additional revenue is more productive than focusing on cutting costs. Red Rooster, the auto-parts retailer, learned that it is not sales but profits that pay the bills. As the company reevaluated its performance measures, it began to use industry operating data for benchmarking. Management also began to share information more openly with employees on performance measures and financials and to allow employee participation.

The importance of metrics, and the lack of them in an ailing company, underscores the role of the finance function as the linchpin of the company. To illustrate, Goodman says that one of the clear signs of trouble in a company is an ill-defined finance function, along with a lack of financial metrics. In a company that is faltering, the finance function does not assume joint ownership of the key performance indicators or responsibility for achieving them. Although other warning signs should never be ignored, for CFOs and other financial executives, it's especially important to recognize what has gone awry in your own backyard.

The Seven Deadly Signs

C. Charles Bahr of Bahr International in Dallas, Texas, maintains that companies do not have to get into trouble in the first place if management is alert to the early symptoms of problems. He has identified seven warning signs:

- Management fails to listen to warning signs and believes only its own rhetoric.

- The management team breaks down. People leave and the remaining employees concentrate on their own agendas. Common purpose, functions, method, and direction dissolve.

- Priorities are disordered because management makes poor choices or no choices at all.

- Form prevails over content as people fail to achieve desired results.

- Management has a poor command of key financial and non-financial numbers (i.e., KPIs) and what they mean to the business. Reports may be too complex, mismatched to the requirements of the business, ignored, or late.

- Management makes misrepresentations to the outside world.

- Customer needs cease to dominate.

Comparison of Financial Turnarounds

The causes of financial difficulty are both external and internal. This study identified four principal external factors: business cycles, market shifts, hostile takeovers, and labor strikes. There are far more internal factors, as table 4.1 shows.

External Causes

Business cycles that caused financial difficulty were both economic and industry specific. The effect of economic business cycles was most severe in the case of two capital-intensive companies in cyclical industries—Navistar in the early 1980s and USG in the early 1990s. In the retailing sector, the U.S. recession in the early 1990s affected clothing sales for Jos. A. Bank. Similarly, Canadian retailing experienced a downturn in the late 1980s before the more general recession in 1991. Hotel occupancy rates for Fairmont Hotel Management also were affected by the general economic slowdown, as were Canadian real estate values and rental income in Cadillac-Fairview's case.

Stephen F. Cooper, managing principal of Zolfo Cooper LLC, a firm that specializes in turnaround consulting, observes that high-fixed-cost industries, such as hotels and paper-product companies, have considerable sensitivity to capacity cycles. When new capacity emerges, producers and managers may see demand slacken. Then they have to adjust prices accordingly or develop promotion or incentive programs to retain customers and maintain profits.

Although the health of the overall economy is an important factor, industry cycles can be just as important to a company's profitability—and they can hit just as hard. For example, with the slowdown in defense spending at the end of the Cold War, revenues from Kollmorgen's

Table 4.1
Principal Causes of Financial Difficulty

External

- Business cycles
- Market shifts
- Hostile takeover attempts/candidates
- Labor strikes

Internal

- General management capability
- Poor or declining margins
- Indecisiveness
- Problems with acquisitions
- Strategy
  - Need for critical mass and market share
  - Overexpansion
  - Overdiversification
  - Under investment
- Marketing
  - Lack of customer/product focus
  - Lack of customer profitability analysis
  - Inappropriate pricing
  - Poor product quality
- Financial Management
  - High leverage
  - Need for appropriate performance measures
  - Deficient accounting, control, and information systems
  - Lack of cash-flow management

periscope and weapon-positioning system lines of business declined. Musicland was affected in the mid-1990s by an unexpected slump in recording sales caused by a dearth of new hits.

In this study, **market shifts** were noticeable in retailing, high technology, consumer durables, and health care. In retailing, both Jos. A. Bank, a company known for tailored men's clothing, and Forstmann & Co., a manufacturer of high-quality woolen fabrics, were affected by a shift toward more casual business attire as well as by the changing economics of garment manufacturing. Sales of Edison Brothers' low-end, private-brand clothing were hurt during the economic boom of the 1990s, when shoppers moved up to more expensive, name-brand merchandise.

High-technology companies are always vulnerable to leapfrogging by competitors. Computervision, once the industry leader in CAD/CAM (computer-assisted design/computer-assisted manufacturing), failed to recognize a key market shift when it turned down an internal proposal to develop three-dimensional modeling software and equipment. The person who developed that proposal left and later started Parametric, the company that eventually acquired Computervision.

Similarly, when Microserv was founded in the mid-1980s, corporate customers were looking for service firms to help them maintain a growing variety of computer equipment from different manufacturers. By the 1990s, those corporations were looking for consulting firms that could provide equipment service and help them use information systems to gain competitive advantage. Computer equipment service firms such as Microserv had to become subcontractors to broader-based consulting and service firms rather than selling directly to end users, as they had been accustomed to doing.

Maytag, a high-end appliance manufacturer, and St. Luke's Hospital, which serves a low-income neighborhood, also needed to develop good responses to their changing business environments. Maytag's challenge was the growing pricing power of large retailers. It responded with innovative products that justified its premium prices. St. Luke's Hospital was affected by the swift and radical shift toward managed care in the early 1990s. As an independent hospital competing with health maintenance organizations, it continually had to cut costs and introduce new services.

Hostile takeover attempts were another major cause of financial difficulty. Two case-study companies were turned around in the early to mid-1990s after surviving hostile takeover attempts in the late 1980s. USG's management did a leveraged recapitalization to avoid a financially motivated hostile takeover by corporate raiders. For Kollmorgen, fighting off a hostile takeover attempt was costly, both because of litigation expenses and because of demands on management attention. The battle delayed a necessary strategic refocusing on core businesses. Maytag was never the subject of an actual takeover, but the potential for that to happen influenced the company's acquisition strategy. Management reasoned that building critical mass would help it avoid becoming a hostile takeover target.

Finally, a prolonged and costly **labor strike** was among the causes of International Harvester's financial difficulty in the early 1980s. However, the company also had other fundamental problems related to market share and profitability.

Internal Causes

The internal causes of financial difficulty in case-study companies outnumbered the external causes. They fit into several broad categories that include general management, strategy, marketing, and financial management.

General management is the area to which experts ascribe many of the problems of troubled companies. According to Raleigh C. Minor, chairman of Allomet Partners Ltd., the economy causes only 10 to 20 percent of company failures; management mistakes cause the rest. A particularly dangerous combination is weak management and a strong personality. CEOs with strong personalities often think they know it all. Unwilling to listen to dissenting viewpoints, they surround themselves with relatively weak, compliant managers and board members. Even a very good CFO has difficulty working effectively in such an environment.

Treleaven of Deloitte & Touche believes the CEO and the board chair should be two different people with complementary capabilities. This allows the chair to act as the CEO's mentor and challenger. A CEO who is a flamboyant visionary, for example, might be matched with a chair who is an advocate of controls. In any event, the most important attribute of a strong CEO or CFO is confidence because confident executives surround themselves with good people. In a turnaround situation, Treleaven says, two-hour interviews with the top members of management quickly reveal who understands the situation and who does not.

As Stephen Cooper puts it, "The only long-term competitive advantage we have ever seen in a company has been its management—not its products, not its markets; just management." Good managers, he explains, are insightful and forceful. They recognize problems and fix them. Bad managers in most distressed companies deal mainly with hindsight. "They consider themselves the victim of circumstances, never the problem. That is the distinction between good management and bad management."

To illustrate his point, Cooper likes to use the acronym OPEC: *organize, plan, execute,* and *control.* Some managers, in both large and small companies, consider these steps tedious and nonessential and prefer to improvise. But companies that ignore these steps suffer because they have no framework to measure whether they are correctly allocating people, time, money, and other resources.

When a management team does not feel responsible for the downside as well as the upside, the company is doomed. Cooper points out, "I cannot think of a single instance in U.S. business over the past 20 years in which financial difficulty was caused by a so-called 'lightning strike' (a sudden, unforeseeable event)." Rather, most distressed companies decline over time. Rarely does a single event take a company from being very good to very bad. (An exception is the occasional catastrophic event, such as the plant explosion in 1984 in Bhopal, India, which severely weakened Union Carbide.)

A series of small mistakes is the more common scenario. In retail, it might be opening too many stores over too many years, not managing rent exposure, or having too many seasons of being behind rather than ahead of current fashions. A retailer does not decline over a 90- to 180-day fashion season but over a longer period because of the compounding of small mistakes.

Eventually, management no longer can bluff, either externally or internally. Cooper says, "One of the characteristics we observe of management in distressed situations is the triumph of hope over experience. There is a steady decline of sales or erosion of gross margin, and expenses are heading north as opposed to south. Management says next quarter will be better, but they are doing nothing different to create the improved results."

Private companies have special management issues of their own. It is common, says Raleigh C. Minor, for an owner or senior manager of a small company to be reluctant to acknowledge problems because the company is an extension of that person's ego. Admitting that the business is in trouble seems like a personal failure. Abraham Getzler, chairman of Getzler & Co., a New York-based consulting firm specializing in advising private businesses, adds that the entrepreneur is running what has become a family business. Every assumption or decision is part of their persona, and it is difficult for the entrepreneur to learn to think objectively. Entrepreneurs often do not realize when they are to blame. Some, for example, blame all their problems on their employees.

Apart from the issue of ego, a CEO of a small company simply may lack the skills to turn it around. Microserv, Pepsi-Cola Bottling, and Sampson Paint were relatively small, private companies when they ran into financial difficulty. Their managements were insular and had not been exposed to current marketing and financial management techniques through experience with large corporations or close working relationships with astute board members or bankers. For example, both GenRad and Microserv were hindered by the engineers or technicians who "ran" the company but did not focus on marketing, profitability, and general management. Microserv in particular had the classic problem of a startup: The company's rapid growth exceeded the founder's ability to manage it.

Likewise, the CEOs of Pepsi-Cola Bottling Company of Charlotte and of Sampson Paint, both small, family-owned companies, had neither the training nor the predisposition for profitability analysis, strategic planning, or human resource management. But because of their well-established products, these companies survived despite their management weaknesses.

Private companies frequently fail to recognize problems because they do not have suppliers who question their balance sheets when deciding whether to extend credit, according to David Steadman, president of a firm that specializes in turnarounds. Nor do they have lenders saying they are not in compliance with covenants or investors concerned with unpredictable earnings. The working relationship between the board and the CEO in a private company is not the same as in a public company. In private companies, the CEOs sometimes see the company as their own and consider the board merely a group of advisors.

Poor or declining margins, which created profitability problems for six of our case-study companies, are one of the unfortunate outcomes of bad management. These problems took several different forms. For example, after Burlington Motor Carriers was taken private in an LBO, its new management did not have the skill to achieve the margins required for profitability. A heavy debt load accentuated the problem. When Computervision was a market leader with high margins, it lacked an overhead benchmark and allowed its expenses to grow. The engineers who ran GenRad were primarily concerned with technical accomplishments and neglected profit-and-loss issues. Red Rooster made the mistake of overcompensating its employees with a system that was based on top-line growth rather than profits, and its cost-control systems were inadequate. Sampson Paint failed to raise its prices periodically as petroleum and other costs rose. International Harvester, with relatively low market shares in agricultural and construction equipment, earned lower margins for those products than the market leaders did.

Indecisiveness was a problem for three case-study companies. Computervision was unwilling to invest in a new technology that could have made it more competitive. To make matters worse, when the company ran into financial difficulty, its management procrastinated about making staff cuts. Forstmann's problem was different. It offered too many products and undertook too many product-development and manufacturing-efficiency projects at the same time. Because the company failed to prioritize, its capital expenditures were disproportionate to its size. Forzani had too much inventory because its assortment of sportswear and sports equipment was too broad. The company also failed to consider the relative importance of fast- versus slow-moving items in stocking its stores. Obviously, this is a major problem for a retailer.

Forzani also ran into some major **acquisition problems,** largely because it tried to gain market share too rapidly. When two U.S. "category-killer" sporting-goods retailers threatened Forzani's market territory in Canada, its management tried unsuccessfully to expand its store network through acquisitions and to improve its information systems and business processes all at once. Unfortunately, in the first few years after the acquisition, it failed to integrate the systems of the acquired stores with its own and to eliminate redundant overhead.

In a similar vein, Ames Department Stores, which was advised by an investment banker with an alleged conflict of interest, took on substantial debt to acquire a discount chain that initially seemed to be a good fit strategically. As it turned out, the chain performed poorly, and its **customer profile and merchandising strategy** was incompatible with Ames' strategies.

Ames Department Stores and Forzani, as well as Red Rooster Stores, now avoid potential integration problems with acquired stores by clearing them out and then custom designing and rebuilding. A retailer with such a strategy, of course, must try not to overpay for the stores it acquires.

Many of Maytag's problems also stemmed from its acquisitions of major appliance companies operating in the U.K., Europe, and Australia. Although Maytag had gained **critical mass** in the North American market in the mid-1980s, it still lacked a meaningful presence outside the U.S. and Canada. To gain that presence, the company expanded its operations overseas through acquisition. Maytag's managers believed the company needed to expand internationally to build volume and become a world-class player. Although the strategy was sound, the assets it purchased were not large enough to give the company a significant presence in Europe, and it was difficult offering single products worldwide due to differences in consumer preferences country-by-country.

While many companies suffer from acquisition fever, **overexpansion** is a closely related problem. Too much growth too fast is a serious weakness because a company's growth can easily outstrip management's abilities. Therefore, it is important for management to guard against the dangers of hubris in a rapidly expanding business, according to consultant Abraham Getzler. Seymour Jones, of the Stern School at New York University, observes that an entrepreneur may well be able to manage a business with $25 million in revenues. Indeed, sales are the strong suit for most entrepreneurs. But when the business grows to $100 million, managing it may be beyond that person's control. Jones cites Gitano, the jeans company, as an example of a company whose sales outgrew its management's capabilities.

Overexpansion is an ailment to which retailers quickly succumb. In our study, this included Jos. A. Bank, Edison Brothers, Forzani, and Musicland. All of these companies kept extending their retail store networks to take advantage of sales opportunities as the economy grew in the mid-1990s. Overexpansion is undoubtedly tempting to retailers because they need relatively little cash to open new stores. The resulting obligations, however, create an immediate cash drain if the sales volume and margins do not develop quickly. All four of these retailers found that when sales did not meet projections, they did not have enough cash flow to service their expansion-related debt.

But overexpansion is not entirely limited to retailers; this also happens to high-technology and service companies. Management does not foresee the need for more infrastructure and controls as the company expands. If it lacks a good budgeting and variance system, management does not know whether the company is making money until it receives financial statements from its accountants. Then, Jones points out, if problems exist, it may be too late to resolve them easily. Another example of overexpansion was Fairmont Hotels, which took advantage of high leverage and available financing to build two new hotels just before occupancy rates declined during the 1990–91 recession. And Burlington Motor Carriers made the mistake of adding trucks, trailers, and terminals before bringing in new sales. The key difference here, however, is that a company in the trucking industry can more feasibly finance asset acquisition with debt.

By and large, asset-heavy companies did not suffer from overexpansion. Perhaps the fact that they must put much more cash up front to finance growth prevents them from falling victim to this problem. Asset-heavy companies, however, were not immune to **overdiversification** problems. In fact, both retailers and manufacturers made this mistake. In all, seven case-study companies diversified through acquisitions outside their core businesses. Maytag, as we mentioned earlier, diversified more than it expected to when it found that the European appliance business was considerably different, not only from the U.S. business, but also from country to country.

For International Harvester (later Navistar), trying to manage too many businesses resulted in low margins and diminished market share in the construction and farm equipment business. Sometimes a company has low market share in a given business for very understandable reasons—perhaps because it needs to correct internal weaknesses in product development and marketing or because it is new in the market. But low market share in itself is a weakness because market leaders often benefit from economies of scale. Since International Harvester was not a market leader in the agricultural- and construction-equipment businesses, it lacked the pricing power, margins, and cash flow to re-invest in new products.

USG diversified away from gypsum wallboard and acquired Masonite and DAP adhesives as part of a strategy of becoming a build-ing-materials conglomerate. Those acquisitions diluted USG's overall return on capital. It should be noted, however, that the conglomerate strategy did not directly cause the company's problems. Rather, the tac-tic attracted corporate raiders, who triggered management's defensive leveraged recapitalization.

As another example of a company that both overexpanded and overdiversified, Burlington Motor Carriers invested in new services, such as refrigerated trucking, that it had not market tested sufficiently for revenue potential and profitability. Likewise, GenRad made acqui-sitions outside its core expertise in test equipment without adequately considering those same factors. This was also true of Kollmorgen, which diversified from motion-control and electro-optical systems into semi-conductors.

On the retail side, Edison Brothers overdiversified when it pur-chased Dave & Buster's, the mall-based restaurant and entertainment concern. The saving grace was that Dave & Buster's was a freestanding, separate business, so it was easy to spin off when Edison Brothers ran into financial difficulty.

For perspective, it is important to recognize that when most of these strategic moves were made, many companies considered conglomera-tion a viable business strategy. The rationale was to diversify into busi-nesses with different economic cycles. But wide diversification often brought poor results, and, with a few notable exceptions such as General Electric, conglomerates fell out of favor. By today's standards, such diversifying moves would be considered early warning signs of financial difficulty because the companies were moving outside their core compe-tencies and trying to manage too many businesses. In the late 1980s, many companies moved to become more narrowly focused "pure plays," concentrating on one or a few related products or services where they had, or thought they could develop, identifiable competitive advantages.

Another key factor for three case-study companies was **under investment** in one form or another. These companies did not reinvest enough money or resources to keep growing. During the 1960s and 1970s, International Harvester's high dividend payout, financed with debt, kept it from reinvesting to enhance its market position. In the early 1980s, a prolonged financial restructuring also prevented reinvestment. Computervision did not invest sufficiently in new technologies, such as solid computer modeling, a classic example of a company's failure to rise to the challenge of "disruptive" technological change. Finally, the founding owner of Pepsi-Cola Bottling Company did not invest enough in plant and delivery-truck maintenance because he planned to sell the business.

Although under investment was an issue for only these three companies, the effects were dramatic: Under investment severely undercut their ability to compete. Over investing clearly is not the right tack, either, but companies that over invested at least had some assets they could convert to cash while they regrouped.

Marketing weaknesses were universal. They included loss of customer or product focus, lack of customer- or product-profitability analysis, poor or declining product quality, inadequate information systems, inappropriate pricing strategies, and low market share. **Customer and product focus problems** extended across all industry sectors. In retailing, Ames Department Stores strayed from its core customers—moderate-income homemakers and senior citizens—by trying to move its merchandise upscale. Jos. A. Bank also lost sight of its core customer, the upscale urban businessman. Also, as styles changed, it found that it could no longer be competitive selling women's clothing.

Other marketing weaknesses among manufacturers emerged. Forstmann, for example, developed too many products. However, this problem was compounded by the company's failure to systematically analyze which fabric products were most profitable. As a result, management did not have the data **to focus product development and marketing efforts** where they would build the most value, and it was unable to prioritize on the basis of profitability.

Edison Brothers was unsuccessful selling private-brand merchandise at low price points in mall-based stores because customers preferred to pay more for higher-priced name brands. The broad assortment of sportswear and sporting goods that Forzani stores carried caused several problems. Many items were not available in a full range of styles and colors, and salespeople were not trained to sell all of the products. In addition, the inventory was difficult to manage and slow to sell.

In the asset-heavy service sector, Fairmont maintained an upscale image with high prices in its hotels, but it did not have targeted marketing programs. It had not categorized and analyzed the profitability of each service its hotels provided, nor had it identified which guests were business travelers, leisure travelers, or members of affinity groups. It also was unwilling to negotiate its high room rates for fear of compromising its top-tier image. Because of its **inflexible product pricing** and **lack of profitability analysis,** its revenue per available room and bottom-line earnings suffered.

On the manufacturing side, Sampson Paint took a different tack with respect to pricing. In contrast to Fairmont, which refused to lower its prices, Sampson's mistake was that it did not increase its prices enough to keep up with inflation and rising petroleum prices.

Kollmorgen saw a **compression of margins** in its core motion-control and electro-optical equipment businesses and diversified into other fields, such as printed circuit boards and semiconductor equipment. GenRad diversified away from its core test equipment business into CAD/CAM and design automation products. Its engineers thought they knew more about customer needs than their customers did.

Product quality problems caused headaches for retailers, manufacturers, and service companies alike. Edison Brothers was unable to control the quality of low-end apparel contract-manufactured overseas; the distance made supervision and personal visits difficult and infrequent. Jos. A. Bank had quality problems in its own Maryland plant, which stemmed from inadequate inspection. Forstmann's fabrics had to meet color, texture, moisture-content, and other criteria. Only 60 percent were ready for shipment the first time through the production process. The remaining 40 percent had to be recycled, doubling the variable cost, delaying deliveries and using up machine time more profitably spent on new production.

While trying to expand, Burlington Motor Carriers relaxed its driver-hiring standards, which caused a costly increase in accidents.

The Pepsi-Cola Bottling Company of Charlotte saw a drop in its production rate because the owner did not reinvest in plant repairs. As a result, customers consistently received fewer cases of soft drinks than they had ordered.

Financial management weaknesses were demonstrated by the case-study companies that included high leverage, insufficient controls, poor accounting systems, and absent or inappropriate performance measures. These financial management woes occurred in companies in a variety of industries.

A number of case-study companies **had more debt than they could support.** Six of them had undertaken LBOs, and one had done a leveraged recapitalization. A large number of LBOs were arranged in the late 1980s, failed in the early 1990s, and turned around by the time we began researching this study. What is remarkable is the range of industries represented by the highly leveraged companies. High leverage generally is considered most appropriate for companies with limited growth opportunities and dependable operating cash flows. Companies subject to either business cycles or volatile revenue streams generally do not fit this category.

Aside from the LBOs, some case-study companies took on high debt for other reasons. Kollmorgen and USG were threatened by hostile takeover attempts. Fairmont Hotel Management, Maytag, and Musicland (after paying down some of its LBO debt) borrowed to finance expansion and acquisitions. International Harvester gradually increased its leverage during the 1960s and 1970s to sustain a dividend payout that its operating cash flow did not support.

Even when LBOs were popular in the 1980s, seasoned lenders believed that most

High-Leverage Companies

- Ames Department Stores

- Jos. A. Bank (LBO)

- Burlington Motor Carriers (LBO)

- Cadillac Fairview (LBO)

- Computervision/Parametric (LBO)

- Fairmont Hotel Management

- Forstmann (LBO)

- International Harvester/Navistar

- Kollmorgen

- Musicland (LBO)

- USG (leveraged recap)

were motivated by short-term profit-making opportunities and were not financially viable throughout the business cycle. Seymour Jones agrees with that assessment; he finds that companies often do not conduct crucial stress testing to see how they could survive with a given amount of leverage under different economic scenarios. Stephen Cooper recalls that some of the LBOs of the late 1980s and early 1990s had more of a leverage problem than an operating problem but still were not top performers. He explains, "If you had fixed the balance sheet, operations would have been okay, but just okay. We always have argued that an LBO cannot be done on a successful company because the spread is too thin between the stock market or other reasonable valuation and what the buyers could do with it." He adds, "Successful LBOs can only be achieved when companies are performing poorly and someone has concluded that there is unutilized, underutilized, or misutilized asset value."

One important exception is the management buyout, a particular type of LBO that often has worked very well. Cooper concedes that sometimes conglomerates have eliminated nonstrategic businesses because they lacked focused strategies for them. An acquirer, often a management team, may turn the business around by providing focus, sweat equity, and financial equity, and by making choices for which it will be held accountable. For Burlington Motors, however, this was still not enough. The management team that participated in the LBO was unable to achieve sufficient operating margins to pay down the debt.

Key performance indicators are crucial in avoiding financial management problems—including those occasioned by an LBO. Clearly, this is easier said than done. Seven case-study companies, ranging across all of our industry groups, either used inappropriate performance measures or did not recognize the need for financial and nonfinancial KPIs to tell the finance function and line management on a daily, weekly, and monthly basis how well the business was performing. Among the KPIs retailers track daily are sales

Lack of Performance Measures

- Fairmont
- Forstmann
- Forzani
- International Harvester/Navistar
- Pepsi-Cola Bottling
- Red Rooster
- Sampson Paint

per square foot, sales per employee, and trends in same-store sales from period to period. Non-financial performance indicators include market share, new product development times, customer-inquiry-response times, business-process cycle times, accident rates, and results of customer surveys.

Regardless of how much the CFO is involved in operations, Stephen Cooper believes a company should produce reports that help management identify where important operating and financial measures are not in sync. He contends that operating information is more important than financial information because financial information tends to lag. In other words, "You can trim an R&D budget and hype your short-term earnings but blow the long-term future of the organization." But even good reports, whether they are operational or financial, describe symptoms rather than causes of problems. If sales are declining, management can't simply increase sales, for example. It might achieve short-term improvements by changing sales compensation, marketing programs, promotion, or advertising, but the real problem often turns out to be poor quality control, purchasing, and overall management. As Cooper points out, it does little good to address the symptoms. Companies must find and address the fundamental problems.

In our study sample, three small, privately held companies—Pepsi-Cola Bottling of Charlotte, Red Rooster, and Sampson Paint—had overall, widespread **deficiencies in accounting, control, and information systems.** Pepsi-Cola Bottling experienced several information-system mishaps, including initially adopting a system that was designed for a different kind of company, switching too quickly from manual to computerized operations, and inadequate training of data processing and accounting personnel. Other related examples are Forstmann and Forzani, both of which had inadequate inventory control systems. Also, Forzani did not have a fundamentally sound management information system because the people who had to use it were not properly trained.

Musicland, on the other hand, had a strong accounting and reporting system that was critical in helping management determine what actions to take during the turnaround. Before deciding to reduce costs in a particular category, management could "drill down" to analyze subcomponents and find which costs were necessary and which were not, which helped management estimate the effects of reducing certain costs.

4

This demonstrates that a company's finance function must establish good internal control systems of its own without relying too much on outside auditors. Auditors are largely concerned with the accuracy of historical financial statements and are sometimes unaccustomed to thinking about a company's future viability in terms of risks and probabilities. As a result, audited statements all too often do not provide early warning signs of financial difficulty. Cooper points out, "Go back and look at all of the recent retailers in the Northeast that have failed and see if they got a clean bill of health from their auditors the year before they filed for Chapter 11 protection."

In any company, and especially in a turnaround, properly **managing cash flow, receipts, and disbursements** is a matter of survival. Forstmann, Microserv, Pepsi-Cola Bottling, and Sampson Paint did not have early warning systems because they did not understand how to forecast and manage cash flow effectively. Forstmann's turnaround CEO, Bob Dangremond, explains that cash flow is not just an accounting change in working capital. Real cash flow is what comes in and goes out today, what is left over, and how that compares to yesterday's cash position.

Wes Treleaven adds that changes in working capital accounts such as cash, inventory, accounts payable, and accounts receivable, which can be prepared for internal use as often as needed, are key to revealing and assessing a company's changing situation. He points to the surprisingly large number of companies that lack fully integrated models with which they can reconcile their income statements, balance sheets, and cash-flow statements. Companies should be able to easily trace their receivable accounts. In other words, they should be able to start by opening their accounts receivable, adding sales, and subtracting cash received, and end with closing accounts receivable.

What happens when CFOs, not internal systems, are to blame? In his experience with three turnarounds, Jeff Goodman has found the CFOs to be among the major stumbling blocks, and he had to replace each of them quickly. Poor technical skills were part of the problem. A more important issue, however, was a strictly accounting mentality, compounded by an unwillingness to move outside the financial arena, to become involved with operating management, and to see the importance of nonfinancial metrics. Both GenRad and Microserv had CFOs who were not capable of effectively working with line management and really understanding their businesses. But to put the issue in perspective, a CFO cannot accomplish this alone; a CFO needs the CEO's full understanding and support, caution Goodman and Robert Sartor, CFO of Forzani.

How Causes Vary by Industry

We found that most causes of financial difficulty are not specific to a certain industry. As Abraham Getzler observes, "People think they and their businesses are unique, but they aren't. Regardless of the industry, business is business. Are you making a product with a price that leaves enough room for overhead and profit? If not, why not? How much money will be required to fix the business? If the amount is more than the profits will justify, you don't have a business."

Although most of the problems seem to be universal, note that retailing has a strong representation in this research—6 of the 20 case studies. That is because retailing is always prone to market shifts. One of the problems with retailing in the United States, says Stephen Cooper, is that there is retailing capacity for 1 billion, but only 280 million people, and this does not even take the Internet into account. The most expensive component of retailing is real estate, a need that e-commerce potentially eliminates. Of course, we have recently seen a major shakeout of Internet retailers with inadequate capital and poor business plans. It is not yet clear what this will mean for the future of retailing, but it seems likely that a retailer will need a coordinated strategy for both traditional and electronic selling to be competitive.

5

Comparison of
Turnaround Methods

Turnaround management can be divided into two categories: short-term crisis management and long-term strategic management. A company in or near bankruptcy needs short-term crisis management to survive. Consultant Abraham Getzler explains, "Our clients often are like patients who just have been wheeled into an emergency room. First we have to stop the bleeding. Until the patient stabilizes, we don't have time for a scientific approach."

Yet, crisis management can solve only immediate problems. Sometimes reorganization is required which can be accomplished informally, i.e., outside the courts, or through the formal bankruptcy process. The causes and ultimate solutions for financial difficulty, however, are usually long term and strategic. Table 5.1 categorizes the methods used in various stages of the turnaround and in addressing typical problems. This section begins by describing how two turnaround specialists approach the restructuring process.

The Turnaround Process

There are three major stages in the turnaround or restructuring process: stabilization, reorganization, and restructuring. But before company management recognizes that a problem exists, it typically goes through a period of drifting during which no effective actions are taken to improve the business. The next stages are awareness, in which symptoms of distress appear, and then denial. Often management does not begin restructuring soon enough because it fails to recognize that the symptoms stem from a larger problem. It also has difficulty acknowledging the problem even after it becomes apparent. Usually, management finds the prospect of restructuring frightening.

Table 5.1
Turnaround Methods

Crisis Turnaround Management

- Management of cash receipts and disbursements
- Asset reduction
- Communication with stakeholders
- Cooperation with suppliers and landlords

Reorganization Methods

- Bankruptcy/informal proceedings
- New ownership
- New management

Strategic Turnaround Management

- Focus on core competencies
- Contraction
- Marketing
  - Market research
  - Customer/product profitability analysis
  - New retailing/merchandising strategies
  - New business models
  - New product development

Financial Management

- Coordination with marketing
- Performance measures
- Capital-structure and dividend policies
- Capital-budgeting disciplines
- Improved inventory management
- Overhead reduction
- Improved information systems
- Equity infusion
- Financial reporting and control systems

Human Resource Management

- Change in culture and leadership style
- Incentive compensation
- Use of outside professionals

Once the turnaround process begins, the stabilization stage involves taking some immediate steps to protect the business, such as fostering open communication, establishing a management team, conserving cash, and identifying and safeguarding assets. Company management may be able to begin this process on its own. More often, however, stabilization requires a new manager or a consultant with turnaround experience. A turnaround specialist can often help to objectively assess the strengths and weaknesses of the current management team. The specialist ensures that the priorities of current managers are aligned to deal with the most critical issues. Often, talented managers are hired to fill gaps in the management structure. It is also important that management establish a system of consistent and credible communications to all stakeholder groups.

Also during the stabilization stage, the turnaround management must assess the company's liquidity problem, establish a system to conserve cash, and identify whether the liquidity problem is surmountable. According to Treleaven, if the liquidity hole is so deep that a company cannot possibly climb out, filing for formal protection may be advisable. The company also needs to identify and safeguard other assets—for example, retain key employees, protect against potential lawsuits, and file business-interruption insurance claims. The CFO must look beyond the obvious to ensure that all of the necessary assets are protected. The CFO also should draft a time line of all the required steps in the restructuring process.

Turnaround Stages

- Stabilization
    - Foster open communication
    - Establish management team
    - Conserve cash
    - Identify/safeguard assets
- Reorganization
    - Assess financial condition
    - Review business strategy
    - Review management processes and support infrastructure
    - Analyze operations
- Restructuring
    - Develop and implement business strategies
    - Choose among the following
        - Informal restructuring
        - Sale of business
        - Bankruptcy proceedings
        - Liquidation

The overall objectives in the reorganization stage are (1) to provide a factual, comprehensive study of the causes of the company's poor performance; (2) to establish a mandate for clear change, designed to force management into action; and (3) to prioritize improvement opportunities. Deloitte & Touche's diagnostic review, for example, typically focuses on four key elements. These are:

1. A value-based financial review of revenue growth, profit margins, and asset productivity;

2. A business strategy review of the company, competitors, customers, and industry dynamics;

3. A review of management processes and support infrastructure, which comprises management information systems, financial management, and other infrastructure, such as organizational structure, human resources and compensation, performance measures, and management processes; and

4. An operations analysis, which assesses the fundamental operating segments within the business, such as procurement, sourcing, logistics, merchandising, and plant or store operations.

The financial review is the most critical element in determining a company's ultimate course of action. The company must determine the amount of the liquidity shortage, as well as its ability to create value through the three key drivers: revenue growth, profit margins, and asset productivity.

The final stage involves developing and implementing a restructuring plan and business alternatives and strategies. The CFO, senior management, and financial advisors decide the best route for the business: an informal, out-of-court restructuring, a sale, a bankruptcy filing, or liquidation. If management finds an informal revitalization plan viable, it may then start to rebuild the business. This can include taking steps such as strengthening its staff support, improving operating procedures, and renegotiating onerous commitments such as property leases and supply contracts. Rebuilding also typically involves developing a plan for short-term business opportunities with a fast cash payback, developing a longer-range strategic plan, and keeping all stakeholders informed of the company's plan and progress.

Treleaven emphasizes that many restructurings fail because management does not correctly implement and control these strategies. But he also believes that many falter because certain conditions for success did not exist in the first place, such as:

- An effective communications program

- A manageable cash shortfall

- New money

- New management

If the company can arrange a restructuring by deferring payments and renegotiating contract terms, an informal process is always preferable. However, if the company needs to terminate its leases or have its debt forgiven, it may need court protection. Creditors often are more willing to ease their terms if they see financial support coming from other sources as well. Finally, creditors are usually skeptical about management's abilities—the same management that got the company into its current predicament—and they are understandably leery of entrusting these players with new money. If management is not entirely replaced, creditors will take comfort in seeing at least a few new key managers with proven track records in restructurings.

Jeff Goodman provides some perspective on the process by outlining the six major phases in a turnaround. First, everyone in the company has to understand the state of the business. Within the first couple of weeks, the turnaround manager should gather all employees, explain the most important problems, and schedule additional meetings to describe the next steps.

Second, the CEO has to audit the company's senior management team to find out how it has been operating, how its performance is measured, and how members are compensated. If they are paid bonuses, for example, what formula or metric determines the amount?

Third, the manager needs to "divide and conquer." Although it may seem counterintuitive, the manager should build silos and solve some of the problems in each area before connecting the silos. In a broken business, problems typically exist in different areas, such as product quality, marketing, and sales. Employees should be aware of activities in other parts of the organization, but at this stage the company needs them to concentrate on problems in their own areas, where they can have the most impact.

Fourth, the management team should build a consensus about what has to be done to improve the business. If the plan reflects just the CEO's ideas, the CEO will be saddled with the responsibility to do it all, without the necessary support from other senior managers, line managers, and employees.

Fifth, the management team must agree to functional objectives, combining and aligning them to form corporate objectives. Finally, the company needs to interlace the silos to form a coherent organization.

Now, having seen an overview of the restructuring process from the turnaround specialist's perspective, we move on to how the case-study companies approached the process.

Crisis Turnaround Management

Management of Cash Receipts and Disbursements
Without cash, a company cannot continue to operate. Therefore, cash is often the first issue a company has to deal with when it finds itself in a crisis. Managing daily cash receipts and disbursements was one of the most important concerns for the CEOs of Forstmann and Microserv, the treasurer of Cadillac Fairview, and the CFO of Forzani when their companies were on the brink. In the crisis turnaround stage, these companies could make only vital payments, and even those had to be prioritized. The turnaround CEO and owner of Sampson Paint Company, faced in the beginning with a cash constraint, called every vendor to introduce himself and explain his payment plans.

Cadillac Fairview developed a cash conservation program that curtailed advisory fees to the firm that arranged its LBO, any payments to shareholders and subordinated debt holders, and interest payments under its syndicated credit facility. Collections also had to be managed carefully. The largest receivables often were negotiated individually. Sometimes discounts were offered for immediate payment. In this way, the portfolio of receivables was converted to cash.

Asset Reduction

A close companion to cash-flow management is selling assets to generate some cash. Companies fighting for survival often must focus on which assets they can sell quickly rather than what makes the most sense in terms of long-term strategy. Edison Brothers, Navistar, and USG sold major subsidiaries to raise cash. Along the same lines, closing selected stores was a crisis turnaround measure for Ames Department Stores, Forzani, and Musicland. Sampson Paint eliminated several product lines and sold the related inventory. Cadillac Fairview considered selling some of its real estate assets, but, in the end, it parted with relatively few because the market was unfavorable and it wanted to protect the company's franchise value over the long term.

Communication with Stakeholders

Faced with the daunting task of stabilizing the company and its cash flow, senior management also needs to remember to keep the lines of communication open with stakeholders. Notably, the CEOs of Forstmann, Forzani, and GenRad were all very forthright with their stakeholders, in a bid to reduce anxiety and enlist their support. For example, immediately after Forstmann filed for bankruptcy, CEO Bob Dangremond, who engineered the turnaround, wrote to every employee, customer, creditor, and stockholder to describe the reasons for filing and to outline the plan for reorganization. Management met regularly with employees at each plant. It prepared monthly progress reports with financial results and kept suppliers current on the company's cash position.

Wes Treleaven, who was involved in the Forzani turnaround, also stresses the need for consistent communication. He worked with management on a careful disclosure plan—truthful but not excessive. This was to ensure that suppliers would not get an optimistic message from the chairman, only to hear from the accounts payable department that their payments would be delayed.

Usually, management needs to strike a calculated balance between emergency and long-term measures, both of which are necessary to ensure the company's future viability. For example, when Jim Lyons joined GenRad as CEO, he had to stabilize a crisis. He resolved to understand and listen to all of the stakeholders before acting and to make no major strategic moves in the first six months. At the same time, however, he had to generate confidence among employees, customers, vendors, and lenders. Despite the gravity of the situation, he thought it was essential to emphasize the positive, and eventually this approach helped restore the company's credibility.

Cooperation with Suppliers and Landlords

This same spirit of optimism is crucial when negotiating and revising terms with suppliers and landlords, a key measure for any company trying to avert bankruptcy. If a company can be salvaged, it is in suppliers' best interests to help it stay out of bankruptcy. Therefore, a company in crisis must quickly develop a plan that will allow it to meet some of its commitments in the short term. This approach worked out well for Forzani, Musicland, and Sampson Paint, all of which found that suppliers would rather receive discounted or delayed payments than lose large customers altogether. Forzani and Musicland also avoided bankruptcy partly because they were able to renegotiate their store leases. Some large landlords had these retailers' stores in their shopping malls and did not want to lose them if they appeared viable in the long run. However, negotiations did not work out as well for retailers Ames and Edison Brothers. Both companies had to file for bankruptcy protection, partly so they could terminate their store leases.

Reorganization Methods

Most of the companies we studied changed ownership and management and required some form of reorganization, either informal or under bankruptcy court protection. The turnaround process generally diverted a huge amount of time and effort and inflicted physical and emotional stress on those who were directly involved.

Ames Department Stores, Burlington Motor Carriers, and Forstmann all declared and successfully emerged from bankruptcy. USG went through a briefer prepackaged bankruptcy process, a process used when the majority of creditors agree on the terms but the court process is still necessary because of a few holdouts. Cadillac Fairview, the Canadian commercial real-estate company, reorganized under CCAA protection.

The restructuring path was a bit different for Jos. A. Bank, Forzani, Musicland, and Navistar; all of them were on the edge of bankruptcy but negotiated out-of-court settlements with their creditors. Edison Brothers emerged from one bankruptcy, partially recovered, and then liquidated after declaring bankruptcy a second time. Forstmann also succumbed to a second bankruptcy and was sold to another fabric company. Computervision was acquired by its competitor, Parametric, while Sampson Paint was acquired by a turnaround investor and manager.

Turnaround specialists and virtually everyone interviewed in the case-study companies agree that a company should avoid bankruptcy unless there is absolutely no other choice. For Ames and Edison Brothers, Chapter 11 protection was necessary to allow them to cancel store leases, and this was also true for Burlington and its equipment leases. Almost every outside party involved with Musicland recommended filing for Chapter 11 protection at one time or another. But at this company, as at Forzani and Jos. A. Bank, management's determination and skill in negotiating with creditors prevented formal bankruptcy.

Paul Hunn, who has many years of commercial loan workout experience, notes that in the past, it was easier for a company and its banks to reach out-of-court settlements. This was largely because bankers were more willing to become involved in financial turnarounds, and they were more willing to make sacrifices, such as taking equity in the borrower as part of their compensation, with a 5- to 10-year perspective. Skilled workout specialists understood a company's business and how to work with other creditors and with accountants. In Hunn's opinion, the best example of an out-of-court settlement was Navistar's predecessor company, International Harvester, in the early 1980s. Two hundred and forty banks, many of them offshore, worked together to accomplish the settlement.

Today, the environment is less conducive to this solution. Securities analysts and investors pressure bankers not to report high levels of non-performing loans. As a result, bankers often prefer to sell those loans at a discount to prime-rate funds and distressed-securities investors. It follows naturally that banks now employ fewer workout specialists. Distressed-securities investors generally have no interest in becoming involved with workouts. They are primarily interested in buying debt at a discount and selling it at a profit. In a restructuring, their main objective is protecting their own position against other creditors. As Hunn observes, "They fight for the last buck."

Bankruptcy is expensive for a company. Top bankruptcy lawyers now charge $450 to $600 per hour, although the cost comes out of collateral. But, adds Hunn, "The environment has changed so that a chapter proceeding is sometimes the only way you can get anything done. With the proliferation of people involved, all with different interests and all wanting to fight to the very end, you need the hammer of a cram-down from the judge." A cram-down forces all creditors to accept terms the court has determined to be fair and equitable.

Current bankruptcy law does, however, give the debtor a chance. Nonetheless a judge should consider—particularly after the first four-month exclusivity period—whether or not the company has the financial or management resources to effect a turnaround. Often, a company's management will press to extend the exclusivity period, to give the company as much time as possible to regain momentum while under Chapter 11 protection.

Creditors, on the other hand, often argue against such extensions, particularly when they fear that their recovery amounts could diminish over an extended bankruptcy. During its first bankruptcy, Edison Brothers received approval for an initial six-month extension and then an additional five-month extension while management developed its reorganization plan. The creditors' committee supported the first extension but not the second because it felt the company had begun to turn around and should hasten its emergence from bankruptcy.

New Ownership

In virtually every turnaround of a publicly held company, there is a significant change in ownership. Existing investors become disenchanted and sell their stock. New investors buy at bargain prices, betting on improved performance. In bankruptcies, of course, the original shareholders usually get a small percentage, if any, of the reorganized company's stock. Edison Brothers was a partial exception. Shareholders recovered a significant amount of value because of an improvement in performance during the first bankruptcy, only to lose their investment in a subsequent downturn—one that led to a second bankruptcy and liquidation.

USG's shareholders were bought out in a leveraged recapitalization. Because of subsequent financial difficulties, the new equity owners lost most of their investment. Debt holders received the majority of stock in final settlements.

Cadillac Fairview, which was bought out in an LBO, had somewhat different circumstances. In addition to common stock, Cadillac Fairview's pension-fund investors owned subordinated debentures with equity voting rights, which they sold at deep discounts to distressed-security investors. Some of these investors earned sizeable gains in the final reorganization. The entire company eventually was purchased by a Canadian pension fund that could view the cash flows and intrinsic values of the company's real estate properties from a long-term perspective.

In four instances, completely new owners undertook the difficult work of pulling the companies out of their quagmires. When the current owners of Burlington Motor Carriers decided they wanted to buy the company, they were able to demonstrate their trucking industry experience to the bankruptcy-court judge and purchased the company out of bankruptcy. After a partially successful turnaround attempt, Computervision was sold to Parametric. Sampson Paint, a company that had been family-owned for a long time, was sold to a turnaround specialist who saw a combined management and investment opportunity. Forstmann was sold to a Canadian textile company in 1999 after its two-year turnaround faltered and it filed for Chapter 11 protection the second time.

New Management

CEOs do not usually keep their jobs after their companies run aground financially. In 10 diverse case-study companies, a successful turnaround required new management with different professional capabilities and a new strategic vision. Shortly after assuming their positions, the new CEOs guided their companies toward new business models and strategies. The turnaround of Forzani is an interesting variation on this theme. When the founder and chairman realized that the company was in trouble—and, perhaps more important, that he needed help—he hired two new executive vice presidents, the current CFO, and the head of operations and marketing. The EVPs worked together to turn the company around, reporting to the chairman and a supportive board.

Strategic Turnaround Management

Focus on Core Competencies

Once management gets the immediate cash-conservation issues under control, it needs to turn its attention to the strategic direction of the company. Five of the case-study companies adopted a renewed focus on existing core competencies as part of their turnaround strategies. Ames Department Stores' approach was to take a fresh look at the moderate-income housewives and seniors who had been the mainstay of its business.

In the high-technology area, both GenRad and Kollmorgen had diversified too far afield from their strengths. GenRad redirected its efforts toward test equipment, then used that business as a foundation for software and diagnostic systems for automobile companies and other large manufacturers. Kollmorgen sold its semiconductor businesses to concentrate on motion-control and electro-optical systems.

On the manufacturing side, International Harvester was forced to sell its agricultural and construction equipment businesses to survive. It stayed in truck manufacturing because that was its strength. USG reached the same conclusion about its business. After emerging from its prepackaged bankruptcy, management realized the company had the resources to be a market leader and grow internationally—but only in wallboard and ceiling systems, its two strongest businesses.

New Turnaround Management

- Ames Department Stores
- Burlington Motor Carriers
- Jos. A. Bank
- Cadillac Fairview
- Edison Brothers
- Forstmann
- Forzani
- GenRad
- Kollmorgen
- Microserv

Contraction

Contraction was a necessary survival measure for most of the companies in this study. It was also a natural byproduct of rediscovering core competencies. Edison Brothers, Forzani, and Musicland closed stores to reduce expenses and raise cash. Musicland also closed a distribution center. Burlington Motor

Carriers allowed trucks and trailers to be repossessed, while Computer-vision and Forstmann exited unprofitable businesses and product lines, respectively. Edison Brothers, Navistar, and USG divested, and GenRad, Kollmorgen, and Maytag undertook both divestitures and acquisitions in the process of readjusting their strategic direction.

Marketing Measures

In seeking this shift in strategy, several of the companies found it helpful to get better acquainted—or reacquainted—with their customer base. Fairmont Hotel Management, for instance, began to group its customers into categories, such as high-income international travelers and corporate travelers. Then it conducted **market research** to better understand their needs. The company also started to treat each feature and service, such as restaurants, room service, parking, banquets, and even telephones and fax machines, as a separate product with its own P&L; then it researched the total markets for those products.

Before the turnaround crisis, Fairmont, like Forstmann and Sampson Paint, lacked any kind of cohesive **customer- and product-profitability analysis** and therefore could not easily sort out in which areas the company was competitive and in which it was not. Instituting formal business analysis helped all three companies accurately gauge where they were making most of their profits and trim off unprofitable products.

Microserv did detailed studies of trends in the computer-services and consulting markets. Based on the results, the company stopped selling directly to corporate customers and repositioned itself as a service subcontractor to large companies such as Dell and IBM. GenRad's shift from test equipment manufacturing to a broader array of integrated test, measurement, and diagnostic solutions for manufacturing and maintaining electronic products was inspired by market research with major customers.

Most of the retailers in our study developed **new retailing and merchandising strategies.** Jos. A. Bank used promotions as its primary selling strategy and discontinued its women's clothing lines because they fell outside its design and retailing expertise. In accord with its renewed emphasis on its core strengths, the company closed its manufacturing operations, switched to contract manufacturing, and focused on retailing.

Forzani also discontinued slow-moving merchandise and it adopted a narrow-and-deep merchandising strategy. In other words, its stores carried fewer items but stocked a good selection of sizes and colors, and the company ensured that its stores were staffed by well-trained salespeople. Ames Department Stores, which was selling apparel and housewares to a different customer base, went in the opposite direction because its moderate-income customers preferred variety to depth.

Finally, in the late 1980s, Edison Brothers shed its staid image as a retailer of clothing and footwear to the over-40 market. In an effort to grow faster, Edison's new strategy targeted menswear for fashion-conscious teenagers and young adults, but the company ultimately did not succeed in repositioning itself.

Although Edison Brothers failed in its attempt to regroup, some companies were more successful in adopting entirely **new business models.** Microserv is probably the best example. The company conducted an analysis of corporate computer-service needs, and, based on those results, it decided to become a subcontractor to large computer companies such as IBM rather than sell its maintenance and repair services directly to corporate users. GenRad likewise gained a fresh focus on its key strengths in the test equipment area and began to pursue growth opportunities in diagnostic equipment, software, and consulting for large manufacturers. This gave it the momentum to embark on an aggressive new product development program.

Maytag and Navistar also started to actively **develop new products** in the wake of newly revamped strategies. Maytag also invested heavily in its core business and product lines. For St. Luke's Hospital, new services such as outpatient programs and neighborhood clinics were part of a strategy to serve the needy and combat intense competition from health maintenance organizations.

Financial Management Measures

As we have repeatedly emphasized, the finance function is a cornerstone of any company—and never more so than in a turnaround situation. In all the companies we studied, finance assumed a very prominent role in the rebuilding process. This encompassed running the business during the turnaround, negotiating with creditors, coordinating with marketing, working with line management to develop new financial and nonfinancial performance measures, and setting new capital-structure and budgeting policies.

In addition, finance improved inventory management, information systems, and controls; reduced overhead, assets, and dividends; and raised new equity. It's also worth noting that for the three small, privately held companies (Sampson Paint, Pepsi-Cola Bottling, and Red Rooster Auto Stores), improved financial reporting and control systems were especially important. This included budgets, monthly financial statements, plan/actual reviews, profit centers, and accountability systems.

Because the hurdles of a turnaround are nearly universal, these measures were not limited to a particular industry. On the contrary, all 20 companies had to go through at least one—and usually several—of these crucial processes to reestablish their fiscal and operating stability.

Role of the Finance Function During a Turnaround

Amidst the chaos that characterizes a turnaround situation, it can be difficult for a CFO to attend to both the restructuring and the company's day-to-day business. For the companies we studied, resolving this conflict often involved some division of responsibility, although each company's perspective was slightly different. During Navistar's turnaround, the finance function essentially ran the daily business. USG bifurcated its top management: The president and operating management ran the business while the finance function focused on the restructuring. Jos. A. Bank's CEO hired a workout specialist to deal with legal and other restructuring details and told the members of the finance function to concentrate on their normal, day-to-day operating responsibilities.

At Forzani, financial matters were intertwined with retailing issues, such as negotiating with suppliers and landlords and devising new merchandising strategies. Therefore, the newly hired CFO and head of retailing worked together on all aspects of engineering the turnaround. The CFO of Burlington Motor Carriers, which was purchased out of bankruptcy, initially spent a great deal of time on residual bankruptcy issues, such as settling unliquidated claims. Later he found more time to work with the CEO on pricing, cost reduction, information systems, deferred maintenance, and other measures designed to restore the company's operating margin.

As a company survives its immediate hurdles and repositions itself for the longer term, the finance function has to solidify its partnership with operating management and assume joint ownership of KPIs. Finance also should help managers prepare their forecasts and review operating and financial results with them to see what went right or wrong, Jeff Goodman advises. But note that a finance person needs to have the stature and the backing of the CEO to routinely ask business managers whether their business units will meet the projected numbers in their plans and, if not, what corrective actions the managers will take.

Coordination with Marketing

Forzani and Microserv are two excellent examples of the **coordination between finance and marketing,** and the synergies they can create. The marketing and finance functions in both companies jointly developed the new business strategies, so they were able to tightly link marketing and financial goals. Forzani's new narrow-and-deep merchandising strategy was designed both to sell what the customer wanted and to improve the turnover of inventory. Previously, the company had not paid enough attention to the high costs of inventory, and it remedied this by focusing on the most profitable items and moving them quickly. The finance function supported and enhanced this effort by working closely with the marketing function in selecting store locations and tracking trends in same-store sales and sales per employee. In addition, one of the CFO's main priorities is reducing selling, general, and administrative expenses, much of which is under store managers' control.

Microserv's new CFO works with his marketing counterpart to estimate the cost of each new service contract and decide how it should be priced. He is also segmenting the company's various businesses, such as technical support and parts support, and comparing their profitability.

Improved Performance Measures

Jeff Goodman suggests that turnaround management teams identify which financial variables are most crucial to a company's operations and use them as a basis for defining KPIs. Once management has selected its indicators, the finance function and operating management must establish joint ownership and use them as a basis for establishing incentive compensation.

Eight of the case-study companies did just that, developing **new performance measures** as part of their efforts to regain control of their destinies. The turnaround CEO of Forstmann and the new CFO of Forzani both emphasized the need for line management and the finance function to establish KPIs, the financial and nonfinancial measures that are the most important gauges of the business' health.

Focusing on the most important performance indicator, revenue per available room (REVPAR), was fundamental to Fairmont Hotel Management's turnaround. Management raised REVPAR by letting the average daily rate for hotel rooms drop, thereby increasing occupancy. In a different industry, Red Rooster restored its profitability partly by shifting from sales-based to gross-profit-based performance measures. As part of its restructuring process, Navistar established return-on-equity and return-on-assets measures. Line managers throughout the company are now trained to understand how these measures are calculated and how they reflect variables under their control, such as revenues, costs, and capital investments.

For every company, it's crucial to "know what can kill you," Steadman warns. For most troubled companies this includes having timely data which enables management to recognize inventory problems, margin problems, and quality problems. This information does not all necessarily come from financial statements. Therefore, when familiarizing himself with a turnaround situation, Steadman begins by analyzing the gap between a company's current situation and the model of how a successful business should work.

Capital-Structure, Dividend and Budgeting Policies

Companies on the mend are especially in need of good **capital-structure and dividend policies** that can provide some much-needed support. After their companies were stabilized, the new CFOs of Ames Department Stores, Cadillac Fairview, Forzani, Kollmorgen, Maytag, and Musicland set capital-structure targets in step with their companies' new or reevaluated strategies and business risks. Used properly, new targets can help reestablish a company's credibility with the investment community. USG is a good example. When the company emerged from its prepackaged bankruptcy in 1993, it announced a goal of achieving a triple-B credit rating within five years. Management reached this goal by improving earnings and steadily repaying debt (establishing the needed credibility to conduct an equity offering) and by gradually increasing investment in growth.

Divestitures helped Kollmorgen and Maytag fortify their balance sheets, and Maytag also reduced its relatively high dividend-payout ratio. The company **tightened up its capital-budgeting practices** as well to ensure that projects earn more than the company's cost of capital. In their capital-expenditure proposals, business managers must support their projected cash flows with information such as sales forecasts, competition, price points, and working-capital requirements.

International Harvester/Navistar's tale bears some similarities to Maytag's. International Harvester likewise paid out too much in dividends, and it failed to earn more than its cost of capital in the 1960s and 1970s, its CFO explained. Navistar now has better capital-budgeting disciplines. One of the most important things the company did to reverse its fortunes was to eliminate its dividend so it could retain cash for reinvestment. Some of the other companies had some notable changes on the capital front, too. Forzani's CFO set hurdle rates for both capital investments and acquisitions. Taking a different approach, GenRad's CEO focused mostly on how a project fit in with the company's overall business plan because, he said, return-on-investment (ROI) projections were usually overly optimistic, particularly for new products.

Improved Inventory Management

Reducing and improving inventory management was essential in the turnarounds of both Forstmann, the textile manufacturer, and Forzani, the sporting goods retailer. Previously neither company had paid enough attention to the high cost of inventory. Both reduced inventory by focusing on products that were most profitable and moved most quickly. Navistar found that inventory management really saved the day, and, by increasing inventory turnover, the company was able to generate more than $1 billion in cash.

Overhead Reduction

To some companies, reducing overhead was purely a matter of survival, especially for those that were contracting their businesses, such as Burlington. Forzani's CFO set an ambitious percentage-of-sales target for SG&A expenses, based on benchmarking studies with some of the best-run retailers. Forstmann fired senior executives who were neither contributing to the bottom line nor trying hard enough to minimize expenses. GenRad's approach was to sell unproductive real estate. Kollmorgen, which had reduced its backlog of work, downsized its workforce accordingly, and it cut an already lean corporate staff in half.

Improved Information Systems

Improved information systems were an important turnaround measure for companies in the retail, service, and manufacturing sectors. Many of these companies previously had not paid enough attention to the need for good information systems. In the turnaround process, revamping their information flows dovetailed with new business models and strategies. Jos. A. Bank developed methods of tracking an individual customer's preferences, as well as the success of its promotions. With Red Rooster's new information systems, management can check each employee's sales and gross profits at any time. Employees in each store can monitor whether the store's monthly sales have reached the threshold for employee bonus awards. For Pepsi-Cola Bottling, improving its information systems meant hiring a qualified data processing manager and installing a system tailored to the bottling industry. Forzani reinvigorated a fundamentally good but poorly utilized system by assigning "ownership" to the head of merchandising and properly training the users.

Equity Infusion

In the course of their turnarounds, both Cadillac Fairview and Forzani raised cash through initial public offerings. Cadillac Fairview also raised cash from a long-term strategic investor who helped the company emerge from its restructuring and is now its sole owner.

Financial Reporting and Control Systems

Improved financial reporting and control systems, including budgets, monthly financial statements, plan/actual reviews, profit centers, and accountability systems were essential to the turnarounds of three privately held case-study companies. In contrast, the quality of Musicland's accounting and financial reporting systems helped management determine which expenses could be reduced without sacrificing business performance.

Human Resource Management

Change in Culture and Leadership Style

At some point in any turnaround, the company needs to undergo some serious soul-searching about its employee philosophy and management style. Are these effective? Do they need to be updated in light of changes in the workforce? Can they be improved to better reflect, enhance and support the company's new business model and direction?

For several of the case-study companies, the answer was an unequivocal yes. Both GenRad and USG began to delegate authority much more extensively and to flatten their organizational structures. Red Rooster's management began to share more financial information with employees. This helped employees understand how they could improve the company's performance and, by extension, their own compensation. Pepsi-Cola Bottling's management style moved along a different path, becoming less paternalistic and more professional.

Fairmont's market research showed that the previous management had been perceived as arrogant, inflexible, unfriendly, and unwilling to listen to customers' needs. This was a major problem for a company in the service industry. Its new management used the characteristics of successful employees, such as self-respect and interest in helping others, to serve as guidelines for improving its interviewing and hiring procedures. Fairmont found such employee training to be an important factor in improving its sales and service capabilities. Interestingly, Forzani reached the same conclusion during its turnaround. Clearly, neither retailing nor service industries, which depend heavily on customer relations, can afford the perception that they are unresponsive to customer needs.

A less tangible but no less important shift occurred in Computervision's management philosophy. Computervision executives who stayed after Parametric acquired the company observed that Parametric's management decision-making process was quicker, more decisive, and less bureaucratic—important attributes for a high-technology company competing in a fast-changing environment.

Navistar had very different human resources issues. The company had a long history of difficult relations with United Auto Workers, the union to which most of its employees belonged. But when Navistar's management stopped blaming the UAW and started to address productivity issues under its own control, the union became more cooperative in discussing the remaining issues. As a result, management began to recognize the need to establish its own relationship with employees, rather than relegating employee communications to the union.

Incentive Compensation

Effective incentive compensation requires sound control and reporting systems. Therefore, it is not surprising to find companies that rebuilt their control systems also revised their compensation plans, usually to spur productivity more effectively. For instance, compensation for Jos. A. Bank store managers now consists of a base salary and a bonus based on achieving targeted quarterly profit goals. Store managers also are required to meet sales quotas. Forzani's compensation scheme has been redesigned to make each of its salespeople behave more like entrepreneurs.

Red Rooster first had to reduce employee compensation, as a percentage of gross profit, to a level closer to the industry average for auto stores. Then it developed an incentive compensation plan that provides bonuses based on company, store, and individual performance. At Navistar, all key executives receive bonuses based on overall company performance. The top 50 must buy company stock in multiples of their salaries, depending on their grade levels.

Use of Outside Professionals

Most companies trying to pull themselves back from the financial brink need a hand from outside advisers at some point. At Cadillac Fairview, lawyers, investment bankers, and financial advisors played essential roles at various stages. However, companies should be cautious in how they represent the advisory role to employees. Cadillac Fairview's treasurer at the time, John Macdonald, acknowledges that the appearance of consultants is often unsettling for employees. This is because consultants are paid top dollar and often seem to have a cavalier attitude, while employees of a troubled company are worried about their jobs, working extended hours, and receiving level or even reduced compensation. But Macdonald believes the company could not have survived without its consultants. They not only provided advice but also lent credibility to management in its efforts to salvage the company.

Musicland's financial and legal advisors also provided solid business advice, such as second opinions, negotiation support, and financial-modeling support to help the company identify which stores to close. But the company's CFO and treasurer warn companies to manage their outside advisors closely to ensure they are accurately reflecting and carrying out management's wishes. During Musicland's turnaround, the advisors often behaved as if they thought their role was to help the company through an orderly bankruptcy-filing process (which would have earned them significant fees) rather than to help it avoid filing. Filing was not management's intention, and it was certainly not the impression it wanted to convey to its stakeholders.

Role of Boards of Directors

Corporate governance can be an important check on management's actions, and there is never a more important time for this function than during a turnaround. Yet, according to Wes Treleaven, boards of directors often do not challenge management's performance in effective ways, such as reviewing management independently or holding CEOs accountable. A well-constructed board offers a spectrum of experience to augment that of the CEO. It is, of course, important to have outsiders on the board but also to have enough insiders to ensure that directors do not hear from the CEO alone, Steadman counsels.

Forzani's board of directors, advised by an independent legal firm, kept in touch with management through weekly telephone conferences and provided useful business advice during the turnaround. The board was comprised mainly of outsiders with business experience. Two were finance professionals who had engineered turnarounds, and two were retailers. GenRad's CEO nominated new board members, primarily CEOs of other technology companies, who were more capable of understanding the company's business strategy. Musicland's board of directors—five outside business people and two members of management—relied primarily on management's initiative in the turnaround but reached its own fiduciary conclusions on major matters, such as whether to file for bankruptcy. Pepsi-Cola Bottling's management benefited from the advice of three outside board members in the 1980s. Eventually, however, management felt that the company had outgrown these directors and replaced them with three inside directors.

The real test of a board occurs when things are not going as planned. As a company approaches insolvency, a board must make complex judgments. It has a responsibility to all stakeholders, not just shareholders. Therefore, Steadman emphasizes that the board must be concerned about the company making commitments it may not be able to meet. However, once a company is in bankruptcy, the board is well protected. The court has so much power that the board of directors really becomes purely an advisory body, while the creditors' committee assumes many of the board's governance responsibilities.

Surviving the Turnaround

As we have said repeatedly, financial turnarounds are not for the faint of heart. By now, you may be wondering how the turnaround specialists and finance executives in our case-study companies survived the inevitable stress and long hours turnarounds entail. Jeff Goodman found that the most difficult aspect was the feeling of being a loser for a long time before the company's performance started to improve. He had to expend a huge amount of energy tutoring, coaching, and mentoring employees and management to bring their professional skills to the required level.

As a newly hired CEO, Tim Finley had a relatively calm attitude toward the turnaround of Jos. A. Bank. He had successfully turned around companies before and saw relatively little to lose in taking on the challenge again. He hired a professional with workout experience to see to most of the restructuring details and encouraged other members of management to concentrate on rebuilding the business.

The process did not go as smoothly for the CFOs of Navistar and USG, both of whom played major roles in their companies' prolonged financial restructurings and turnarounds. Both found that the experience involved almost unbearable working hours and fatigue over several years. Rebuilding their companies diminished their family and social time and created tension and confrontation as they worked with suppliers, lenders, investors, and other outside constituents on survival missions, with uncertain prospects for success.

6

Preventive Medicine for Healthy Companies

Virtually all the lessons that the case-study companies had to learn the hard way also apply to healthy companies. Most of the problems stemmed from a lack of attention to business basics. That's exactly why financial officers of sound companies need to keep a sharp eye on the fundamentals, such as business strategies, capital structure, KPIs, controls, and cash management.

In "Turnaround Management Every Day," John O. Whitney points out that turnarounds are not limited to financially troubled companies. To the contrary, turnarounds occur regularly in product lines, divisions, and subsidiaries within most large corporations. Whitney believes that many of the methods that turnaround managers use can restore a company's vitality and prevent financial difficulty from taking root to begin with. For example, turnaround managers generally try to flatten organizational charts (just as GenRad and Forstmann did), streamline decision making, and improve their companies' flexibility and mobility.

As several of the case studies show, these specialists emphasize cash generation and cash forecasting, and they typically find opportunities to raise cash by selling assets and reducing accounts receivable and inventory. For some senior managers, questioning cash forecasts and requiring sensitivity analyses is a way of understanding and monitoring day-to-day business activities. Turnaround managers talk to all the important stakeholders, such as bankers, customers, vendors, middle managers, and other employees. With due respect for established reporting relationships, these are just the people senior managers must talk to daily to stay informed, have a feel for the business, and reduce their dependence on subordinates, who may report only what the boss wants to hear.

Stephen Grace, president of a firm that advises companies on turn-arounds, and Robert Sartor offer some additional guidelines for CFOs of healthy companies. Although some of this may seem basic, companies ignore the fundamentals at their peril.

- **Management focus.** A clear, crisp management focus on fundamentals cannot be emphasized strongly enough. These fundamentals include opportunities for growth created by trends in the market and industry environment as well as opportunities to improve the company's market share, adjust capital structure, and strengthen management.

- **Business plans.** The management focus is the foundation of a good business plan, and it is equally critical for management to develop a balanced business plan in which all stakeholders participate.

- **Budgets and targets.** To achieve the objectives of the business plan, management needs to develop financial and operational budgets, set targets, and pursue good operational tactics to achieve them.

- **Cash-flow management.** The finance function must manage day-to-day cash receipts and disbursements and develop very good cash-flow forecasting capabilities. The importance of concentrating control of the purse strings in the hands of a few people cannot be overemphasized.

- **Metrics, metrics, metrics!** Balanced scorecards of financial and nonfinancial measures are the "report cards" for crucial functions like cash-flow management. Balanced scorecards include the key performance indicators that measure the fundamental health of the business on a daily basis, and they are absolutely vital to any company's long-term profitability. No lesson stands out more in our analysis.

- **Accountability.** The inescapable light of accountability is another key ingredient to success, whether in a healthy company or a turn-around. It is one of the fundamental attributes of corporate health.

- **Financing.** CFOs must understand what drives the company's cash flows and monitor those factors. They must also understand the inverse relationship between industry volatility and debt capacity. Grace says such an understanding is essential for running the business and explaining it to lenders and investors.

- **Stakeholders.** On the less tangible side, "Understand your protagonists," Sartor advises. Appreciating the viewpoints of lenders, suppliers, shareholders, and other stakeholders is always critical. Come crunch time, however, CFOs must do what they think is right for the company.

- **Bargaining position.** Similarly, bargaining position is a key factor in any negotiation. The CFO and treasurer should identify the relative strengths the company and the lenders have and how each side might counter the other's leverage.

- **Lending syndicates.** The CFO or treasurer must be alert to problems within and among lending syndicates because lenders are always competing, Grace points out. Certain lenders may not mesh because of different corporate policies or personal animosities. But the CFO or treasurer should be prepared to intervene on behalf of the company if relationships within or among the syndicates appear to be bogging down.

- **Covenants.** Covenants are critical, too, and the time to negotiate them is at the beginning. The company should be aware of different lender proclivities and retain the right to approve buyers of syndicated interests. In a troubled situation, for example, the policies of foreign banks may be far different from those of U.S. banks. The company also has to watch out for "progressivity," that is, covenants whose requirements change over time. For example, a company just emerging from a restructuring has to guard against covenants that require its financial performance to improve at an unrealistic rate. It needs breathing room.

- **CFO Role.** Most important of all, remember that "The buck stops here!" Sartor reminds CFOs that they must always be prepared to deal with critical issues. Passive CFOs who allow themselves to be "bullied" by CEOs in times of actual or imminent crisis are open to legal consequences. CFOs have to do what they think is right, even at the risk of losing their jobs.

By the same token, the CFO can't bear this weight alone. The CFO and the finance function should have the CEO's full support in assuming joint ownership of KPIs and financial targets with operating management. And the CFO must have an explanation from operating management any time it cannot achieve those targets. A prospective CFO who does not sense that the CEO would provide this kind of support should not even consider taking the job.

Manufacturing Sector

Maytag Corporation

In 1980, Maytag was a high-end niche manufacturer of clothes washers, dryers, and dishwashers. The company grew by acquisition through the mid-1980s, becoming a full-line manufacturer of major appliances. Late in the decade, Maytag added overseas acquisitions for international growth. While that strategy helped diversify the corporation's product lines, the overseas businesses did not meet its internal profitability standards. Maytag subsequently sold off its poorly performing European and Australian operations. Maytag used the proceeds to pay down debt and strengthen its balance sheet, reinvest in its core North American business, and initiate a share-repurchase program. Maytag once again performed as a high-margin producer with strong synergies among its laundry, dishwashing, cooking, and refrigeration lines.

Background

The company began in 1893 as a manufacturer of farm machinery. It introduced a hand-cranked clothes washing machine in 1907, replaced the hand-cranker with a wringer and pulley in 1909, and replaced hand operation with electric power in 1911. Gradually the company evolved to manufacture a broad line of home appliances, including washing machines, clothes dryers, dishwashers, refrigerators, cooking appliances, and floor-care products that carry the Maytag, Hoover, Jenn-Air, and Magic Chef brand names. It also makes commercial appliances, including laundry, vending, and cooking equipment.

Maytag historically had a conservative approach. It was not the first with a new technology, and it maintained high margins and no debt. Most of its earnings were paid out in dividends. But in the 1980s the industry was consolidating, and Maytag looked like an attractive target for LBO investors. Management also believed that the company needed to become a full-line supplier of major appliances to remain competitive. In the early 1980s, Maytag extended its product lines into cooking and refrigeration by acquiring Hardwick Stove in 1981; Jenn-Air, Inc., an innovator of the electric downdraft grill range, in 1982; and Magic Chef, including the Admiral brand, in 1986. These acquisitions increased the company's size and allowed it to compete in middle- and higher-price markets.

As a result of these and other mergers, 80 percent of the U.S. appliance industry became concentrated in four manufacturers: Whirlpool, General Electric, White Consolidated Industries, and Maytag. Consolidation was motivated partly by economies of scale and partly by pressure from large retailers for full product lines.

Management believed that the company would have to grow not only domestically but internationally to become a world-class player. In 1989, Maytag bought Chicago Pacific Corporation for $950 million, primarily to acquire the Hoover brand of floor-care equipment and its European and Australian major-appliance businesses. The acquisition was financed with a combination of stock and debt. As it turned out, the European and Australian appliance businesses did not meet Maytag's expectations and were sold in 1994 and 1995.

Causes of Financial Difficulty

Problems with the Acquisitions
The acquired companies generally were not as profitable as Maytag and did not meet its cost and quality control standards. Imparting Maytag's culture and methods to them was more difficult than anticipated. While Maytag's management knew how to run its own highly profitable operation, it was not experienced in turning around less successful companies.

Hoover had a high-quality vacuum-cleaner business in the United States and good brand presence in the United Kingdom; it also had a weak white-goods (large home appliances) business in continental Europe. Because product preferences differ substantially among European countries, local manufacturers usually have the strongest market share. Further, in 1993, the European operation was overwhelmed by the effects of an expensive promotion program that awarded round-trip airfares to purchasers of Hoover appliances. Fulfilling these promotional commitments cost the parent company more than $70 million.

The Company Turnaround

Sale of European Business
Following the appointment of Leonard Hadley as CEO in 1993, Maytag realized that Hoover lacked a pan-European product line that could serve as a foundation for greater market penetration. Therefore, the goal became to make the operations more profitable and prepare to divest them. Maytag sold Hoover's Australian and European operations in 1994 and 1995, respectively, at about a 40 percent discount from their purchase price. Going forward, Maytag remains interested in selected overseas business opportunities.

Capital Spending
Maytag's long-term debt grew from zero in the early 1980s to 57 percent of capitalization in 1992. Until 1991, the company maintained a generous dividend payout despite the increasing demands of its acquisition program. Such a capital structure and dividend policy might have been suitable for a company with strong cash generation and few investment opportunities, but Maytag was suffering reduced cash flow from spending to repair its European operations. As a result, its domestic businesses were starved for capital. To generate the cash for increased domestic capital spending, management secured the board's approval to cut the common stock cash dividend in half. It used proceeds from the sale of the European operations to reduce its relatively high-cost debt, further freeing cash flow for capital spending.

Product Development
Even as the company's financial performance suffered overall primarily because of the unprofitable international operations, Maytag continued to invest in new product development in its core U.S. businesses. In 1993, Maytag began to articulate a premium-brand strategy and invested in new product platforms in dishwashing, cooking, laundry,

and floor care for the North American market. The next year, the company approved an investment in a new platform in refrigeration. Then, by 1995, the overseas businesses were sold, the proceeds were used to pay down debt, and the earlier investments in new products were taking root in the United States.

Investment Discipline

Maytag followed the general principles of economic value added in comparing project returns to the cost of capital. Capital-spending proposals at Maytag fell into three categories: projects that create value by earning more than the cost of capital; projects that retain value; and infrastructure and other essential projects (e.g., roof repairs) that do not directly contribute to corporate value. Projects such as the Maytag Neptune and the Hoover Extractor are expected to earn far more than the cost of capital.

The corporate-value-added discipline helped Maytag's engineers hone their business skills. A proposal to invest in a new product had to show how it fit in the total product line, the product's competitors, its target price points, and its working-capital requirements. Domestic projects were required to cover more than the cost of capital, and international projects had to cover a risk premium as well.

Investment Priorities

Maytag is focused on three areas for its use of cash. First to invest in its existing businesses to support brand positioning and product performance. These projects have the best chance of earning a good return because management is in control of factors such as product development, production, and marketing. Second, to pay shareowner dividends and to buy back stock. Many companies view share repurchases, which tend to increase capital gains for shareowners, as more tax efficient for shareowners, because investors can realize those gains when they choose for tax purposes. The third use of cash is to invest in new businesses and product lines.

Maytag has three most important criteria for acquisitions: (1) they must be within the company's core competencies; (2) they must have strategic importance, including synergy with the company's other businesses; and (3) they must be accretive (adding to shareholder value) within two years—preferably within one. An acquisition that did fit these criteria was Blodgett, the maker of commercial cooking equipment. Despite its relatively high price and the fact that it had been run as a cash-cow business without significant reinvestment, the company fit with Maytag's long-term product-development strategy. Building on its significant presence in residential cooking, Maytag will use the Blodgett acquisition to gain a foothold in the commercial cooking market. It will take advantage of synergies between residential and commercial cooking. Once established in commercial cooking, Maytag will have an opportunity to expand into other areas related to its competencies, such as commercial refrigeration and dishwashing.

Intelligent Innovation

For Maytag, removing the management distraction of underperforming international operations and relieving the financial constraints created by high-cost debt created the opportunity to focus once again on its core North American business—major appliances and floor-care products—and to invest more aggressively in new product development and brand advertising. Maytag is more willing to be a product innovator than it was in the past. Management has made several significant financial bets on new products, including the Neptune washer and the Extractor carpet cleaner.

By starting with the consumer for insight, Maytag focuses its expenditures on product innovation and development and remains competitive even though the two dominant players, General Electric and Whirlpool, are much larger. Product innovation also helps Maytag achieve higher selling prices. Since about 1989, appliance manufacturers have not been able to raise prices significantly. Prior to release of the Neptune model, the average price of a top-loading washing machine was about $450, and many said a $1,000 washer could not be sold in high volume. Neptune redefined the game by giving consumers benefits they were willing to pay for, such as larger capacity and a tumbling rather than an agitation cycle, which is gentler on clothes and saves on electricity. Similarly, the performance of the new Hoover Wind Tunnel vacuum cleaner justifies a price of more than $200 at Wal-Mart, a higher price point than Wal-Mart would normally carry for such a product.

Financial Results

Thanks to management's turnaround efforts, Maytag achieved a 51.2 percent return on equity and a 11.2 percent return on assets in 1998, a level of performance the company had not realized since the late 1980s. The company has been more than able to cover capital expenditures with earnings before interest, income taxes, depreciation, and amortization (EBITDA).

Key Findings

- It is difficult for a company to grow and develop new products while maintaining high debt and a high-dividend payout.

- Companies that grow through acquisitions often inadvertently find themselves in the turnaround business.

- In-depth market research and an understanding of consumer needs are the foundation for successful product innovation.

- In today's environment, it is difficult for a consumer product company to maintain premium prices and high margins if it is not an innovator.

- Product innovation helps a manufacturer achieve pricing leverage.

- Acquisitions to broaden a company's product line must be done with great care, especially if they will take the company into unfamiliar markets.

Navistar International Corporation

In the 1960s and 1970s, International Harvester was in the farm equipment, construction equipment, truck, and gas turbine businesses. It paid a high percentage of profits in dividends and earned less than its cost of capital in most years. The combination of a strike, high interest rates, a recession, and deregulation of the industry nearly bankrupted the company in the early 1980s. During a five-year, multistage restructuring of bank and insurance-company debt, it closed a dozen plants and sold its farm equipment, construction equipment, and solar turbines businesses. Renamed Navistar, it focused on becoming a world-class competitor in trucks and diesel engines.

Background

In 1903, J. P. Morgan combined Deering Harvester, the agricultural equipment maker that traced its roots to Cyrus McCormick's invention of the reaper in the 1820s, with the International Wagon Company to form International Harvester. Navistar, the corporate successor to International Harvester Corporation, is a leading manufacturer of medium- and heavy-duty trucks and school buses and a supplier of midrange diesel engines to other vehicle manufacturers. Its subsidiary, Navistar Financial, provides financial services to dealers and customers. Navistar trucks still carry the International brand name.

Causes of Financial Difficulty

In the fiscal year ended October 1979, International Harvester earned a record $370 million on record sales of $8.4 billion. Underlying problems, however, weakened its ability to weather difficult conditions. For years, its return on assets and operating and net profit margins trailed those of competitors such as Deere in agricultural equipment and Caterpillar in construction equipment. This situation affected the company's ability to reinvest in the business and remain competitive. According to a later study by Robert C. Lannert, now Navistar CFO, International Harvester earned more than its cost of capital in only one year between 1960 and 1979. During that period, the company paid out 60 percent of its book income in dividends and increased debt from near zero to $6 billion for the parent and International Harvester Credit Corporation (IHCC) combined. A substantial portion of the debt was commercial paper, which had an average maturity of 18 days.

In the early 1980s, International Harvester was nearly bankrupted by several important economic events: a six-month strike by members of the United Auto Workers Union, record high interest rates, a recession, and deregulation of the U.S. truck industry. From 1980 to 1985, the company lost $3.3 billion.

The Company Turnaround

As part of one of the largest out-of-court restructurings in history, Navistar sold several major businesses and focused on becoming a world-class competitor in trucks and diesel engines.

Financial Restructuring

Commercial paper provided a large portion of short-term borrowing for IHCC. Each commercial bank or investment bank that acted as a commercial paper dealer had a defined limit it could have outstanding at any time. The commercial paper facilities were fully backed by lines of credit through separate agreements with 200 banks. The company could draw on the lines of credit if it was unable to sell its commercial paper. Those lines were available to either International Harvester (IH) or IHCC. Unlike a revolving credit facility, which is legally binding through a signed loan agreement, a line of credit is usually "confirmed" for one year, but a commercial bank concerned about a borrower's creditworthiness can withdraw the line at any time.

Starting in 1980, the company incurred substantial losses and worried about continued support from its banks. It therefore drew down a large portion of its available commercial paper backup lines. The treasury function had increasing difficulty persuading banks to roll over the 90-day promissory notes under the lines. Finally, in October 1981, one leading bank refused to roll over its outstanding amount unless the company promised not to repay any other bank.

Bankers believed that if the company filed for Chapter 11 protection, they would recover 90 percent of amounts lent to IHCC but only 10 percent of amounts lent to the parent. On the day the company announced it would make no further repayments, a given commercial bank was either lucky or unlucky, depending on how much IH and IHCC owed it. This led to bickering among the banks. Some claimed they consistently had lent to IHCC and their loans to the parent on the day of reckoning were an aberration.

During the ensuing months, many of the banks passed responsibility for their IH loans from regular commercial lenders and relationship managers to their in-house workout specialists, who were more experienced in dealing with these issues and, in Lannert's opinion, more objective. Creditors' committees were established for both IH and IHCC.

IH needed cash to survive, and the only place it could get cash was IHCC. For such a cash transfer to occur, some banks had to exchange IHCC liabilities for IH liabilities. A number of banks with loans to IHCC considered themselves "money good" and did not care whether the parent survived. Others, particularly those with large exposures to both borrowers and those with large exposures to overseas IH subsidiaries, were more willing to try for a plan that would be best for all concerned.

First Restructuring

In November 1981, with $3.8 billion of IH and IHCC short-term debt outstanding, the company reached a standstill agreement with 200 banks. The agreement was intended to give management breathing room to downsize the company and survive the recession. In Lannert's words, all the battle lines were drawn in the first restructuring.

The finance function worked with line management on operating measures to improve the company's cash position. The promising Solar Turbines Division was sold in 1981 for $505 million in cash. Inventory liquidation generated additional cash. Unfortunately, the economy did not pick up.

Second Restructuring

A continued decline in sales, book losses on asset sales, and operational restructuring costs caused IH to lose $1.6 billion in 1982, eliminating its book net worth. Net worth covenant violations triggered a second restructuring in mid-1982. Lenders agreed to relax some covenants, make some retroactive interest concessions, and exchange $350 million of debt for preferred stock and common stock warrants to cure the net worth violation. "Sharing the pain" was the operative concept in the restructuring, and bank concessions were keyed to the scale of concessions from trade suppliers and dealers who accepted some equity for amounts due or extended their payment terms.

Third Restructuring

In December 1982, the company agreed to a third restructuring that provided for repayment of $125 million in debt, rescheduling the maturities of $900 million of term debt, conversion of $500 million debt into convertible preferred stock, and rescheduling most of IHCC's debt.

The banks' willingness to convert debt to equity hinged on a plan giving them collateral during a preference period, which protected them from the danger that the company would file for bankruptcy right after the banks converted to equity. At this time, dealers accepted preferred shares of $75 million in exchange for trade discounts they would earn from IH in 1984.

Fourth Restructuring

In January 1984, shareholders approved a fourth restructuring of $4 billion of IH and IHCC debt and a doubling of common shares outstanding from 100 million to 200 million. At the end of the restructuring, IH had four times as many shares outstanding as at the beginning of 1980.

The final restructuring of the parent's $1.4 billion in debt contained three core elements:

- Lenders received $160 million in cash payments, most of which came from IHCC.

- Lenders agreed to convert the $500 million principal amount of preferred stock and 22 million common stock warrants, most of which they had received in the 1983 restructuring, into a newly issued class of preferred stock that would be convertible into about 60 million shares of IH common stock.

- Lenders were left with about $800 million in secured medium- and long-term loans, including a $400 million secured revolving credit maturing in 1987 and $200 million of 12-year notes. The lenders were allowed to replace this outstanding debt by selling new debentures with attached warrants later in 1984. This provision helped lenders who wanted to reduce their 12-year exposure but still allowed IH to add long-term debt to its balance sheet while keeping the coupon below 15 percent. These agreements and reduced sinking-fund requirements reduced IH's debt-service burden, including interest and amortization of principal, to about $200 million per year over the next six years. IH was not allowed to issue new securities on its own until October 1985 and then only under strict conditions to safeguard the lenders.

IHCC lenders received $348 million in cash and converted the remainder of the $3.6 billion debt into a revolving credit due in 1987.

They made an additional $600 million revolving purchase facility for retail receivables available to IHCC.

In the end, the banks that sold their equity securities relatively soon recovered their principal and some earnings. Those that waited in the hope their securities would appreciate lost a small amount of their principal.

To File or Not to File

During the debt-restructuring period, there was a difference of opinion among members of the management team and members of the board as to whether the company should file for bankruptcy. Before one crucial board meeting, eight board members were believed to be in favor of and four against filing. In the meeting, those against filing cited the company's underlying strengths and argued that all parties would be better off if the company continued as a going concern. One board member who held this position was J. Patrick Kaine, executive vice president in charge of the truck business. He was not involved with either legal team. He told the board that if the company filed, the dealer distribution system would evaporate, a Chapter 11 would turn into a Chapter 7, and the company would cease to exist. His argument turned the board around, and the vote was eight to four against filing.

Cost Reduction and Divestitures

In 1979, International Harvester had 33 plants. Between 1981 and 1984, it closed a dozen of them, reducing its break-even point by about one-half, to between $4.5 billion and $5 billion in sales. It sold its axle and transmission business, a sheet metal plant in Ohio, a truck manufacturing unit in England, and a farm-equipment manufacturing unit in Mexico. It sold its Solar Turbines business to Caterpillar for $505 million in cash in 1981, sold its construction equipment business to Dresser Industries in 1982, and sold its agricultural equipment business to Tenneco (which already owned J. I. Case, another farm-equipment manufacturer) in 1986. Selling the construction equipment business was a relatively easy decision because International Harvester did not have enough scale in the business to be a significant player. Selling the agricultural equipment business was more difficult because it was part of the company's heritage. But viewed objectively, the agricultural equipment business seemed incapable of generating cash and operating profitably throughout a business cycle.

One way to achieve critical mass might have been to buy J. I. Case from Tenneco, but this would have required cash and was deemed too risky, especially considering a declining market and Deere's strong market position. The agricultural equipment market had grown steadily in the 1970s, reaching $11.8 billion in 1979 and allowing most manufacturers to do well. But it declined in the early 1980s, reaching a low of $7.4 billion in 1984, because of high interest rates, the recession, and declining farm commodity prices (the result of a strong dollar and the Soviet grain embargo).

In previous years, while International Harvester remained diversified and invested in new areas such as solar energy, Deere focused on farm equipment, consistently reinvesting 5 percent of every sales dollar in research and development. Between 1979 and 1984, while International Harvester was conserving cash to restructure, Deere continued to invest in product development, increased its sales force, and developed a leasing program that reduced the burden of high interest rates on its buyers. During that period, Deere's share of the market increased from 26 percent to 33 percent, while International Harvester's share declined from 20 percent to 15 percent. Despite a long history in this market, International Harvester had lost its competitive advantage in farm equipment.

Rebuilding the Company

In 1985, Navistar's truck business had $3.5 billion in sales, an estimated 26 percent of the U.S. medium- and heavy-duty truck market, and 850 dealers nationwide. In 1986, Navistar earned its first full-year profit since 1979. The next year, improved performance allowed the company to raise $471 million through an issue of 110 million shares of common stock. The proceeds reduced long-term debt from $736 million to $222 million, lowering the company's debt-to-capital ratio from 93 percent to 29 percent.

Between 1986 and 1991, Navistar continued to operate in survival mode. Sales were flat, then rose in 1988 and 1989, before the Gulf War and the ensuing recession. In 1992, Freightliner, a Daimler-Benz subsidiary, overtook Navistar as the market-share leader for heavy trucks.

Health Care Buydown

In the early 1990s, the cost of Navistar's health care benefits was an unusually high 7 percent of sales. This was the chief cause of the company's losses from 1990 to 1993. Because of downsizing in the 1980s, the company had 40,000 retirees and 23,000 dependents, 3.3 for every active employee. In July 1992, Navistar filed a declaratory judgment in U.S. District Court affirming its right unilaterally to reduce retiree health care benefits. The United Auto Workers (UAW), among others, countersued. In June 1993, shareholders approved a plan to give employees and retirees half ownership in the company in return for reduced health care benefits. The present value of the benefits was reduced from $2.6 billion to $1 billion. The vehicle for their ownership interest was a voluntary employee benefit association, a type of tax-free trust set up to fund continuing health care costs.

The health care buydown allowed Navistar to reduce its benefit costs by $150 million per year. As part of the agreement, it also negotiated productivity gains with the UAW that reduced overhead by an additional $50 million. The primary cost of this plan was in dilution of existing shareholders' interests. The company was required to double the 255 million common shares then outstanding. At the same time, because its common stock price was in the $2 to $3 range, the company did a one-for-ten reverse stock split.

Next-Generation Vehicle Program

In 1996, Navistar began a program to reengineer its trucks, the most extensive product redesign it had undertaken in 20 years. To achieve the target 15 percent return on assets, the company did not need wage concessions from its UAW workers, but it needed work rule changes, including the ability to downsize its plants. When management and the union failed to agree on those changes, management postponed the program and wrote off its initial $35 million investment. It did not want to jeopardize its target return on the overall program investment, estimated at $600 million. The next year, management reached an agreement on a slower program whereby some jobs would be lost in the short term, but only through attrition. In the course of these discussions, management helped the union understand that it was not trying to profit at the workers' expense. It needed an appropriate return for the capital it invested and continually needed to adjust to a changing market environment to stay competitive. At this time, the company gave a course on shareholder value to top managers and a briefer version to all employees.

Working with the Union

In the past, management believed the company was not competitive because the UAW's wage structure was too high and there were too many work rules. When John R. Horne became chairman and began to encourage a growth rather than a survival mentality, management reexamined the company's operations. It concluded that there would always be disputes with the union, but those disputes were a fraction of the company's problems. There were other ways to make the business more productive and cost effective that management had overlooked because it was so fixated on the union problem. When management stopped blaming the union and started to address more productivity issues under its own control, the union became more cooperative. Also, it became apparent that management had previously relegated employee communications to the union; it needed to establish more direct relationships with employees and rebuild its credibility.

Other Recent Initiatives

Navistar cut the number of diesel engine models in production from 70 in the early 1980s to 3 in the early 1990s. It then replaced one of those models with a larger engine. The company has gained market share continuously in recent years and is now the world leader in the sizes it produces.

Navistar closed several plants in the 1980s and consolidated production in the remainder. As a result, one plant manufactured 19 truck models. Recently, production has been realigned so most factories focus on a single product line.

Internal experts nicknamed "black belts" address product quality issues on the factory floor. They saved the company an estimated $17 million in 1998.

Market Share

Until the mid-1980s, Navistar had the leading market share, with 20 to 25 percent of the Class 8 heavy-truck market. In the early 1990s, Navistar, Freightliner, and PACCAR each had 20 to 25 percent of the market. Since then, Navistar has fallen to third place behind Freight-liner and PACCAR. In the early 1990s, Navistar was slightly behind Ford and General Motors in Class 5, 6, and 7 medium-size trucks. Navistar is now the clear market leader, with 36 percent of the market. Ford and General Motors both have less than 20 percent. Navistar has led the bus chassis market for the past 20 years. Since 1990, the company has increased its market share from 45 percent to 60 percent; its nearest competitor has less than 20 percent.

Cash Reserves

Truck and engine manufacturing is a cyclical business. Since its financial difficulty, the company deliberately has run with negative working capital. Navistar sells receivables to Navistar Financial the day they are created. In periods of rising sales, Navistar generates cash by liquidating receivables immediately and paying suppliers on trade terms. In periods of declining sales, cash is drawn down as fewer receivables are liquidated, but payables continue to come due. Unlike most companies, Navistar generates cash when sales are robust and loses cash during downturns.

Financial Performance Measures

Navistar's principal financial targets are a 17.5 percent return on equity and a 15 percent return on assets in its business units, after taxes and over a business cycle. In an average year, the total truck market is 308,000 units. Each year, management plots a return on equity (ROE) curve to show Navistar's adjusted ROE target for different industry volume levels. ROE is measured as net income divided by book equity with minor accounting adjustments. The ROE target was 6 percent from 1993 to 1996. It has been raised incrementally to its current level. In the year 2000, the volume forecast for the market is 405,000 units; Navistar's ROE target is 29.9 percent.

The advantage of the ROE and return on assets (ROA) performance measures is that managers throughout the company can understand both how the ROE and ROA are calculated and the consequences of their own actions. Management realizes that ROE and ROA are simplistic goals that could take the company in the wrong direction if not managed carefully. But Lannert says, "We are after improvement in operations, not utopia."

Incentive Compensation

Line managers' bonuses depend on meeting financial targets. Horne and Lannert set aggressive targets and allow line managers considerable autonomy to develop plans to achieve them. All key executives receive bonuses on the basis of overall company performance, based on the company's ROE curve.

About 50 key executives also are required to buy Navistar stock in amounts ranging from 75 percent for grade-nine managers to 300 percent for the CEO and CFO. (The company has 13 employee grade levels.) Management believes it essential for managers to commit part of their personal net worth and see returns if the company's financial goals are achieved.

Capital Structure

Navistar's long-term debt is currently about 40 percent of capitalization, a level Lannert considers appropriate. Despite capital expenditure and development programs in the range of $500 million to $700 million per year, the company generates more cash than it chooses to reinvest. Net income in excess of $100 million generally is returned to shareholders in the form of stock repurchases. Navistar has no plans to pay dividends. It prefers stock repurchases over dividends because of the tax advantage to shareholders. Lannert notes that mutual funds own an increasing portion of shares. Their managers have made it clear they do not want dividends.

Culture Change

A culture change has enabled Navistar's recent initiatives. In a paper titled "Climate for Performance," management has encouraged communicating openly, facing reality, and finding value in diversity of thought. People should come to meetings prepared, speak their minds, understand what decisions are reached and why, and support those decisions. Management encourages everyone to be on one team. This change minimizes the difference between line and staff.

Role of the Finance Function

Finance staff members are part of the team, responsible for helping deliver results. The role of the finance function has evolved through three phases since the 1970s. Prior to 1979, International Harvester's finance function was involved primarily in generating money for line management's priorities. From the time of the UAW strike in 1981 until the restructuring was completed in 1987, the finance function ran the company in survival mode, negotiating with banks and creditors, selling off inventory, receivables, property, and entire businesses to avoid bankruptcy. Cash was required to survive and was the basis of virtually all operating decisions. After 1987, the finance function developed a more normal relationship with line business units, working with them to set financial targets.

Today, according to Lannert, operating managers view the finance staff as partners rather than police. The finance staff helps line managers set and achieve their business units' financial targets. Lannert says, "We keep score and make sure everyone knows the score." Part of the finance function's role also is to understand what type of capital structure and what type of debt and equity instruments will attract the funds needed to run the business. These requirements must be explained in detail to the 50 executives on the senior management team, but employees at all levels must understand how the company builds shareholder value. A study course helps employees understand the basics of corporate finance.

The finance function helps line units formulate plans to achieve Navistar's financial goals and communicates those plans internally and externally. Once those plans are formulated, the finance function is less involved in capital budgeting and other day-to-day activities at the business-unit level than it had been in the past.

Key Findings

In Lannert's opinion, the most important lessons were that International Harvester became all sales and no profit during the 1960s and 1970s. Management did not understand that it was growing the company too quickly and that growth had to slow so it could be financed; it did not sufficiently understand the need to earn more than the cost of capital. Today, Lannert and Horne believe that no matter how much a manager may feel a project is needed, it is inappropriate to invest shareholder money unless there is a clear plan for generating a 17.5 percent return over a business cycle. All employees must understand this logic.

Lannert says, "If you don't know how to invest in the business to get the desired rate of return, either you haven't thought and planned enough or you need to get a different team." Not grasping if and how these return goals are being met is a form of denial, which management cannot allow itself to practice.

USG Corporation

USG is the world's largest producer of gypsum wallboard, under the brand name Sheetrock; the world's largest producer of ceiling suspension grid; and the world's second-largest producer of ceiling tiles. In 1988, the company had a conservative balance sheet and a long-established, leading market position selling essential building materials. It had used excess cash to diversify into other building-related products. A hostile takeover attempt put the company in play. Management responded with a leveraged recapitalization. The combination of high leverage and a poor housing market in the early 1990s caused USG to default on several loans and to undergo a complex financial restructuring that culminated in a prepackaged bankruptcy. Fortunately, the company's underlying business was worth saving despite its balance-sheet problems. Since then, USG has focused on gypsum products, ceiling products, and building-materials distribution. It has regained an investment-grade credit rating and developed a less hierarchical, more entrepreneurial and team-focused corporate culture.

Background

Gypsum is a white mineral used in plaster, plasterboard, cement, and fertilizer. Sewell Avery founded United States Gypsum Company in 1902. In 1905, Avery consolidated 38 plaster mills in what was then called a trust (it would be called a roll-up today). As a conservatively managed, low-cost producer, the United States Gypsum Company survived the Depression. At that time, the company introduced wallboard, a labor-saving substitute for traditional plaster walls. United States Gypsum had no debt from 1921 to 1965.

In the 1980s, the company was renamed USG as it diversified from its gypsum base and developed a conglomerate building-materials business strategy. That strategy was partly the result of perceived antitrust limitations on its gypsum market share. USG purchased Masonite, a manufacturer of wood-fiber siding; DAP, a manufacturer of adhesives and caulks; and Donn, a manufacturer of ceiling grid with a strong international presence. As a result of the Donn acquisition, USG became the first company capable of making and marketing complete ceiling systems.

As a stable, risk-averse market leader, USG was a comfortable place to work. Many employees spent their entire careers there. As a result, the corporate culture was somewhat insular.

Causes of Financial Difficulty

The primary causes of USG's financial difficulty were a leveraged recapitalization that followed a hostile takeover attempt and unfavorable economic conditions that prevented it from servicing its extraordinary level of debt.

At the end of 1987, USG's financials appeared normal for a strong cash generator in a cyclical industry. Long-term debt was 55 percent of book capitalization and just 27 percent of market capitalization. The cash dividend payout was about 30 percent of earnings.

But the late 1980s were not normal times. Granted, there had been sensible reasons for some LBOs and even some hostile takeovers, but the availability of junk-bond financing encouraged highly leveraged transactions designed expressly to achieve short-term profit. In this environment, USG's prudent balance-sheet management and conglomerate structure became liabilities. The company was an attractive target for a hostile takeover because of its low debt and its potential breakup value.

Hostile Takeover Attempt

Recognizing USG's vulnerability, management began a stock-repurchase program to increase leverage and reduce the number of shares outstanding. But these measures were not sufficient to fend off raiders. The Belzberg group of Canada made a hostile investment in 1986 that USG bought back at a premium as part of its overall stock-repurchase program. Two weeks before the 1987 stock market crash, Cyril Wagner, Jr., and Jack E. Brown—two rich Texas oilmen who called themselves Desert Partners—made another hostile investment in USG, causing its share price to rise by 40 percent. Wagner and Brown had made substantial profits in other takeover attempts, teaming with other raiders such as T. Boone Pickens. They did not seem interested in operating the company but rather were willing to pay a substantial premium to take control of it and sell it in parts.

Following the 1987 crash, Desert Partners suffered a paper loss on USG stock; their takeover financing fell through. But in 1988, they secured a half-billion-dollar loan commitment from Wells Fargo National Bank and made a tender offer of $42 per share for 51 percent of USG's stock. The offer was two-tiered: Investors would receive cash for the first half of shares tendered and junk bonds for the second half. Thus, shareholders had an incentive to tender as quickly as possible.

Leveraged Recapitalization
Management could not fight off Desert Partners. USG was in play. More than half the company's stock was in the hand of arbitrageurs. Whether management accepted an offer from Desert Partners or another entity, the company faced a radical change. Rather than allow USG to be dismantled, management, advised by Goldman Sachs and Salomon Brothers, responded with its own offer to shareholders for a leveraged recapitalization. For each common share, USG would pay a cash dividend of $37 (85 percent of the share price at the time), a $5 junior pay-in-kind (PIK) subordinated debenture, and one share in the company after recapitalization. The recapitalization would be financed with $2.5 billion in bank and high-yield-bond debt. The high-yield bonds, maturing in the year 2000, paid 13.25 percent, 4.25 percent over the prime bank lending rate.

Management's offer was marginally below the Desert Partners offer, so the issue became who was more qualified to run the company. Management won a shareholder vote at a cost of completely changing USG's financial risk profile. Bankers Trust, Citibank, and Chemical Bank syndicated a $1.6 billion term loan. At the end of 1987, the company's balance sheet reflected $610 million in book equity and $745 million in long-term debt; at the end of 1988, it had negative book equity of $1.5 billion and long-term debt of $2.5 billion. USG's annual interest expense rose from $70 million per year before the recapitalization to $360 million afterward. In his book, *Money of the Mind—Borrowing and Lending in America from the Civil War to Michael Milken,* James Grant describes the transaction as ill-conceived but also, in some sense, inevitable. Grant cites an investment banker's observation that finance had not really mattered to USG when it was the low-cost producer and market leader in wallboard. Now, according to Grant, almost nothing mattered but finance.

Sale of Businesses and Cost Reduction
To manage its high debt load, USG sold assets and reduced costs and capital expenditures. It sold Masonite, Kinkead—a manufacturer of shower and tub enclosures—and other assets because the expected synergies among the products were minimal, netting about $550 million. Through a combination of divestitures and internal cost cutting, employment was reduced from 24,000 in 1988 to 13,400 in 1989. The company's debt shrank by about $800 million between 1988 and 1990.

Economic Conditions
In the recapitalization prospectus, management forecast a steady rise in sales and earnings for USG's remaining businesses. An unfavorable economic environment, however, prevented USG from realizing that forecast. At the time of the recapitalization, about 46 percent of USG's revenue was tied to residential construction. Although housing starts had declined by 11 percent from 1987 to 1988, many thought the construction industry was near its trough and that interest rates would be cut soon, stimulating demand.

That was not to happen. Housing starts declined by 14 percent in 1989 and kept falling until 1992, when they reached their lowest point since World War II. Rather than falling, interest rates rose, increasing USG's interest expense and further softening the housing market.

The decline in housing starts caused wallboard prices to fall by one-third between 1988 and 1990, from about $116 to $78 per thousand square feet. Each dollar decline in the price of wallboard reduced USG's pretax profit by $7 million. In the fourth quarter of 1990, USG's interest expense began to exceed its profit. That year, USG posted the first loss in its 88-year history. Citibank transferred its USG loans to its workout group. A borrower's relationship with a bank workout group is more pressured and less collegial than a normal corporate/bank relationship. Richard H. Fleming, now USG's executive vice president and CFO, remarks, "These aren't the guys who invite you to Chicago Bulls games."

The economic environment was ominous. A decline in real-estate prices caused crises in both the savings-and-loan and commercial banking businesses. USG's competitor, National Gypsum, an LBO, declared bankruptcy. Trade creditors began to fear that USG would do the same.

Loan Defaults

Poor operating performance caused a cash shortage. As a result, management foresaw that the company would have to default on a principal payment due at the end of December 1990. Knowing such a default would preclude further bank advances, it drew down $140 million under its revolving credit facilities. The drawdown increased USG's cash to $175 million at the end of 1990, a level management hoped would be sufficient for the forthcoming restructuring. At that time, the company moved its lockboxes from credit to noncredit banks to prevent credit banks from exercising their right of set-off and seizing incoming deposits.

Trade Credit

During the restructuring period, USG had trade-credit problems, including raw-material supplies, corporate credit cards, payroll, workers' compensation insurance, freight carriers, and utilities. Some vendors required cash up front. Some would not accept cash for fear that the bankruptcy court would require them to return it. Each state where the company operated required a standby letter of credit to secure workers' compensation coverage. Some banks would not accept cash from USG as security for issuing standby letters of credit. A large California bank refused to continue processing USG's payroll, forcing the company to make separate arrangements with community banks for each plant in California.

The Company Turnaround

USG turned around through a lengthy and complex financial restructuring that culminated in a prepackaged bankruptcy, an orderly deleveraging process focused on achieving an investment-grade credit rating, and refocusing the businesses for competitive advantage.

Restructuring Plan

In December 1990, Fleming, who had joined USG through the Masonite acquisition, was promoted to treasurer. His first official act was to warn a group of 80 bankers that USG expected to default on a $150 million principal payment due at the end of December. He and then-CFO J. Bradford James explained that USG wanted to negotiate a debt restructuring outside bankruptcy court.

Management had considered four options:

- Seek a quick out-of-court settlement based on cash-flow improvements

- Secure an equity infusion from an investor

- Try to survive a full in-court bankruptcy reorganization

- Negotiate an out-of-court settlement followed by a prepackaged bankruptcy

Because of the recession, cash flows were not improving fast enough for a quick, out-of-court deal. Negotiations with one possible equity investor fell through. An in-court bankruptcy proceeding would have been long, painful, and expensive. And USG faced possible asbestos claims from a previously discontinued product. A bankruptcy court might quantify these claims and place them as superior to the senior lenders' claims. Thus, an out-of-court settlement followed by a prepackaged bankruptcy seemed the best solution. Little did management know how long it would take.

Fleming observes that commercial lenders usually prefer a temporary fix to a permanent fix in such a restructuring. Although this may seem counterintuitive, he explains that lenders usually want to maximize their debt claims and minimize their "haircut," and this dynamic can lead to a temporary solution.

Prepackaged Bankruptcy

Management's overall objectives for a debt restructuring were for all creditors and shareholders to be treated fairly, given their position in the capital structure and USG's prospects; for consensus rather than confrontation; and for a long-term solution within a reasonable time that would involve all stakeholders, reduce leverage, and increase flexibility. In October 1990, an investment banker predicted that Chicagoans would be putting away their winter coats by the time the deal was done. The only problem, recalls J. Eric Schaal, assistant general counsel, was that the investment banker didn't specify the year.

Extended negotiations between management and creditors ensued. The number of creditor groups was large and their relationships complex, which was the principal reason negotiations that began in December 1990 were not finalized until January 1993. The lending syndicate consisted of 70 banks, led by three agent banks and seven steering-committee banks. The bank group had both legal and accounting advisors. And there were five major issues of senior debt. Fidelity Mutual Funds, Trust Company of the West, and Goldman Sachs were among three large debt holders. There were committees for both the senior- and the subordinated-debt holders, each with legal and investment banking advisors. Stockholders were at the bottom of the totem pole.

Further, USG's total enterprise value declined during the recession. The "pie" available for all the creditors, explains Fleming, shrank because of lower earnings. As a result, all the liabilities were subject to "haircuts." Fleming says, "It takes a while for people to agree on the amount of the shrinkage and how to allocate the haircuts. The dynamic is finding the intersection between fear and greed. They all have to feel they have pushed as hard as they could to get the best deal. We went right to the wall with all the lenders."

Members of USG's crisis team acted as shuttle diplomats, maintaining simultaneous conversations with all creditors. After the team developed a rough notion of where consensus might exist, it started to lock in the broad outline of a plan for each group, starting with the senior debt and rolling down the capital structure. After reaching a tentative agreement with each group, the team developed a more detailed plan that was subject to further negotiation and trade-offs before all parties were satisfied.

Threat of Bankruptcy

At many points during negotiations, the deal nearly collapsed. Each time, the crisis team thought it would have to file for Chapter 11 protection. Filing papers for each subsidiary stood ready in Federal Express pouches. Investment bankers advised the team that it had to be willing to file because if the creditors thought it was bluffing, the deal would never get done.

Changing Players
Distressed-security investors were careful not to receive confidential or inside information in order to avoid becoming insiders. As a result, they were free to sell their investments at any time. The crisis team had to deal with this uncertainty throughout the restructuring. After months of negotiation, several key lenders in the bank group simply sold their claims and disappeared. The team quickly had to establish relationships with the new investors who bought USG's debt.

Most Influential Investors
Fidelity and Trust Company of the West, both of which had acquired significant positions at deep discounts in several levels of senior and subordinated debt (including the bank debt), helped resolve intercreditor issues. They agreed on a letter of intent in spring 1992. The letter was passed on to the bank group, which accepted the proposal with some modifications after about four months. Then the letter went to the subordinated-debt committee. By fall 1992, the basic deal among the different levels of the capital structure was put together. It entailed restructuring the bank agreement, rescheduling some of the senior debt, exchanging $1.4 billion of subordinated debt for 97 percent of the common equity, and a one-for-fifty reverse stock split.

Fulcrum Security
The agreement by the senior-subordinated-debt holders to accept all equity was a milestone. The senior-subordinated debt became what is known as the fulcrum security—the security that receives the bulk of the equity. The party that wielded the most influence in reaching agreement on this class was a distressed-security investment fund that had bought half of the outstanding senior-subordinated debt for 50 cents on the dollar and wanted to receive equity in the restructuring.

Bank Debt
The principal amount of the bank debt was honored with a nominal 100 cents on the dollar but received a net-present-value haircut in the form of extended maturities and reduced interest rates. The bank debt was bifurcated. One tranche was converted to public bonds with a 10-year

maturity and a coupon of 10¼ percent. The other tranche became a bank revolving credit that funded into a term loan.

Equity Allocation
Senior-subordinated debt holders received 82 percent of USG's equity as a result of the restructuring. Junior-subordinated debt holders received 15 percent. Common stockholders received 3 percent. This was accomplished by a one-for-fifty reverse stock split before the new shares were issued.

Junior Subordinated: The Free Rider
Prepackaged bankruptcies usually are an alternative when the majority of the creditors agree on a restructuring, but the bankruptcy court process is required to force one or two classes with minority positions to go along. The most important reason for USG's prepackaged bankruptcy was to prevent the junior-subordinated debt class from becoming a free rider. Holders of junior-subordinated debt, trading for about 10 cents on the dollar, had an economic incentive not to vote on the restructuring plan. If their debt had remained outstanding after the senior-subordinated debt became equity, they could have sold their claims for perhaps as much as 80 cents on the dollar. USG had to deal with this possibility by going to court and applying the bankruptcy standard, which requires two-thirds of the total dollar holders and half of the unit holders to agree to a deal.

Venue Selection
After researching possible venues for the prepackaged bankruptcy, the crisis team decided Delaware was the best available jurisdiction. USG knew who the judge would be because only one judge worked in that area. She had overseen several prepackaged bankruptcies and clearly understood all the issues in the case.

Sharing the Pain
All stakeholders had to share the pain. As management asked senior lenders for concessions, it had to show its own willingness to sacrifice. Twenty-five percent of the company's workforce was released between 1987 and 1992. Employees' 25 percent ownership stake in USG would be almost wiped out. Eugene B. Connolly, chairman, fought hard for

existing shareholders to receive a small piece of the equity after restructuring, which turned out to be 3 percent—more than in most similar deals.

Management During the Restructuring Period

For a company to be run properly during a restructuring, some duties have to be split. Fleming believes one of management's best decisions was to bifurcate the office of the CEO. The chairman and the crisis management team—James, Fleming, and Schaal—worked almost full time on the restructuring, logging incredibly long hours. The president ran the company with a mandate to maximize earnings. Naturally, the CEO, CFO, and treasurer also had to spend time with the ongoing business.

Incentive to Maximize Enterprise Value

The dynamics of running a company during a restructuring vary considerably depending on whether the restructuring is in or out of court. Under an in-court bankruptcy proceeding, the tendency is to be conservative in projections of financial results to keep the post-bankruptcy debt load as low as possible. In contrast, the out-of-court restructuring gave USG every incentive to maximize enterprise value. By showing how well it could run USG during a cyclical trough, and thereby providing an idea of how well the company might perform when wallboard prices rose again, management helped convince creditors to take equity in the restructuring. USG's competitor, National Gypsum, took the opposite tack in its bankruptcy proceedings, leading to an interesting range of outlooks for the financial community to consider.

Professional Services

Management hired investment banks that had been involved with the company before its recapitalization, investment banks that had not been involved at that time, the company's normal general counsel, another law firm as bankruptcy counsel, and a financial-communications firm for proxy solicitation. In all, the fees to complete the reorganization, including bank fees, were $55 million. Although that may seem high, management estimates an in-court bankruptcy settlement would have cost twice as much in professional fees.

Emergence from Bankruptcy

The Delaware court confirmed the prepackaged bankruptcy plan in just 38 days. USG emerged from bankruptcy on May 6, 1993. USG's debt, which had risen from $743 million to $3 billion as a result of the recapitalization, was reduced under the bankruptcy plan to $1.5 billion. As a result, USG's annual interest expense declined from $334 million to $143 million. In Fleming's words, USG had progressed from "hyperleveraged" to "walking wounded." The company still resembled an LBO with an all-debt capital structure. Interest expense, although dramatically reduced, still was not much less than current EBITDA.

New Goals after Bankruptcy

When USG emerged from bankruptcy, the organization was weary; however, management believed it was important not just to declare victory. The company needed to set new goals. First, USG could not continue to exist with an all-debt capital structure. It needed a plan to reduce leverage as operating cash flow increased. Second, because capital would be expensive, USG needed to focus on the businesses where it had a competitive advantage and could earn substantially more than its cost of capital: gypsum and ceilings. Aside from its related distribution subsidiary, USG did not want to be in any other businesses. But to grow these businesses and build shareholder value, the company would have to reduce its cost of capital.

Plan to Achieve Investment Grade

At this time, Fleming announced a five-year plan for USG to achieve an investment-grade credit rating, targeting 1996 for a double-B rating and 1998 for a triple-B, investment-grade rating. Achieving this goal would create value through a huge reduction in borrowing cost. It also would increase the company's financial flexibility, allowing consistent access to capital and diversification of funding.

Management planned to start by accelerating the repayment of debt to create credibility early on. That would allow USG to raise new equity. Then it could identify new opportunities to invest for growth while moving toward investment-grade status.

To communicate the strategy to bondholders and employees, Fleming developed a formula. While USG had a single-B rating, it would allocate 75 percent of free cash flow to debt repayment and 25 percent to capital expenditures. When the rating was raised to double-B, the allocation would be 50-50. Finally, when USG reached investment grade, it would use 75 to 80 percent of free cash flow for capital expenditures and the remainder to fine-tune the balance sheet through dividends or stock repurchases.

The company never wavered from its plan. In August 1993, it exchanged $139 million in bank-loan payments due between then and 1996 for 10.25 percent bonds due in 2002. Management also modified a cash-sweep provision of its bank credit agreement to allow repayment of other senior debt. Later that year, it completed an $18 million sale and leaseback of a research facility to raise cash for debt repayment.

Early in 1994, USG began a $93 million strategic investment program to add wallboard capacity at nine plants. As the year progressed, management replaced cash and notes due in 1996 and 1997 with 9.25 percent senior notes due in 2001, increased its revolving credit facility to $70 million, and completed a 7.9-million-share common stock offering with proceeds of $224 million, most of which was used to reduce debt. It also modified the cash-sweep provision of its bank credit agreement to allow cash flow to be used for capital spending. In fall 1994, Fleming initiated quarterly conference calls with securities analysts on the mornings earnings are released.

In 1995, USG applied $132 million in cash generated by operations to reduce debt further, established a $500 million bank revolving credit facility, redeemed the remaining $268 million of 10.25 percent senior notes, and issued $150 million in 10-year, 8.25 percent bonds due in 2005. The *Wall Street Journal* described the issue as a "crossover credit," a high-yield security that investors expect will rise to investment grade. In March 1997, the company's bank credit facility was amended to eliminate collateral on all bank- and senior-debt obligations. In December 1997, Standard & Poor's upgraded USG's debt to triple-B. Since then, the company's credit rating has been fortified by a continuing increase in book net worth. Fleming believes triple-B-plus is about optimum for USG.

Improvement in Performance
During this deleveraging, USG was blessed with a steady increase in wallboard prices, from $75 per thousand square feet in early 1993 to $124 in early 1998. EBITDA increased steadily, from $159 million in 1992

to $572 million in 1997. Total debt fell from $1.5 billion in May 1993 to $620 million in December 1997. USG's stock price rose from $13 in June 1993 to $48 in December 1997. Total enterprise value rose from $2 billion in May 1993 to $2.9 billion in December 1997. By this point, the distressed-security investors who bought USG's senior-subordinated debt at a deep discount, and received common stock in the restructuring, could have sold their investment for 5 to 10 times the purchase price. Most had sold earlier.

Amortization of Fresh Start Charge

When USG was recapitalized in 1993, it in effect was sold to the bondholders, who received 97 percent of the equity. The total enterprise value was $2 billion, the sum of the equity the bondholders received and the $1.6 billion debt remaining on the balance sheet. The book value of the company's assets at that time was $1.2 billion. The difference between the enterprise value and book value was accounted for as excess reorganization value, similar to goodwill. This recapitalization required a so-called "fresh-start" charge against earnings, similar to a goodwill charge. USG petitioned the Securities and Exchange Commission (SEC) for permission to write off the entire amount in one year or less. The SEC would only allow an amortization schedule between 5 and 40 years, similar to the schedule for goodwill charges. USG chose a five-year schedule to coincide with its time line for deleveraging, rebuilding cash flow, and qualifying for an investment-grade credit rating. Once that financial restoration process was complete, management did not want the burden of a noncash fresh-start charge that caused net income to understate earning power. USG then accelerated the five-year amortization schedule by six months because of a gain on a prerestructuring liability booked in 1993.

Refocused Business Strategy

In 1991 and 1992, Eugene B. Connolly, then chairman and CEO of USG, developed a business plan to focus the organization after the financial restructuring. He wanted to have more grassroots involvement in strategic planning and to retain key personnel. With these objectives in mind, he convened a strategy development council composed primarily of nonofficer business managers. The leader of this planning effort was William C. Foote, the current chairman and CEO.

The strategy development council concluded that USG had core competencies in continuous-process manufacturing, construction systems, and building-products distribution. The company's two natural businesses were gypsum in North America and ceilings worldwide. With an established international presence in ceilings, it made sense for the company to tap a relatively undeveloped market for wallboard in countries that employed modern building methods. USG would develop the natural linkages among the gypsum, ceilings, and building-material distribution businesses. Both gypsum and ceilings entailed manufacturing and marketing engineered panels. Research, development, and distribution channels could be shared. The products had mutual customers.

Recent Priorities
In the gypsum business, USG recently has focused on geographic expansion, capacity addition, cost reduction, and branding. In 1997, the company announced a plan to be implemented over several years to shut down older, high-cost plants—some dating to 1935—with 1 billion square feet per year in capacity. It is adding 3 billion square feet of capacity in new, lower-cost plants that are about twice the size of the older plants. The new plants will manufacture wallboard at a cost of $40 to $45 per thousand feet, roughly half the cost of the oldest plants. Higher-cost plants that remain in service can be run at full speed or slowed, depending on demand. Through this plant rationalization program, USG has kept pace with the expansion of Home Depot and other store chains and reinforced its position as the lowest-cost producer of wallboard in every region of the United States. USG's Sheetrock branding campaign is creating a value premium over the normal market price. L&W, USG's distribution company, is the largest customer for both of USG's product areas, absorbing about 25 percent of gypsum output and 15 percent of ceiling output. L&W is expanding in the United States to create distribution around new gypsum plants, often by buying out small distributors.

Corporate Valuation
Fleming observes that astute, value-oriented investors get to know USG well enough to do detailed projections for each of its businesses, discount them at the company's weighted average cost of capital, and compare the resulting intrinsic value to market value. Management

uses a similar process. If there is a value gap between market value and intrinsic value, management consciously addresses issues that will close that gap, such as lowering the cost of capital, increasing the growth rate, making sure each project earns more than the cost of capital, and minimizing any discount associated with unpredictable earnings.

Cultural Changes

The financial restructuring forced USG to take a new look at its strategy and also introduced welcome changes in its corporate culture. Throughout its history, USG's leadership and organizational structure had been hierarchical. In restructuring, management took the opportunity to move toward team-based leadership and organization. It initiated a culture that encouraged people to be risk tolerant, flexible, and creative. Strategic planning is now more bottom-up than top-down. Rather than being debt averse, USG is now debt tolerant to the extent it can maintain its optimum triple-B-plus credit rating. USG can never pretend its business is not cyclical. Someday there will be another downturn. Securities analysts worry about the combined effect of increased plant capacity and falling wallboard prices in a recession. Management's job is to plan for that possibility and create value by managing better than investors expect.

Key Findings

- Growth without focus, such as conglomerate strategies, can be fatal. Such strategies usually do not create much value. And the appearance of being unfocused can subject a company to takeover threats from investors who see an opportunity to earn a profit from breaking it up.

- Strategic and cultural change can be accelerated in a crisis. Even without the crisis induced by the takeover threat and leveraged recapitalization, USG would have been well advised to narrow its focus to gypsum and ceilings, to flatten its organizational structure, and to create a more empowered, team-oriented culture.

- Handled properly, a crisis can strengthen a company's competitive position.

- To ensure a fair restructuring when many parties are involved, management must be prepared for lengthy negotiations. Success in these may require setting up one management team to run the company and another to handle the negotiations.

Forstmann & Company

Forstmann & Company, a manufacturer of high-quality woolen fabrics for the garment industry, filed for Chapter 11 protection in September 1995 and emerged from bankruptcy in July 1997. The company filed for Chapter 11 protection again in July 1999, and a Canadian competitor purchased its assets under bankruptcy-court proceedings in November 1999. The principal causes of financial difficulty in 1995 were an unfocused sales strategy and capital expenditure program, a lack of product-profitability analysis and cost controls, poor inventory management, and high leverage. The principal elements in the turnaround were communication with all stakeholders, reorganization of management, development of a business strategy, product rationalization, overhead reduction, and establishment of systems for cash-flow management, cost analysis, quality control, and customer service. The 1999 bankruptcy was caused by management's failure to react soon enough to a precipitous decline in market demand.

Background

The Forstmann family imported woolen fabrics from Germany in the nineteenth century and built a factory in Passaic, New Jersey, in 1904. J. P. Stevens, one of the country's largest, most diversified textile manufacturers, acquired Forstmann in 1947 and shifted its operations to a mill in Dublin, Georgia. In 1985, the company was spun off and reassumed the Forstmann name. Manufacturing remained in Georgia. Administrative offices were in New York City. With sales of $222 million in 1995, Forstmann & Company was the largest U.S. manufacturer of high-quality woolen fabrics for the garment industry.

Following the spin-off, Forstmann experienced a turbulent decade. It was threatened with a takeover in 1987 and sold to Odyssey Partners in an LBO in 1988. The company went public again in 1992 and embarked on a major capital-investment program. Throughout that period, it increased its borrowings and encountered frequent difficulties meeting the terms of its debt.

Business Characteristics

The principal competitive factors in the wool fabric business are fashion (product selection), quality, service, price, and credit. Because the industry is specialized and capital intensive, Forstmann had only about four direct competitors. The company had approximately 700 customers, virtually all in the United States, with the largest customer accounting for roughly 10 percent of the company's business.

Historically, Forstmann's core products were fashionable apparel fabrics. In the 1990s, the company positioned itself as a market-driven supplier, responding to target niches, customer demands, and shifting consumer trends. Starting in 1992, Forstmann began to produce other textiles with complex technical specifications for applications such as sports apparel, uniforms, upholstery, billiard tables, and wall coverings. These fabrics offered higher profit margins than the company's traditional products. Late in 1992, Forstmann entered a partnership to distribute fabrics of an Italian designer and manufacturer and later to manufacture those fabrics under license in the United States. The partnership helped the company enter the high-end designer market and keep abreast of the latest European technology and finishing processes.

The Manufacturing Process

Forstmann processed approximately 27 million pounds of wool in 20 different grades and 4 million pounds of other fibers each year. Raw material accounted for 40 percent of the cost of goods sold in 1995. The company converted the fibers into yarn, which it then wove.

Fabric designers demand variations on the amount of twist, number of piles (yarn loops), diameter, fiber content, and color of the yarn, all of which contribute to the texture, weight, and appearance of the finished fabric. A fabric such as a velvet-finish wool for women's coats may require as many as 30 mechanical finishing operations.

Production is primarily to order because of the difficulty of accurately predicting what the customer will want. Textile manufacturing is seasonal. Most orders are placed between December and April for manufacture between February and July.

Forstmann purchased 75 percent of its wool in Australia and the remainder in the United States. Even though foreign purchases were denominated in U.S. dollars, the price of wool was still volatile. Wool prices in Australia increased from a low of $1.60 per pound in 1993 to a high of $3.00 in 1995.

Market Changes
In the mid-1990s, consumers started to spend less on apparel, moving toward casual wear as business dress codes relaxed. At the same time, retailing was undergoing fundamental shifts. Mass-market retailers were becoming a more powerful force. To respond to rapidly changing consumer tastes, they demanded shorter lead times and production cycles from their manufacturers. Computer-driven "quick-response" programs were developed to collect information on shipments, inventories, and purchases and disseminate that information to manufacturers, distributors, and retailers.

Capital Investment Program
Forstmann began a six-year, $100 million capital-investment program in 1992 to reduce manufacturing costs, improve product quality, provide greater manufacturing flexibility, and improve technical capabilities for the production of new blends, styles, and colors. By mid-1995, the company had spent $64 million under that program.

Financial History
Between the 1985 spin-off from J. P. Stevens and the 1995 bankruptcy, Forstmann substantially increased its debt to cover capital expenditures, sales growth, and erratic financial performance. The company frequently violated its loan covenants and had either to renegotiate or to replace its borrowing facilities. In 1987, it resisted a financial takeover with the help of a "white knight." The next year, after the company exceeded a revolving credit line with GE Capital, it was sold to Odyssey Partners in an LBO. Citibank replaced the GE Capital line and provided bridge financing to Odyssey Partners. After

the company defaulted in July and December 1989, Citibank renegotiated and extended its loans. The company defaulted on all of its loans in 1990. In 1991, it executed an exchange offer and completed a $100 million refinancing. Between 1991 and 1994, Forstmann took out three loans totaling $7.5 million under an equipment facility with CIT to purchase textile machinery. The company went public again in 1992.

In October 1992, the company entered into a five-year, $100 million senior-secured credit facility with GE Capital, consisting of a $15 million term loan and an $85 million revolving credit scheduled to mature in November 1993. The facility was secured by liens on virtually all the company's assets. In April 1993, Forstmann issued $20 million of senior secured notes, and in March 1994 another $10 million; all were due in October 1997. The proceeds were used to repay the GE Capital term loan and part of the revolving credit.

Forstmann's sales increased from $209 million in 1992 to $237 million in 1994, and then declined to $222 million in 1995. Between 1993 and 1994, Forstmann's debt-to-equity ratio almost doubled, from 2.3 to 4.4, and its debt-service coverage ratio fell from about 1.2 to near zero. The gross profit margin, historically about 20 percent, declined to 11 percent in 1995, causing the company to estimate a $25 million loss for the year. The company had to seek a waiver of covenants under both the GE Capital and CIT facilities because of a liquidity shortage and declining balance sheet ratios.

Chapter 11 Filing
In September 1995, just a month after he became CEO, Bob Dangremond saw no alternative to filing for Chapter 11 protection in the U.S. Bankruptcy Court for the Southern District of New York. Forstmann's outstanding debt included $30 million in senior-secured notes, $51 million in subordinated notes with an interest rate of 14.75 percent, and $7.7 million that remained past due under the CIT facility. A principal payment of $4 million and an interest payment of $633,937 on the senior secured notes were due in October 1997. The company was required to redeem half the subordinated notes in 1998 and half in 1999. It had been unable to renegotiate or extend the working-capital facility from GE Capital. Its cash flow appeared to be insufficient for principal, interest, and supplier payments due in the coming months.

Market conditions resulting in increased raw material cost and reduced finished product demand seemed unlikely to change.

Causes of Financial Difficulty

Forstmann's financial difficulty was brought on by a combination of high leverage, an unfocused sales strategy, a cash drain caused by poor inventory management, an excessive and unfocused capital-expenditure program, and poor operating results. Forstmann had a cost structure inappropriate to the level of business under market conditions at the time. Management had made a commitment to be the largest producer of décor products in the world without analyzing the market's ability to absorb those products. It favored the largest possible production runs to minimize unit costs, thereby accumulating huge inventories of unsold goods. Other problems included deficiencies in cash-flow management, product-cost analysis, quality control, and customer service.

The Company Turnaround

Despite the problems he observed, Dangremond surmised that Forstmann could be salvaged. As the company filed for Chapter 11 protection, the immediate issues on his mind were how to communicate with employees and other stakeholders, how to ensure that the company had enough cash to survive, and who should be on the new management team.

Communication with Stakeholders

Dangremond believed clear and forthright communication would reduce anxiety and help enlist support from all stakeholders. Immediately after the company filed for bankruptcy, he wrote to every employee, customer, creditor, and stockholder, describing the reasons for filing and outlining the reorganization. Management met with employees at each plant and provided contacts, telephone numbers, and a confidential fax line to Dangremond for questions and concerns. It sent monthly progress reports with financial results. It assured suppliers that the company had sufficient cash to meet its short-term obligations. And it placed particular importance on ensuring that the Australian wool suppliers understood the U.S. bankruptcy process and how it could help a company survive.

Cash-Flow Management

Another early priority was setting up a system to manage cash receipts and disbursements. The $100 million capital-expenditure program was curtailed. In Dangremond's judgment, such a program is, by its very size, out of proportion for a company with $200 million in sales. There appeared to be no sense of priority in the program; managers seemed to get whatever they wanted. No one followed up after projects were implemented to see if they met projected returns.

At first, capital expenditures were allowed only for essentials such as repairs, limited to $5 million per year. Even with this cap, the company spent more because of prior commitments, including "pet projects" that were then unknown to the CFO and CEO. Dangremond notes, "Egos of senior managers sometimes circumvent what you are trying to do." Management also had to encourage people at all levels to report problems and opportunities.

Dangremond observes that Forstmann and other companies with which he has worked did not have an early warning system because they did not understand how to manage cash flow. For many CEOs, cash flow is an accounting change in working capital, but that is only words. Real cash flow is what comes in and goes out today, what is left over, and how that compares with yesterday's cash position. It is a simple definition, but many managers have never thought about it. Cash is a limited resource that must be managed. In a turnaround, managing receipts and disbursements is a matter of survival. Financial difficulty creates increased cash demands, such as suppliers' requirements for cash in advance or customers' requirements for cash deposits to protect warranties. Receipts and disbursements must be forecast for the next week, month, and quarter. Dangremond believes such a forecasting model must become part of the management culture.

Management Reorganization

Dangremond says one of the challenges in turning a company around is identifying as quickly as possible which managers can recognize what has to be done and make the transition to the new company. Sometimes early impressions are reliable; sometimes there are surprises. Managers three or four levels down may appear with energy and ideas they have not had a chance to implement. Others may have been part of the problem. If no one has listened to a given manager's ideas, it is important to learn why.

Aiming to reduce the layers in top management, Dangremond consolidated various departments into six groups led by managers reporting directly to him:

- Marketing, styling, and product development

- Manufacturing, product design, and industrial engineering

- Production planning and customer service

- Operations, including technical service, corporate engineering, procurement, warehousing, and shipping

- Human resources, payroll, and benefits

- Finance, management information systems, treasury, credit, and analysis

As a result, several senior executives left, and management costs went down.

Shortly after Dangremond became CEO, he faced his first management problem. The CFO presented demands that would have to be met for him to stay if there were a bankruptcy. Knowing he would need a dependable management team, Dangremond accepted the CFO's resignation. He appointed a new CFO, Rodney Peckham, who previously had been Forstmann's controller and treasurer and was committed to managing a turnaround. Peckham had worked with the company for nine years before leaving earlier in 1995 to pursue another opportunity. The company's lenders saw his departure as a red flag. When he returned at Dangremond's request, it calmed the lenders to have this experienced and knowledgeable CFO in place.

For certain high priorities, Dangremond commissioned FAST (focus, accountability, simplification, and teamwork) teams of managers and employees selected for their initiative as well as their people and problem-solving skills. The product-line rationalization team assessed the company's product offerings on an economic basis with the objective of a more focused, profitable product line. The throughput/customer-service team focused on simplifying manufacturing and business processes and reducing order-to-delivery time without increasing inventory. The yarn-reduction team focused on reducing the company's excessive yarn inventory. The cost-reduction team, led by the CFO, focused on reducing overhead and manufacturing costs.

Dangremond implemented a management incentive plan based on the company's earnings before interest, income taxes, depreciation, amortization, and restructuring charges (EBITDAR), which would have to be greater than $21 million in 1997 for any bonuses to be paid. In the past, management had been measured primarily on sales and earnings per share.

Business Strategy Development

Dangremond observes that every product or service is sold based on some combination of quality, service, price, and credit, in that order of importance. Quality is the most profitable basis of competition. Extension of credit is the least profitable and highest-risk way to compete. Forstmann lost money in several customer bankruptcies, including that of apparel maker Leslie Fay, because it sold primarily based on price. Dangremond's objective was for Forstmann to move away from competition based on price and credit toward competition based on quality and service.

The new business strategy recognized that it was unrealistic for the company to compete in every segment of the fabric market. Management decided to protect lines of business where it was strong and relinquish others. The first step was a cost analysis of product and customer profitability.

Cost Analysis

Dangremond observes, "You can't spend a sales dollar." Growing revenue is a top priority for many turnaround managers, but such a strategy often fails. Many companies don't know what their costs are and therefore don't know which lines of business are profitable and which are unprofitable. Management undertook an activity-based cost study of 40,000 products, which was not as hard as it sounds because many products were similar. Management worked with supervisors and hourly workers in the plants to identify all of the steps required to produce each type of fabric and to account for all direct and indirect costs. Contrary to management's earlier belief, larger-volume commodity products turned out to be more profitable than lower-volume, higher-value-added products. The latter had special requirements that had not been factored into the allocation of direct and indirect costs. For example, the cost of filling a vat with dye is the same for a small batch of fabric as for a large batch. As a result of the analysis, management determined that market prices could not justify the costs of the Italian fabric line. Some commodity products were profitable because their volume made the company a low-cost producer.

Product Rationalization
The cost analysis led Forstmann to eliminate about 30 percent of its stock-keeping units (SKUs). The company exited businesses in which it did not have a competitive advantage. This reduced revenue but increased cash flow.

Inventory Management
The product-line rationalization reduced inventory requirements commensurately. Finding common yarns that could be used for multiple products also reduced inventory requirements. Production managers were weaned from the mentality of running plants at capacity to minimize unit costs. They started to produce just enough fabric to meet customer orders. Reducing the production lots did increase unit costs, but there were savings from holding less inventory. Management worked with plant supervisors to reduce in-process inventory such as undyed yarn stored temporarily on the factory floor. And the yarn-reduction team found opportunities to sell excess inventory at whatever discount was required.

Customer Service
Management assigned a service representative to every customer. At any time, a customer could call to find out when a product would be shipped or to resolve a question concerning an invoice. Other customer-service measures included new product development targeted to specific customers and market segments, a 50 percent reduction in sample lead times (the time from a customer's request for a sample to delivery of the sample), and a 30 percent reduction in production-delivery times (the time from receipt of order to delivery of the product).

Quality Control
If a fabric at the end of the production process meets shade, texture, moisture-content, and other requirements, it is ready to be shipped to the customer. If it falls short on any of these criteria, it must be recycled. The first time Dangremond began measuring "pounds in versus pounds out," only 60 percent of production was ready for shipment the first time through; the remaining 40 percent had to be recycled, doubling variable cost and tying up capacity. Dangremond offered production managers incentives based on reducing rejects.

Overhead Reduction
Forstmann's SG&A (selling, general and administrative) expenses fell from 12 percent of sales prior to the 1995 bankruptcy to 7.5 percent afterward. While the company was in bankruptcy, management closed one Georgia plant, reduced office space in New York, and eliminated company cars. Dangremond needed to create a cost-saving culture and mentality. During the first six months of his tenure, he terminated several senior staff members who earned high salaries and had generous expense accounts but contributed little to the company's profitability. The company also eliminated substantial associated costs, some of which became apparent only after the managers left.

Key Performance Indicators
Management developed a monthly report of KPIs, including financial results and measures of timeliness, quality, and safety. The budget and actual results were compared in the following categories:

- Monthly sales
- Year-to-date sales
- Total inventory
- Orders received to be produced (backlog)
- Percentage of orders produced on time
- First-quality percentage (yards with no defects as a percentage of total production yards)

- First-quality/first-time percentage (yards with no defects on the first production run, with no rework required, as a percentage of total production yards)

- Labor cost per pound

- Safety incident rate

Financing and Capital Structure

In November 1995, two months after Forstmann filed for Chapter 11 protection, GE Capital agreed to modify the terms of its $100 million senior secured credit facility and extend the maturity through October 1996. At that time, Forstmann also arranged debtor-in-possession (DIP) financing to borrow up to $85 million under a borrowing-base formula, less prepetition advances and outstanding letters of credit under the previous revolving-credit facility. This allowed Forstmann to meet its trade obligations and pay employee wages, salaries, and benefits. Late in 1996, both the senior-secured and the DIP facility were extended for another year.

In January 1997, the bankruptcy court approved the sale of the Forstmann's plant in Tifton, Georgia, for $1.25 million. Proceeds from the sale were used to reduce debt. In February 1997, Forstmann negotiated a new financing package with its two existing lending institutions—GE Capital and CIT—and Bank of America, which provided a line of credit Forstmann needed to emerge from bankruptcy.

Financial Reorganization Plan

Forstmann's financial reorganization plan affected each class of claim holders differently, depending on seniority. As table 7.1 shows, only a few of the claims were unimpaired.

Second Bankruptcy Filing

When Forstmann emerged from bankruptcy in 1997, it employed about 2,400 people. In 1998, the company realigned its manufacturing facilities, closing its Louisville, Georgia, plant and eliminating 450 jobs. It also exited the top-dyed men's suiting and government fabrics businesses.

Table 7.1
Financial Reorganization Plan

Class 1. Allowed Priority Claims—Unimpaired

These claims, worth $11,400,000, represented the amount the company had been unable to pay into its pension plan. The company paid down this claim and continued to sponsor and operate the pension plan in compliance with the Employee Retirement Income Security Act of 1974 (ERISA).

Class 2. Note Holder Claims—Impaired

Senior-secured note holders received cash equal to the outstanding principal amount and a deferred interest note equal to the value of all interest payments in arrears.

Class 3. CIT Claims—Impaired

CIT received the outstanding principal amount and all accrued but unpaid interest after confirmation and acceptance of the reorganization plan.

Class 4. Miscellaneous Secured Claims—Unimpaired

This class was primarily lessors under capital leases. They were reimbursed under the original terms of their leases.

Class 5. Unsecured Claims—Impaired

Members of this class received 77 percent of their original claims based on the market value of new stock issued in kind for unsecured debt.

Class 6. Convenience Claims—Unimpaired

This class was a subset of Class 5 whose claims were unimpaired.

Class 7. Holders of Old Preferred Stock—Impaired

This class received warrants to purchase 0.5 percent of new common stock.

Class 8. Holders of Old Common Stock—Impaired

This class received warrants to purchase 0.5 percent of new common stock.

Class 9. Holders of Old Options—Impaired

This class received nothing.

In May 1998, Forstmann acquired the Arenzano Trading Company, which made moderate-price women's suits under the Oleg Cassini trademark, and created a subsidiary called Forstmann Apparel. This was part of an effort to diversify and reduce the company's reliance on the wool fabric business.

Despite continued efforts to downsize and reduce operating costs, Forstmann lost $7 million in 1997 and $19 million in 1998. In February 1999, the company's auditors said, "The company's recurring losses and related matters raise substantial doubt about its ability to continue as a going concern."

In a quarterly filing with the SEC, management noted that the volume of fabric it sold was down 40 percent for the quarter, that the average price per yard had slipped from $7.43 to $7.26, and that its February 28 backlog was $34 million, compared with $55 million a year earlier. It said lenders had waived certain financial covenant defaults arising from fiscal 1998 results and set new covenants for 1999, but the company might fail to meet requirements under the amended credit facilities. Management reported that the company's lenders had cut its revolving credit facility from $85 million to $70 million, reducing the company's unused-commitment fee by about $75,000 per year. The amended facilities also required the company to repay some of its outstanding loans if orderly liquidation values of its property, plant, and equipment fell below 83 percent of outstanding loans. In the second quarter of 1999, the company failed to meet amended EBITDA covenants in its revolving credit agreement.

On July 23, 1999, Forstmann filed for bankruptcy for the second time in four years, listing assets of $88 million and liabilities of $59 million. Management said the company had exhausted its borrowing capacity under the $85 million revolving credit from the bank group led by Bank of America.

Rodney Peckham, formerly CFO, and president and CEO at the time of bankruptcy, said in an affidavit filed with the petition that the company would immediately cut 50 percent of its workforce, which was then 1,100 people, 900 full time. He said Forstmann had exhausted its availability under its revolving-credit facility. A liquidity problem, he explained, arose from restructuring efforts over the past year and costs associated with the start-up of Forstmann Apparel. He also said the company was hurt by excess capacity in the marketplace; financial problems in Asia, which caused some Asian producers to dump wool fabrics; the popularity of synthetics; warm weather trends; and the continued popularity of more casual dress.

Before filing, the company reportedly reached an agreement with a group of buyers for the apparel subsidiary, which then fell through. At the time of filing, the subsidiary listed assets of $2.3 million and liabilities of $55.6 million, including an unsecured claim of $29.2 million for licensing fees from Oleg Cassini.

Forstmann hired an investment banking firm to identify possible buyers, merger partners, or investors, and a turnaround consultant as interim CEO. The trade press identified two of the company's direct competitors as merger candidates but also said these companies might not want to make acquisitions with an oversupply of fabric in the market.

Forstmann management stated that while in bankruptcy, it would try to transform the company into more of a niche player, relying more on selling fabrics to the baseball cap and billiard-table markets, in addition to the coat business. Forstmann was following other textile companies looking to the industrial and home furnishings markets to reduce their reliance on cyclical apparel fabrics.

In August 1999, Forstmann received approval for a $50 million DIP facility with Bank of America as agent for the bank lending syndicate. Terms of the approval allowed funds to be used for operating expenses and salaries and provided a $450,000 carve-out for professional fees and a $547,000 employee retention and severance program. Also in August, a newly appointed unsecured-creditors committee hired a public accounting firm to analyze Forstmann's financial operations prior to and after the petition date; prepare and submit a report helping the committee to analyze the reorganization plan; verify physical inventory of merchandise, supplies, and equipment as well as any other material assets and liabilities; assist in the evaluation of cash flow, collections, or other projections; and scrutinize both prepetition and postpetition cash disbursements and transactions with affiliated companies.

In September, the company won approval for an employee retention and severance program designed to retain 22 critical management personnel. The program required covered employees to remain with the company for up to six months from the petition date.

On November 4, 1999, Victor Woolen Products Ltd. of Montreal purchased Forstmann's assets under bankruptcy-court proceedings for $16 million. The purchase price included machinery and equipment and the Forstmann trademark but excluded two plants in Georgia and the Oleg Cassini license. The company, renamed Victor Forstmann, planned to continue operating from Forstmann's New York offices.

Key Findings

These are Dangremond's observations on managing the turnaround process:

- A turnaround moves with uncontrollable speed. Decisions have to be made quickly from available information. Because of time pressure, even the most capable managers sometimes make mistakes. As an organization perceives internal difficulty, so do other constituents such as lenders, shareholders, and employees. As a result, management is besieged with demands for information and assurance. The greater the difficulty, the more time compresses. One of the turnaround manager's most important roles is to control the time constraint. The manager has to be willing to tell a constituent, "You'll get it, but not today. Don't panic."

- Management's first priority must be to focus on cash, regardless of how much cash is being generated. If it does so, the company will never go into bankruptcy, despite market forces. It may have to arrange a joint venture, merger, or buyout on a friendly basis, but it will never face a potential liquidation.

- The turnaround manager has to establish a communication process and reward system so ideas are conveyed and, if reasonable, implemented. The last thing a manager wants is to quash a good idea.

- The finance function is pivotal in communicating among all stakeholders during a Chapter 11 process because the jargon related to bankruptcy is loaded with financial terms. Financial officers have to help others understand what is going on.

- Restructuring an independent company in a cash-constrained environment when employees are resigning and banks are pulling lines of credit is very different from restructuring a division of a large corporation where, despite political and other management pressures, the cash is there.

- It's easier to file for than to get out of Chapter 11, and filing is a last resort. Some people who have lived through bankruptcies are grateful for the learning experience but will do everything in their power to make sure it doesn't happen to them again.

- Turnaround management has a brief time to establish credibility with lending officers who are betting their careers on whether the company will survive. Ethically, management must be truthful to its lenders as well as to itself.

- As a company emerges from bankruptcy, equity and subordinated-debt holders may press for the highest possible valuations in the final reorganization plan. This sometimes results in unrealistic "hockey stick" sales and earnings projections that the company must meet to comply with the covenants of bank exit-financing packages. A company needs flexibility and maneuverability in its exit financing.

- Although market growth started to flatten in 1995, Forstmann's first bankruptcy was mainly related to poor management. Its 1999 bankruptcy was more market driven. Management should have been more attuned to the realities of the marketplace. Management might have been able to avoid bankruptcy and arrange a merger under more favorable circumstances if it had downsized more quickly.

Finally, Gary Schafer, who worked in Forstmann's finance function from 1990 to 1999 and was CFO after Dangremond left in 1997, remembers the period when the company was heading into its first bankruptcy as the most difficult. He sensed danger in the lack of control in costs and capital expenditures but did not feel sufficiently empowered to change the culture at the root of the problem. He felt there was "no roadmap through the wilderness." After Dangremond started to spearhead cost controls and other changes, Schafer began to feel "good stress rather than bad stress." Schafer believes if he were to find himself again in a situation comparable to Forstmann in 1994 and 1995, he would resign.

Pepsi-Cola Bottling Company of Charlotte, N.C.

When the current CEO of this family-owned company assumed control in 1981, the company was nearly bankrupt. Production facilities and trucks were in poor shape. Customers were undersupplied, morale was low, and employee turnover was high. There were few internal controls. The company was in danger of losing its Pepsi-Cola franchise, the foundation of its value. The new CEO and chief operating officer worked together to build a management team and restore production, sales, distribution, financial management, and data processing. As a result, case volume has increased two and a half times and profitability has quadrupled.

Background

Pepsi-Cola Bottling Company of Charlotte, North Carolina, owns the Pepsi-Cola franchise for a seven-county area. The company also distributes several other soft drinks. It has a bottling plant adjacent to its headquarters in Charlotte and three distribution centers in nearby counties. Canned soft drinks come from a nearby cooperatively owned cannery. There are about 350 employees.

The company, founded in 1905 by Henry B. and Sadie Clarkson Fowler, is one of the original Pepsi-Cola franchised bottlers. The Fowlers were among the few franchisees who continued bottling and selling Pepsi-Cola during the Depression and kept the brand alive. Mr. Fowler maintained control over the company until the early 1970s, when he was more than 90 years old. In his later years, however, he reinvested very little into maintaining plant facilities, trucks, and vending machines because he intended to sell the business. The current president and CEO is Dale Halton, granddaughter of the founders.

Causes of Financial Difficulty

Dale Halton became CEO and controlling shareholder in 1981 after the previous CEO—another member of the family—left by mutual agreement. According to current management, that CEO was bright but unwilling to listen to managers, share information, and delegate authority. As a result, personnel turnover was four times the average for bottlers in North Carolina.

Because of the previous CEO's management style, Darrell Holland, executive vice president and chief operating officer, had considered leaving the company. However, he had a good working relationship with Dale Halton, who had been responsible for the company's advertising. Holland therefore agreed to stay on when Halton became CEO. They have worked together ever since. When they assumed their positions, they persuaded other managers and employees who had planned to leave that the company would be a better place to work under their management. Among those who stayed are the current managers of sales, production, and personnel.

Accounting and Cash Management
When Halton assumed control, she knew little about the company's financial situation. She had to force the outside accountant to turn over current tax records under threat of legal action. It was impossible at first to tell how much the company owed; hidden bills kept appearing. There was no system to report and forecast receipts and disbursements. Bookkeepers were unable to describe how cash was collected from customers. Because there was virtually no accounting system, there were no monthly P&L reports, and an annual P&L was not available until the audit was completed, months after the end of the year.

Production and Warehouse Facilities
Halton's grandfather had intended to sell the company and therefore did not reinvest in the plant and equipment. As a result, production machinery that should have produced 600 cases per hour was producing only 250. Retailers received fewer beverages than they ordered; in fact some called on Friday afternoons asking, "Where's my Pepsi?" The bottling machine was called a gang machine because a gang of men was required to run it. As for the warehouses, Holland believes the state health department could have closed them all down. And the delivery trucks were in such poor shape that the standing joke was that the company needed to send a wrecker behind each one.

Security
Up to 10 percent of the company's production was pilfered, which is a common problem in the bottling industry. Even one corrupt guard can cause a significant loss.

The Company Turnaround

The new management team turned the company around by reinvesting in the plant and equipment and improving marketing, personnel management, and information and control systems.

Accounting and Cash Management

When the new management assumed control, it had a cash balance of about $200,000, enough for a half week's operations, and had to figure out where to start in the turnaround process. Because of Pepsi-Cola Bottling's thin cash position and uncertain needs, Halton requested a line of credit from the company's principal bank soon after she became CEO. But to everyone's surprise, she never needed to use it. For the next 10 years, Holland maintained personal control over all expenses except minor truck repairs.

Management started to organize the receipts and disbursements process. Working with customers and bookkeepers, it determined that cash generally was collected from stores six weeks after delivery on a weekly basis. Management also replaced the company's accountant and outside counsel.

Data Processing and Reporting

The company's first computer system, installed in the late 1970s, had been designed for a beer distributor. It was a poor fit and not implemented properly. There also was considerable turnover in data processing managers. Now the company is on its third computer system, which runs software adapted specifically for the bottling business. Beyond a detailed, line-item P&L for each department, management does not require budgets and forecasts. The reports it does receive include a daily cash balance, sales the day before compared to the previous year, and sales for the month to date. Management questions any unusual changes in these critical variables.

Production

In the beginning of the turnaround, the production manager had to run the bottling plant as efficiently as possible under severe cash constraints. He had to establish priorities for repairs and improvements and work down the list as funds became available. Gradually, production machinery was overhauled and restored to top condition. Fortunately, bottling equipment lasts a long time if properly maintained. When production improved, sales began to expand and cash flow increased. The plant now produces enough for a week's sales in three and a half days in winter and four and a half days in summer.

Personnel

Restoration of employee morale was very important. Management wanted to show concern for employees without reverting to the paternalistic style of the founders, so it had to adopt a more businesslike approach to handling people. For example, the personnel manager developed policies so employees knew the rules. Management also adopted a policy that no employee could be terminated without the personnel manager's approval. Termination of employees who had been with the company for more than five years required approval of the executive vice president. Turnover has dropped to only about 5 percent a year.

Another important aspect of personnel management was keeping close control over the number of employees. Holland is careful not to get overstaffed because he believes layoffs hurt morale very seriously.

Compensation

Halton's objectives were first to make the company profitable and then to provide more to the employees. She now considers salaries and benefits excellent compared with those of similar-sized companies. Management makes a contribution to each employee's 401(k) plan and awards end-of-year bonuses to every member of a department based on a combination of the department's and the company's performance for the year. People who sell and deliver beverages by truck are compensated with a combination of base salary and percentage commission. Routes are balanced so that each driver has both large and small accounts.

Distribution

Distribution in the 1980s was the responsibility of two long-term employees who knew how to take customer orders but not how to manage people and systems. Recently, bulk distribution has reduced costs, and tractor trailers now deliver pallets of soft drinks to store chains.

Fountain Sales

In the early 1980s, the company had minimal sales through fountains in retail establishments such as restaurants and drugstores. Paybacks for the fountains it had installed were as long as 20 years. A manager of fountains and vending machines, new to the business, turned around the fountain business by focusing on sales and return on investment.

Vending Machines

Pepsi-Cola Bottling invests about $600,000 per year in new vending machines. It now has 6,000 machines, versus about 1,500 machines in 1974. A new machine costs $1,000 to $1,500. In the past, the company had a problem with cash pilfering. Now, a computer system gives management a report of sales and, for security purposes, the number of times the machine is opened. The sales report can be reconciled with cash receipts for each machine. In addition to selecting its own vending-machine locations, Pepsi-Cola Bottling works with other companies that provide total vending-machine services to hotels, office buildings, and factories.

Schools and Special Events

The key to building the schools and special events business was a full-time salesperson who developed a good relationship with the schools. The justification for reinvesting about $80,000 per year in this business is to create brand loyalty among schoolchildren.

Market Share

Market share for each territory is tallied by IRI, an independent organization known throughout the industry. During Halton's and Holland's tenure, the company's market share in its territory has increased from 25 to 32 percent, while that of the competing Coca-Cola distributor has declined from 40 to 32 percent. Pepsi-Cola Bottling's raw case volume has moved from 3 million to 8.5 million cases per year. The company does not plan to expand its geographical territory, but it will continue to grow by further penetration into its existing territory. Plant capacity is sufficient for more business, and the company could consider selling products to, or even buying, other distributors. However, Holland believes that would put the company on a "whole new pressure track" and that its current size provides a good living and working environment for the owners, management, and staff.

Management Style

When Halton and Holland first assumed control, the company's organization and working relationships seemed close to anarchy. Halton and Holland had to become—against their nature—strict disciplinarians. Now they describe their management style as more hands-off, with occasional checks on each manager. They prefer in-person meetings to written communication and try to limit any meeting to one hour. They are willing to talk directly to any employee but insist that employees resolve specific problems with their supervisors. In a company of this size, management learns what it needs to know through informal communication. Holland visits each plant about once a week to show that management is interested in everyone and willing to listen to any problems.

Key Findings

Because Pepsi-Cola Bottling had a valuable franchise, sales opportunities were waiting once production was restored, and cash flow followed sales. If run properly, it is a "cash cow" business. The most important factor in the turnaround was getting the right people in key management positions and allowing them latitude to do their jobs. Halton, Holland, and the managers of personnel, production, and sales have worked as a team throughout the turnaround process. Because the company is privately held and seldom borrows, management was able to be more patient about the amount of time needed for the turnaround than it could have been if it were publicly held or highly leveraged.

Summarizing the turnaround experience, Holland points out that knowing what you want to do in business is essential but knowing how to do it is more difficult. In 1981, the company had a good franchise area and a good product, but its organization was weak and its capital investment was sadly lacking. First, management had to set goals, which were growth and profit. Second, it had to choose its management team, a difficult task that took three to five years of trial and error. Third, as the team took shape, it had to select subordinates to do the necessary jobs. Training, pay scales, benefits, capital investments, morale, and customer service were built into the system as fast as possible.

Sampson Paint Company

The net worth of the family-owned Sampson Paint Company eroded from about $6 million in 1970 to near zero in 1980 because of inappropriate pricing, poor marketing, poor financial controls, high overhead and manufacturing costs, and a lack of product- and customer-profitability analysis. Its turnaround required a new owner with management experience and fresh insight. With financing from an asset-based lender and the previous owners, turnaround specialist Frank Genovese restored profitability by reducing overhead; rationalizing and repricing the product line; and establishing a marketing strategy, operating procedures, and financial reporting and controls.

Background

Sampson Paint Company, based in Richmond, Virginia, was started in 1899 and purchased by Frank Sampson in 1926. When Sampson died in 1967, his two daughters became joint owners and his son-in-law became CEO. The son-in-law died in 1972 and was succeeded by the company's sales manager. In turn, he was succeeded in 1977 by the former treasurer, who remained CEO until the company was sold to Frank Genovese in 1980. In 1979, Sampson had purchased the Alcatraz Paint Company and had run it as a separate company. The Sampson sisters sold the Sampson company in 1980 because it was performing poorly and they did not have the abilities to initiate and oversee a turnaround.

Sampson uses a small-batch manufacturing process. Raw materials are combined in "pebble mills," where pigment is crushed, moved to a mixing tank, and then mixed with an oil or water fluid base. After the paint is mixed and tested, it is piped to a filling machine, where it is automatically poured into cans, labeled, and packed. Mixers and grinders are sturdy and not subject to obsolescence; they last a long time if properly maintained.

Sampson's sales were $5.2 million in 1980, having grown at a compound rate of 13 percent during the previous five years. Alcatraz's product growth had been relatively flat. Approximately 80 percent of the combined companies' sales were their own manufactured products, and 20 percent were products from manufacturers of other products such as wallpaper, brushes, and stains distributed through the company's sales force and retail outlets. Four direct salespeople sold to independent paint dealers and three company-owned retail outlets. Paint contractors accounted for more than half of retail outlet sales.

The company had more than 850 active customers for its products in 1979. The top 10 accounted for 40 percent of sales and the top 60 for 60 percent. The remaining customers averaged annual sales of only $3,000 per year.

Architectural paints, the fastest-growing segment of the market, accounted for 65 percent of sales. The other 35 percent consisted of sundries and special coatings, mostly industrial asphalt and aluminum-based coatings. Sampson had a 4.7 percent share of the Virginia architectural paint market, competing with the top 10 nationwide producers and Duron, a strong regional brand.

Annual shipments for the U.S. paint industry during 1977 were $5.1 billion. The industry consisted of approximately 1,300 firms, with 1,500 plants employing 50,000 people. Only 700 companies employed more than 20 people, and only 50 employed more than 250. Twenty firms accounted for 62 percent of shipments. The average sales level for the remaining companies was about $1.5 million per year. Few companies sold nationwide because the product is heavy and thus expensive to ship and distribute. Proximity to local markets helped small paint companies compete with large ones.

In Virginia, 23 paint-manufacturing companies shipped products worth $50 million in 1980, $25 million of which were architectural-paint products. Only two national firms had manufacturing locations in the state. The total 1980 consumption of paint products in Virginia was $172 million, indicating substantial imports from other states.

Causes of Financial Difficulty

Sampson Paint Company, as Genovese found it in 1980, suffered from a lack of professional management:

- **Accounting and financial reporting.** The owners received no monthly P&L statements, only audited annual statements, which they did not understand. Because, until 1979, they continued to receive their dividends and the previous management did not explain the company's deteriorating financial performance to them, they had no reason to suspect financial difficulty.

- **Budgeting.** The company had done no budgeting.

- **Customer- and product-profitability analysis.** The previous management had never done a customer- or product-profitability analysis.

- **Product lines.** Sampson sold paint under four brand names. It maintained a large variety of paint and stain colors, several purchased from outside sources, in inventory.

- **Pricing.** Following its historic patterns, Sampson raised prices only 2 to 3 percent per year throughout the 1970s, failing to keep up with inflation and rising petroleum prices.

- **Cost structure.** Sampson's paint formulas had not changed in 10 years. Most of it was of top quality and durability, while many of its competitors were producing lower-quality paint at lower cost.

- **Marketing.** During the past decade, consumer purchasing had accounted for an increasing portion of paint sales, while Sampson continued to emphasize direct selling to paint contractors.

Comparative Ratios

Genovese compiled the figures for 1980 (table 7.2), comparing Sampson with other paint manufacturing companies of similar size.

Table 7.2
Sampson Compared with Other Manufacturing Companies

	Sampson	Companies of Similar Size
Gross Profit Margin (% of sales)	22.5%	34.9%
Selling, General, and Administrative Expenses (% of sales)	32.9%	28.3%
Inventory Turn	5.7 x	6.8 x
Sales per Employee	$55,532	$88,100
Material Cost (% of sales)	71.4%	50.7%
Direct Labor Cost (% of sales)	7.0%	4.5%

The Company Turnaround

Buyer's Background

Frank Genovese believed he was well suited to own and manage a business. He started holding odd jobs at age 12 and worked his way through college. After earning his master of business administration degree, he turned down offers in banking to work for the Continental Group, a container manufacturer, because he wanted a position with the quickest possible opportunity for P&L responsibility. He became controller of the poorest-performing plant in the corrugated division in eight months and was instrumental in turning the unit around. Subsequently, he started a general business consulting practice in Coopers & Lybrand's Richmond office and helped an owner turn around a campground business. As he looked for the opportunity to buy and run his own company, Genovese established a list of 10 criteria (not ranked in order of importance):

- Proprietary product or service

- Poor management

- Poor operations compared to the industry

- Potential for improved profit through better operations

- Opportunity for price increases

- Good public reputation

- Established and growing market for product

- Inexpensive purchase price

- High quality products

- Competitive advantage

The Buyout

When Genovese was introduced to the Sampson sisters, he had substantial bargaining leverage. The company was beginning to lose money, and the sisters had neither a capable management team nor the ability to run the company themselves. Genovese, with his turnaround experience and vision, offered them the best opportunity to salvage value.

Given the company's disorganization, Genovese offered to purchase its net operating assets at a discount to book value. He paid $100,000 cash and financed the remainder with a subordinated seller's note in an amount equal to 37.5 percent of the net purchased assets and liabilities, subject to a minimum of $300,000 and a maximum of $400,000. Starting in April 1982, Genovese made quarterly payments that were the greater of $6,250 or 12.5 percent of cash flow (net income minus principal payments on other indebtedness). The final payment, including accrued interest and the remaining principal balance, was due in April 1994. The better the company performed, the faster Genovese would pay the previous owners. The note was subordinated to any additional debt of up to $1,000,000 required to finance the turnaround. To further facilitate the sale, the Sampson sisters retained ownership of the company's manufacturing plants, leasing them to Genovese until he had the cash to buy them.

Personnel
Upon assuming control, Genovese laid off one-third of the company staff and froze salaries. Funds were not available for severance pay. Employees who remained did not know about the company's financial difficulty, so Genovese explained where the company stood and what they might expect during the turnaround process. Over the following year, he hired a sales manager, industrial chemist, and vice president of manufacturing.

Pricing
In gradual increments, Genovese raised prices about 20 percent the first year and another 20 percent the second year. Because the company's prices had been so far under the market, it did not lose a single customer.

Vendor Negotiations
Genovese called every vendor to introduce himself as the new owner and to explain his payment plans. He said he did not have enough cash to pay them but was trying to raise additional financing and hoped to pay all of them in two or three months. Wanting Sampson to survive as a customer, all but one supplier agreed. That one, owed $6,000, hired a collection lawyer—for a fee of $2,000—to obtain the payment.

Genovese agreed to pay the invoice in full, over the period initially offered, and the vendor was out the $2,000 collection fee.

Working-Capital Reduction
A liquidator bought the remaining inventory of discontinued paint and stain lines, helping the company create $500,000 in working capital. This, combined with $1,000,000 in new bank debt, allowed Sampson Paint to pay its suppliers in full.

Capital Expenditures
Because mixers and grinders do not quickly deteriorate or become obsolete, relatively few capital expenditures were required during the turnaround period. Motors and pumps were routinely repaired or replaced. Two new forklift trucks and a panel truck were purchased.

Production
With the help of the new vice president of manufacturing and the new industrial chemist, Genovese set out to improve production efficiency. Manufacturing locations were consolidated, cleaned, and repaired. The production team began an ongoing effort to reduce raw material and overhead costs and to develop master scheduling and standard costing systems.

Marketing
Genovese consolidated four product lines into one, under the Sampson brand name. He developed a new corporate logo, new product packaging, and a promotion and advertising program. He began to work on improving the customer mix and channels of distribution.

Financial Reporting and Controls
When Genovese assumed control of the company, the financial staff consisted of an accountant, with the title of assistant controller, and an accounts receivable person. After a year, Genovese promoted the assistant controller to controller but continued to spend one-third of his time developing the company's reporting and control systems. Genovese cleaned up past-due accounts payable and improved credit-approval and accounts-receivable collection procedures. He then implemented daily sales reports and monthly financial statements. Over the

next two years, he established a budgeting system, improved and consolidated the purchasing function, developed an inventory control system, and reduced the level of inventory. Genovese and the controller worked together to install a new computer system and profit-center and accountability systems.

Because Genovese did not view the controller as a planner or strategic thinker, Genovese himself remained CFO and retained responsibility for banking relationships. Because he had to hire a head of manufacturing (an area in which he did not have expertise), he could not afford to hire a CFO as well. He therefore taught the controller how to close the books efficiently by 10 days after the end of the month, how to prepare financial statements, how all the financial statements tied together, and how to prepare budgets. After the second year, Genovese spent about 20 percent of his time as CFO and hired an accounts-payable employee. A year later, he hired a purchasing specialist.

Personnel Management and Employee Benefits
Immediately after the purchase, Genovese replaced an unusually generous health-insurance plan with a more modest, standard plan. During 1981, his first full year as owner, Genovese established a personnel system and evaluated employee-benefit packages to provide reasonable benefits at reduced cost.

Sale of the Company
By his fourth year, Genovese had implemented most of his improvements and the company was essentially turned around. But having completed his self-appointed task, he began to feel less challenged and searched for a buyer. A manufacturer of paint colorants that wanted to vertically integrate purchased the company. The Sampson brand survives today.

Key Findings

Commenting on what it takes to be a turnaround manager, Genovese says, "If you cannot live with yourself when you have to fire people or owe large amounts of debt, or if you are not comfortable making hundreds of instant decisions every day that could be right or wrong, then turnarounds are not for you." He cites the following lessons learned from his experience in buying, turning around, and selling Sampson Paint:

- Don't trust the numbers. Learn the truth through due diligence.

- Don't overpay. Genovese usually would not recommend paying more than book value, particularly for a company that needs to be turned around. He comments on the risk-reward relationship in a turnaround. If one buys for the right price, the rewards can be enormous. A $50,000 investment in Sampson Paint in year one was worth $1,400,000 in year four.

- Buy a company that has a quality reputation. The internal operations that support such a reputation are easier to fix than market perception.

8

Retailing Sector

Ames Department Stores, Inc.

Ames Department Stores, Inc., the fourth-largest national discounter and the largest regional discounter in the United States, had to declare bankruptcy after it made an ill-advised acquisition and lost sight of its core customer. A new CEO and his team accomplished the turnaround by refocusing on the core customer and establishing a market niche that allowed Ames' stores to coexist with the larger Wal-Mart and K-Mart stores.

Background

Ames began operations in 1958, opening a store in the former Ames Worsted Textile Company building in Southbridge, Massachusetts. The company's business strategy was to bring discounting to the smaller towns and rural areas of the northeast United States. By 1974, it had 46 stores with annual sales of nearly $80 million. At that time, Ames began acquiring other retailers and store sites of failed retailers such as W. T. Grant. By 1983, the company had 160 stores. Its strategy of serving a largely rural customer base in smaller, relatively uncompetitive markets resulted in consistently good performance. Between 1970 and 1985, Ames achieved a 15-year compound annual growth rate of 23 percent in sales and 25 percent in net earnings. Its return on equity averaged more than 20 percent during this period.

Causes of Financial Difficulty

Several factors contributed to the company's financial difficulties. First, Ames lost sight of its traditional core customers by changing its merchandising strategy. In addition, it made an ill-advised acquisition that placed it under a huge financial strain.

G. C. Murphy Acquisition

Ames grew initially by gaining financial strength through good performance. In 1985, it acquired G. C. Murphy Company, a Pennsylvania-based operator of discount and variety stores. This acquisition doubled the company's sales and number of stores, expanded its geographic presence in the Northeast, and provided access to more competitive, urban areas. Ames' consistent earnings growth ended in fiscal 1986—the first full year following the G. C. Murphy acquisition—when it reported a 33 percent decline in net income caused in part by substantial inventory losses from employee theft. In 1987, the company increased operating expenses by more than $5 million for controls to reduce the inventory shrinkage rate from 2.7 percent to 1.6 percent, which was still above the industry average of 1.2 percent.

By 1988, Ames had 8,000 employees and operated 348 discount department stores and 161 other self-service stores under the Ames, G. C. Murphy, and Murphy's Marts names in 20 northeast and mid-Atlantic states and the District of Columbia. The stores offered apparel, housewares, home furnishings, appliances, hardware, and garden and auto supplies. Most also had jewelry and leased shoe departments. The company had plans for expansion into other product lines such as arts and crafts, specialty items, and even discount office supplies. Ames continued to target its traditional customer base of housewives and blue-collar workers, but it had to spend more on marketing in urban areas, where it competed with other discount stores. The company also began its first television advertising campaign.

Zayre Acquisition

In 1988, Ames doubled its size again by acquiring 392 Zayre discount stores from Zayre Corporation, now known as the TJX Companies. Ames had financed its previous acquisitions mostly with internally generated funds, but it financed the Zayre acquisition largely with debt. Ames paid approximately $443 million in cash, gave Zayre a $200 million subordinated promissory note, and issued to Zayre 400,000 shares of 6 percent cumulative convertible senior-preferred stock with a stated value of $200 million.

To finance the acquisition, Ames and its subsidiaries entered into a $900 million credit agreement with a group of banks led by Citibank. The credit agreement consisted of a $425 million term loan and a $475 million revolving-credit facility. Citibank received from Ames and its subsidiaries various guarantees of the obligations of other entities within the Ames group, pledges of the stock of Ames' first- and second-tier subsidiaries, and pledges of intercompany indebtedness owed to the parent by its subsidiaries.

Ames later attempted to reduce and stretch out its debt service. In April 1989, it refinanced part of the Citibank term loan with $38.5 million in guaranteed first-mortgage notes of three subsidiaries. In May 1989, it refinanced the $200 million subordinated promissory note with $200 million in senior-subordinated-reset notes due in 1999. In September 1989, it sold 130 G. C. Murphy stores and 25 Bargain World stores to E-II Holdings, Inc., parent of the McCrory Variety Stores, for $78 million. (The G. C. Murphy stores were considerably smaller than most of the Ames stores and therefore had not been a good merchandising fit.) In October 1989, Ames refinanced more of the Citibank term loan with $155 million in $7^1/_2$ percent convertible subordinated debentures due in 2014.

Bankruptcy Filing

Ames' increased debt burden and the cost of converting Zayre stores to Ames stores was compounded by the failure of sales—particularly in the Zayre stores—to meet unrealistic projections made at the time of the acquisition. The stores became overstocked with seasonal merchandise, and cash from operations decreased, straining the company's liquidity and forcing it to file for Chapter 11 protection on April 25, 1990. The bankruptcy surprised vendors because management had not been candid with them about the company's deteriorating condition. Just days before the filing, one national-brand vendor was assured there would be no problems and shipped several million dollars' worth of merchandise.

Problems with Zayre

Zayre turned out to be a poor fit for Ames for two primary reasons. First, Zayre was a bad retailing match. Even though Zayre and Ames both were discount stores, Zayre had a different target customer, product mix, and pricing strategy. Many of its stores were in high-density urban areas where Ames stores tended to be less successful.

Second, Zayre was in bad financial shape because of declining retail performance.

To compound its bad business decision, Ames significantly overpaid for what it received, assuming a huge debt burden. And both Ames' chairman and its investment-banking firm later were alleged to have had a conflict of interests in advocating the Zayre purchase.

The postacquisition integration was not smooth. In the 15 months following the acquisition, Zayre stores' sales were 12.5 percent below projections made at the time of the acquisition; the gross margin was 2.9 percentage points below projections. Ames had trouble integrating management information systems and was slow converting Zayre stores into Ames stores, partly because it was constrained by heavy debt. In the end, Ames closed about three-quarters of the 392 Zayre stores it acquired. It sold leases for about 30 stores in desirable locations and rejected the rest. The ability to reject leases was one of the benefits Ames realized from declaring bankruptcy.

The Company Turnaround

After Ames emerged from bankruptcy, a new management team restored its performance by refocusing on the company's traditional core customers and carving a viable niche in the increasingly competitive discount retail market.

Emergence from Bankruptcy

Ames' bankruptcy was slowed by the complexity of its debt and subsidiary structure. There were separate committees for creditors of the parent company and the subsidiaries, as well as committees for employees, bondholders, and bank lenders. Alliances among creditors constantly shifted. The lenders and other creditor constituencies, such as bondholders and unsecured creditors, argued over whether the bank debt was properly secured and whether it had priority over the other debt. There were arguments over whether Ames operated as one company or a consortium. Most of these issues were resolved out of court.

David H. Lissy, senior vice president, general counsel, and corporate secretary, describes the bankruptcy case as a process of trading back and forth among the creditor groups. In the end, the creditors tired of fighting. They concluded that they were never going to agree, that the litigation process was expensive, and that their best solution was to take a chance on Ames' revival. In the settlement, the common shareholders lost their investment, the bondholders received little or nothing, the unsecured creditors received about 10 cents on the dollar, and the commercial bank lenders came close to being made whole. The prepetition bank group funded the postpetition revolver for about two years before a new bank group took over.

In Lissy's opinion, a key question for a company in bankruptcy is whether it pares down enough. It is human nature for management to believe that with a little more effort it can turn around a poorly performing store. For example, because results failed to improve for several stores in the Rochester, New York, area, Ames closed them about two years after emerging from bankruptcy. It would have been less expensive to recognize earlier that those stores were problems and close them while the company was still under the protection of bankruptcy law.

Living Through Bankruptcy

Lissy observes that bankruptcy, an unpleasant, thoroughly consuming experience, allows participants little time for anything else. Management should not casually decide to file because it thinks bankruptcy will solve some of its problems. A company in bankruptcy is not free to do anything on its own. Someone always looks over management's shoulders, second-guessing every decision. And the second-guessers often come from different directions because they are fighting with each other. Even if management and staff concentrate on running the business while specialists work on the bankruptcy, the business cannot run normally. The court must approve every major expenditure. If management makes a case for a systems upgrade, for example, creditors must decide whether the expenditure will help the company survive or reduce the amount they can recover in a liquidation.

Wertheim Suit

In 1992, Ames filed a suit against Wertheim Schroder & Co., the investment banking firm that arranged the Zayre acquisition, and James A. Harmon, who had served as chairman of both Wertheim Schroder and Ames. The suit alleged that the defendants had breached their fiduciary duty to Ames, had a conflict of interests in advocating the Zayre acquisition, and were motivated to recommend the Zayre purchase because of substantial fees Wertheim would earn from the transaction and subsequent debt offerings and refinancings. It further alleged that the Ames board of directors received unrealistic financial projections for Zayre and that no one in Ames' finance function except the CFO was involved in analyzing the Zayre acquisition. Finally, the suit alleged that Bear Stearns, the investment banking firm, had only 24 hours to render a fairness opinion before the board was scheduled to vote on the acquisition, was instructed to rely only on projections provided by a Wertheim model, and was precluded from speaking to Zayre's management. According to Ames, both Wertheim and Drexel Burnham Lambert (another investment bank) had valued the Zayre discount division for substantially less than Ames paid. Ames alleged that Harmon had pressured two dissenting directors, including one of the founders, who had preceded him as chairman. When Ames' board of directors voted on the transaction, each member was asked to provide his opinion and to disclose his vote. The two directors most likely to dissent were deliberately scheduled to speak last. The suit was settled in Ames' favor for $19 million.

Merchandising Strategy

Ames began to lose focus in 1985, at the time of the G. C. Murphy acquisition. The 1988 Zayre acquisition represented a flagrant disregard for the merchandising strategy and customer focus responsible for Ames' earlier success. Then, two successive CEOs tried new, ultimately unsuccessful merchandising strategies. From 1990 to 1992, when Ames was under Chapter 11 protection, Stephen L. Pistner tried to abandon the traditional discount-store format and established seven specialty stores under one roof linked by a home-and-leisure theme. Pistner was succeeded as CEO by CFO Peter Thorner. Between 1992 and 1994, Thorner tried a "narrow and deep" apparel strategy similar to that of The Gap stores, carrying fewer items in more sizes and colors, thus justifying a higher price with higher quality. Thorner's strength, as might be expected from a former CFO, was in financial restructuring and streamlining operations. He did not have a real vision for how Ames' merchandising strategy should evolve and therefore delegated most of that responsibility.

The essence of the Ames turnaround story is the way it carved a niche for itself under the leadership of Joseph R. Ettore. Ettore became president and CEO in 1994, replacing Thorner. He had previous experience as CEO with two other discounters, Stuarts Department Stores and Jamesway Corporation. Ettore describes retailing as a simple business: First, a company must decide who its customer is and use that profile as the basis for its strategy. Then it must assemble a unified team.

As he assessed Ames' strengths and weaknesses, Ettore noticed that home lines—including housewares, domestics, ready-to-assemble furniture, crafts, and home entertainment—were successful throughout the bankruptcy period, when customers were practically chased away. The reason for the success was that the merchandise appealed to Ames' core customers, working mothers with families and senior citizens with household incomes in the range of $25,000 to $35,000 per year. Ettore considers this market segment underserved; other discounters are raising their price points to attract middle-income customers who, they believe, have more spendable income. Ames customers have less spendable income and fewer stores in which they can afford to shop, but they still want nice things.

To Ettore, it made sense to apply to other lines, such as apparel, the retailing strategy that made home lines successful. He explains that a narrow-and-deep approach does not work in Ames' market. If a woman has only a few choices in knit tops, for instance, and everyone she knows shops in the same store, she fears she will, in Ettore's words, "see herself coming and going" in the same top. Ames' core customer prefers more choice.

After deciding the narrow-and-deep merchandising strategy was inappropriate, Ettore acted, canceling orders for merchandise he thought would not sell. That decision cost $19 million. He believes Ames could have been back in bankruptcy within six to eight months if it had not quickly changed its merchandising strategy.

To help satisfy the needs of the core customer looking for a variety of apparel, Ames embarked on its "special buy" program, purchasing less in advance and taking advantage of closeouts and overruns. The special buy program helps Ames benefit from both current trends and other people's mistakes and helps the company stay liquid. From Ames' central-Connecticut headquarters, its buyers can easily go to New York City several times a week to make opportunistic purchases. For example, a large retailer canceled 5,000 dozen rayon-blend, private-label sport pants. Ames bought the pants and sold them within two weeks at less than half the original retail price. This tactic works because Ames' customers are more interested in values than brands. Now, the only apparel items Ames buys far in advance are basics it knows will sell.

One important strategic issue is how to compete with larger discount chains. It is in direct competition with about 240 Wal-Marts and 175 K-Marts. Ames' stores average about 60,000 square feet. An average Wal-Mart or K-Mart is about 120,000 square feet and therefore has a wider selection in most departments. Ettore's strategy is not to compete head-on but to coexist. Many of Ames' customers prefer Wal-Mart for specific merchandise where it has a better selection but visit Ames stores more often because their smaller size makes shopping easier.

Recognizing that much of Ames' customer base is senior citizens with limited income, the company established a senior citizen discount program called "55 Gold," in 1995. Anyone 55 or older who applies for an identification card gets 10 percent off on Tuesdays, whether the merchandise is on sale or not. Tuesday used to be the worst sales day in the week; now it is the second best. Senior citizens regularly bring family members with them to take advantage of the discounts. With a new point-of-sale system and bar-coded membership cards, Ames captures information on what sells best to this customer segment and targets its merchandising accordingly.

Ames also does micro-marketing, tailoring a store's merchandise mix to its particular location and customer base. A store in a beach area, for example, carries bathing suits, towels, suntan lotion, and pails and shovels through Labor Day rather than trying to clear out that merchandise earlier, as most stores do. Stores in Hispanic neighborhoods feature Hispanic music and videos. Those in college towns offer apparel and supplies for students.

Ames designed its "A+ service" program, in which employees win awards, to encourage store associates to deal with customers in a friendly way. And Ettore sees the results in sales and customer comment cards. To help store managers and associates succeed in the A+ service program, the headquarters office had to provide prompt, friendly support in all aspects of operations giving quick responses to questions, providing good systems support, and making sure advertised items were in stock.

Ettore believes other regional retailers have failed not because they are regional but because they did not find a niche. Ames' answer was not to lower prices to meet Wal-Mart on easily compared items, such as Crest toothpaste. Ettore points out that once the shopper gets beyond those recognizable items, the larger retailers often have higher markups. For example, Ames tends to have thinner margins and better prices in apparel than Wal-Mart.

In Ettore's opinion, what Ames has done is not rocket science. Another retailer could have done the same thing, but Ames has a good management team executing its strategy. He quotes Denis T. Lemire, executive vice president of merchandising, who says, "This is nothing complicated; it's retailing 101. You give customers what they want, when they want it, at the price they are willing to pay, and that's what we're doing."

CFO's Role
In Ettore's opinion, Rolando de Aguiar, executive vice president and chief financial officer, not only has the requisite accounting and control skills, but is a visionary and a strategic thinker. His predecessor was a good accountant but lacked strategic dimension. Ettore says, "A CFO needs to help drive the everyday business with an eye toward where we are going to be next month, next year, five years from now—if we take these actions, here is where we are likely to be."

Ames was attractive to de Aguiar because Ettore and his merchandising colleagues had a strategy and needed a financial expert to integrate financial and operating disciplines. One of de Aguiar's priorities is to work with operating management to improve margins and thereby increase shareholder value.

SG&A Expenses
As of October 1998, Ames' selling, general, and administrative (SG&A) expenses were about $600 million, or 25 percent of sales. De Aguiar's objective at that time was to keep SG&A expenses at the same level while sales grew from $2.4 billion to about $2.6 billion, thereby reducing SG&A expenses to 23 percent of sales. Assuming that Ames' stock was selling at a price-earnings multiple of nine, such an expense reduction could cause its stock price to rise by about $20. Three-quarters of SG&A expense is in the stores. Reducing the staff by one full-time

equivalent per store could increase earnings per share by 40 cents. This type of analysis is useful for people in store operations, who are in a position to help reduce costs and who can realize the results of their efforts through stock options. In de Aguiar's opinion, an equity stake is a stronger motivator than a big salary or bonus.

Another way to reduce SG&A expenses was through supply-chain management and the effective use of technology. Ames is not trying to copy Wal-Mart's information systems but to use technology to manage its own store network and business strategy. Point-of-sale devices transmit sales of each stock-keeping unit (SKU) to Ames' headquarters every night, allowing buyers to check distribution center stock first thing in the morning and order replenishments, if necessary. That reduces the time from merchandise order to receipt in the stores and therefore improves Ames' trade terms. It also lets Ames reduce its inventory by ordering smaller quantities more frequently. The inventory burden thus shifts partly to the vendor.

Expansion Plans
Part of Ames' strategy to increase shareholder value has been to expand its store network from its current base of 19 contiguous states in the Northeast, mid-Atlantic, and Midwest. The company has a niche retailing strategy that clearly works with the right demographics and could expand to other areas. De Aguiar foresees a shakeout among second-tier retailers in which Ames could emerge a leader, growing by acquiring other chains. Ames plans to expand through contiguous states, facilitating distribution systems and name recognition, which calls for a rational march west and south. It would be premature, for example, for Ames to start doing business in Oregon today because its name is not yet known there; the company would incur the extra expense of either running a separate Oregon distribution center or transporting goods from an eastern distribution center. A contiguous expansion strategy should protect Ames from being "landlocked" in key connector states by a competitor that serves the same customer base.

Capital-Structure Strategy

As of October 1998, Ames had no long-term debt, and management had no desire for high leverage. However, de Aguiar believed that if the right acquisition opportunities arose, the company comfortably could carry about $750 million in debt. Ames does not pay dividends because it needs the cash to reinvest in growth and investors hold its stock for price appreciation.

Hills and Caldor Acquisitions

Ames agreed to buy Hills Stores Company in November 1998 and completed the merger at the end of the year. Given Ames' marketing and expansion strategies, this acquisition appeared to be particularly opportune. At the time of the acquisition, Hills operated 155 discount department stores in 12 states within or contiguous to Ames' geographic region. The Hills stores were of a similar size in communities with similar demographics and served a similar target customer. Ames thus increased its presence in five states and entered five new ones. After a review of Ames and Hills stores that operated in the same market areas, Ames decided to close only 10 stores. The cost of the acquisition was $330 million, which involved $130 million in cash, the purchase of $51 million in outstanding senior notes, and the assumption of $149 million of capitalized-leasehold and financing obligations. Bank facilities financed the cash portion.

Under turnkey agreements, Ames retained Gordon Brothers Retail Partners and the Nassi Group to operate all the acquired Hills stores and to conduct liquidation sales before remodeling or closing stores. Ames was delivered "empty boxes" after the liquidations. It had learned to keep its staff focused on core merchandising operations and to delegate the liquidation process to specialists.

As a result of the Hills acquisition, Ames became the fourth largest national discounter and the largest regional discounter in the United States. In March 1999, the company agreed to buy eight Connecticut stores, two Massachusetts stores, and a state-of-the-art distribution center in Massachusetts from Caldor Corporation, a long-troubled discount retailer winding up its operations under bankruptcy-court supervision.

Financial Communications

With the benefit of earnings that have increased every quarter for the past four years, positive cash flow, and moderate long-term debt, Ames is in a favorable position to intensify its financial communications. Ames has turned around, carved its own niche in the retailing market, and now coexists with Wal-Mart in many communities. Telling the story should help the company's price-earnings multiply.

Key Findings

- A retailer should never lose sight of its core customer.

- The finance function must support line management in implementing its basic business strategy.

- By delegating the liquidation of merchandise from the Hills Brothers stores to specialist firms, Ames could concentrate on the growth of core merchandising operations. The year-over-year increase in same-store sales was 7.3 percent in 1998 and 6.2 percent in 1999. This is a typical example illustrating the use of outside experts to avoid unproductive distraction of the company's management from the firm's core business.

Jos. A. Bank Clothiers, Inc.

When turnaround specialist Timothy Finley became CEO of Jos. A. Bank in 1990, he saw its biggest problem as heavy debt from an LBO, although the company had other operating and marketing problems as well. To avoid bankruptcy, Finley persuaded the bondholders to accept equity. Restoring Jos. A. Bank to profitability over the longer term required refocusing on the target customer and redefining the company's merchandising, sourcing, selling, store design, and store location strategies.

Background

The company traces its roots to Charles Bank, a Lithuanian immigrant tailor, his grandson Joseph Albert, who joined the family firm in 1898, and his great-grandson Howard, who led the firm into retailing. In 1981, the family sold its business to Quaker Oats Co., which then was building up a specialty retailing division. At that time, Jos. A. Bank had 10 stores, a catalog division, and a line of women's clothing. Quaker Oats expanded the business over the next five years to 29 stores with $112 million in sales. In 1986, Quaker Oats decided to exit specialty retailing and put Jos. A. Bank up for sale. The winning bidders were McKinley Holdings and Eli S. Jacobs, then owner of the Baltimore Orioles, who purchased the company through an LBO.

Jos. A. Bank is an upscale menswear retailer that sells through catalogs and retail stores in major metropolitan areas. Its strategy is to sell classic apparel with a slightly more contemporary look at prices 20 to 30 percent below topline competitors such as Brooks Brothers. Its merchandise is designed through the coordinated efforts of the company's merchandising and buying staffs, who work on an order-by-order basis with contract manufacturers. Management believes that effective sourcing through contract manufacturers is an important factor in helping it maintain its pricing advantage. Stores are located in a variety of urban and suburban locations convenient to the target customer—the professional man, age 25 to 55, who is well educated and relatively affluent. The company distributes about 11 million catalogs per year and has a database of about 1 million prospects and customers who have purchased through its stores, catalogs, or Web site. Mailings are targeted to specific customers based on their buying histories.

Causes of Financial Difficulty

McKinley Holdings and Jacobs bought Jos. A. Bank in 1987 for a purchase price of $105 million and total costs of $120 million. They financed $96 million with high-yield bonds and bank loans. Institutional investors, mainly insurance companies and thrifts, bought $36 million in senior-subordinated notes yielding 13 percent and $20 million in subordinated debentures yielding 13.5 percent. A commercial bank provided $40 million at 1.5 percent over prime. The commercial bank took liens on the company's assets and, together with the bondholders, liens on the company's manufacturing subsidiary. McKinley Holdings and Jacobs received 18 percent of the common stock, high-yield bondholders received 36 percent, preferred shareholders received 18 percent, and Jos. A. Bank management received 10 percent.

The LBO was predicated on substantial growth, which was expected to justify 20 new stores over the next five years and a new corporate headquarters. A constant growth in sales volume was required just to meet interest obligations of $1 million per month. Instead, however, sales softened over the next two years. In May 1989, the company restructured for the first time. All shares of common stock were written off as worthless. The bondholders forgave $7 million in accrued interest and exchanged their old bonds for new ones. The principal-payment schedule was extended by one year, and interest was forgiven until June 1992 on the new subordinated notes and until June 1994 on the new subordinated debentures. The bondholders received all the company's preferred stock and the majority of its common stock for agreeing to the new payment structure. Jos. A. Bank's directors replaced most of senior management, including the CEO, in 1990.

The Company Turnaround

Jos. A. Bank was turned around through an out-of-court restructuring, a change in merchandising mix, a new promotion strategy, a switch to contract manufacturing, new inventory systems, and improved inventory and cost management.

New Management

Timothy Finley, a turnaround specialist who began his career as an accountant, was hired as the new CEO in 1990. In recent years he had acted as interim CEO in turning around or liquidating several other companies. As he began his new job, Finley acknowledged that the high level of debt was Jos. A. Bank's principal problem, but he also saw fundamental operating and marketing problems that would require further investigation. For example, product quality was inconsistent, so the market perception was no longer as positive. Some stores were too elaborate for the company's cost-conscious image, and in general there was not enough traffic in the stores.

Knowing that if a troubled business has the potential to recover, a case can be made to lenders and bondholders for restructuring its financing, Finley made developing a business strategy for the company to survive and grow his first priority. Debt holders are always better off with a going concern than with a company in bankruptcy. Part of Finley's challenge was to convince the bondholders that he needed a substantial marketing budget to implement his strategy.

Financial Restructuring

Finley did not have time to turn the company around before a second financial restructuring was required in early 1991. One of the LBO equity investors considered but rejected his lawyers' suggestion to make a $20 million equity investment to keep the company running and offer to settle with the bondholders at a discount. Finley finally convinced the bondholders, who included many of the prominent holders of high-yield debt at the time, that they had just two choices: liquidate the company or convert all of their holdings to equity. They chose to convert their holdings. Finley resisted pressure from lawyers to file for Chapter 11 protection because he did not believe that a company could be run effectively in bankruptcy.

In May 1991, the company completed a debt and capital restructuring. Under this restructuring, it issued a combination of new preferred stock and common stock in exchange for all outstanding preferred stock and common stock, senior-subordinated notes, and subordinated debentures issued in connection with the 1986 LBO. The restructuring also created JAB Holdings, Inc. (JABH), a Delaware corporation. JABH issued $47.4 million aggregate principal amount of 8 percent secured notes due December 31, 1998, to the company's former debt holders. There were no cash proceeds from the issuance of the notes. During its existence, JABH had no operations and did not incur any costs on behalf of the company. As a result of this restructuring, JABH became the holder of 90 percent of the company's common stock.

A commercial bank made a $28 million revolving credit available. Finley personally opened a $2 million standby letter of credit in the company's favor to provide financing beyond the bank's $28 million limit. Because he had a good working relationship with the bank, the loan was assigned to the bank's commercial loan division rather than to its workout group. According to Finley, a secured lender can be a turnaround company's best friend. As long as the lender is confident that the loan will be repaid, it can have a good working relationship with the company.

As a final requirement to complete the restructuring, Finley and three other equity owners opened a $4 million standby letter of credit to indemnify Quaker Oats in case a tax-loss carryback was disallowed and insured against Quaker Oats' contingent liability through Lloyd's for a premium of about $250,000. The matter was settled after several months, and part of Finley's and the three other equity owners' premium was returned. Although several accountants and lawyers considered this contingent liability remote, refusing to protect against it was a potential deal-breaker in the negotiations with Quaker Oats, so it had to be resolved.

In January 1994, Jos. A. Bank and JABH completed a further capital restructuring. JABH provided JABH common stock to holders of its 8 percent secured notes in exchange for return of the notes. Concurrently, JABH entered into an exchange agreement with Jos. A. Bank. All existing shares of Bank's common stock were canceled. Bank's preferred stock and JABH common stock were converted to Bank's common stock. JABH was merged into the parent.

By 1994, Jos. A. Bank had become sufficiently profitable for a public stock offering. As a condition for approving the public offering, the board asked Finley to stay on as CEO. A five-year employment contract, renewable for successive one-year periods, was executed. It provided Finley with a base salary and a performance bonus based on company and personal performance goals. In May 1994, Jos. A. Bank sold 2 million shares of its common stock for $10 per share in connection with an initial registration with the SEC. The net proceeds of $17 million were used to pay off approximately $8 million in long-term debt and to open new stores.

Shortly after going public in 1994, the company ran into more financial difficulty because of poor sales in women's wear and a market shift toward more casual clothing; it incurred an operating loss of $15.1 million in 1995. In 1996 it was able to turn around, reporting operating income of $3.1 million. Management attributed the improvement to higher margins driven by strong suit sales; the elimination of unprofitable, lower-margin women's wear; a 9.3 percent increase in same-store sales of men's merchandise; lower operating expenses; and the closing of several unprofitable stores.

The company also restructured several leases, adjusted its manufacturing capacity, relocated three stores, and lowered its store selling expenses. Average inventory levels were $5.6 million lower than for the prior year because of better inventory management and product selection. In fiscal 1997, operating income increased to $6.6 million. During that year, management decided to eliminate its final manufacturing operation and focus only on retail activity. As a result, the company reported a $1.8 million after-tax charge related to discontinued operations.

Merchandise Mix

Important to Jos. A. Bank's turnaround were several changes in the merchandise mix. Finley found in 1990 that Jos. A. Bank's principal selling strength and its highest profit margins were in men's tailored clothing—suits, slacks, and sport coats. Reversing the course of the previous management, which had moved more toward casual clothing during the 1980s, Finley shifted the merchandising mix toward tailored clothing.

In the early 1990s, women's wear, such as skirts, suits, and blazers, accounted for 15 to 20 percent of the company's sales. The Bank family had sold women's clothing in its stores for years, partly to take advantage of extra plant capacity. But when styles changed, the women's clothing business changed with them, and the requirements for success no longer matched Jos. A. Bank's merchandising strengths. Also, women could sell men's clothing in the company's stores, but it was more difficult for men to sell women's clothing. Management decided to discontinue women's wear and liquidate the inventory. Most of the space that had been devoted to women's wear was used for the increasingly important men's business-dress casual clothing. The shift toward more casual men's business clothing became apparent around 1995. Business-dress casual clothing now accounts for about 15 percent of sales.

Promotions and Inventory Management

Shortly after coming on board in 1990, Finley decided that price promotions would be a central element in Jos. A. Bank's sales strategy. Price promotions helped the company reverse a declining trend in same-store sales over the next year. It was a critical decision because once a company starts doing price promotions, the market expects it to continue. Over the past eight years, a substantial part of Jos. A. Bank's sales have been in response to special discounts offered through catalogs and radio and television advertisements. The company has $199-suit sales; end-of-season clearance sales; wardrobe sales, in which a customer buying a certain amount of merchandise receives an additional amount free; and trade-in sales, in which a customer receives a fixed amount off the purchase price of a suit by "trading in" an old suit, which the company donates to charity. Hand in hand with price promotions, inventory management was a high priority. If an item didn't move, it was quickly marked down. If necessary, the company published a clearance catalog once or twice a year to clear out excess inventory.

Information Systems
Between 1991 and 1994, the company replaced virtually all of its management information systems with updated technology. The new systems provide for automatic stock replenishment and distribution, integrated accounts-payable and general-ledger maintenance, purchase-order management, forecasting and planning, human-resource and payroll administration, and extensive management reporting capabilities. In 1993, a new mail-order system was installed and integrated into the merchandising system and later into the warehouse-management system, also installed that year.

Manufacturing
Management found that the company could not manufacture its own clothing in the United States at a competitive cost, so it shut down and sold all of its plants. Except for two name brands of shoes, Cole Haan and Allen Edmonds, the company buys all of its merchandise from contract manufacturers, many of which are overseas.

Cost Structure
Sales and marketing expenses were reduced from 37 percent of sales in 1995 to 33 percent in 1996 and remained constant over the next several years. During that period, general and administrative expenses remained between 10 and 11 percent of sales. The company still has relatively high sales and marketing expenses compared with other retailers because it is still opening new stores and increasing its customer base through catalog and other promotions. It can justify high

sales and marketing expenses by relatively high margins and a $200 average ticket price on merchandise sold.

Store Design and Expansion

The company has developed a standard store design that balances its quality and value images. Store sizes had averaged 8,200 square feet, but now the new prototype is about 4,000 square feet. Selling activities occupy 80 percent of the floor space, and the remainder is for support functions, such as tailoring and the stockroom. There are plans to open new stores and relocate existing ones over the next several years.

Internet Sales

The company's success with catalogs made the development of online selling a natural move. Sales over the Internet began in August 1998. By early 1999, hits to the Web site had grown to 14,000 per month.

Store Sales Staff

Depending on their size, stores normally employ five to 25 full-time sales associates. Each store has a store manager and two or three department managers who are also sales associates. Store managers receive a base salary and a bonus based on achievement of targeted quarterly profit goals, and they also are required to meet sales quotas. Sales associates receive a base salary against a commission.

Management attributes part of the company's success to its customer-service policies. Sales associates assist customers in merchandise selection and wardrobe coordination, thereby encouraging multiple purchases. They seek to develop one-on-one relationships with customers. Sales associates maintain personal business planners containing information on customers' sizes, favorite styles, and colors, and they call customers when new items arrive or when special promotions are beginning.

Role of Finance Function

Finance professionals on Finley's management team manage the business on the basis of key performance indicators such as store-operating costs, store-opening costs, margins on products, quality inventory (measured in percentage of returns from customers and returns to contract manufacturers), and year-to-year same-store sales growth.

A lower priority for finance professionals is financial engineering expertise, which can be hired at any time.

Cost of Financial Difficulty

Because the bondholders hired financial advisors during the restructurings, the company had to retain its own advisors at considerable cost. However, this was a small expense compared to a Chapter 11 filing. Finley believes that his focus on turning operations around and avoiding bankruptcy saved the company huge financial-distress costs.

Surviving the Turnaround

Finley survived the stress of the turnaround partly because he had been through many other turnarounds and workouts. His philosophy is that a turnaround specialist starts in a new assignment with nothing but upside potential because many people don't expect the turnaround to work. But he recognizes the hardship on younger staff members who may have growing families and mortgages. He has learned the importance of keeping people informed but not with all the details of workout negotiations. Finley took care of those details with the help of a workout specialist who had the experience and patience to deal with the lawyers. Finley told other people to concentrate on their normal responsibilities in running day-to-day operations. He said "If we have a good business plan and we make money, someone will finance it."

Key Findings

Finley highlights the following observations:

- Most LBOs in the late 1980s were predicated on inflation exceeding true interest costs. But at the end of the decade, the reverse occurred. When true interest costs exceed inflation, it is difficult for a company to earn its way out of a highly leveraged financing, particularly in a capital-intensive industry. At the time of the LBO, Jos. A. Bank was more capital intensive than it is today because it still owned and operated manufacturing facilities.

- Managements of many companies in trouble spend too much time deciding whether to file for Chapter 11 protection and not enough time on their reorganization and recovery plans.

- Filing for Chapter 11 protection should be avoided if at all possible because the process requires huge legal fees and delays the company's turnaround. Bankruptcy lawyers' concerns have little to do with turning a company around. An exception may be a prepackaged bankruptcy designed to clean the balance sheet of specific liabilities.

- Workout details should be delegated to specialists, allowing others to run the business.

- A secured lender can be a company's friend in a workout. If the secured lender is confident that the loan will be repaid, the lender and the borrower can have a good relationship.

- Boards of directors of troubled companies sometimes are reluctant to incur marketing expenses. However, if Finley had not convinced the board of the need for a substantial marketing budget, he could not have turned Jos. A. Bank around.

Edison Brothers

Edison Brothers was a low-end, private-brand operator of mall-based stores with a retailing strategy geared to price points. In the late 1980s, this once-stodgy group of chain stores targeted trendy young clothing for young men as a growth area. It overexpanded and suffered from a glut of mall-based stores and a shift in consumer tastes toward more expensive name-brand merchandise. The company filed for bankruptcy in 1995 and reemerged in 1997, making creditors whole. Despite efforts to improve merchandising and systems, it faced heavy competition from better-known stores after emerging from bankruptcy and filed for Chapter 11 protection again in March 1999. At that time, it began an effort to sell its store chains and liquidate its remaining operations, a process that was largely completed by summer 1999. This case study illustrates a failing retailing strategy, the nature of intercreditor issues, and how growing enterprise value during a bankruptcy can help a company pay creditors a high percentage of their claims.

Background

Edison Brothers was a St. Louis-based retailer of clothing and shoes. The company operated mall-based concept stores. In menswear it had five store banners: J. Riggings, Jeans West, Oaktree, Zeidler & Zeidler, and Repp Ltd. Big & Tall. Each sold private-brand merchandise to a different market niche. The company's marketing strategy was based on price points. If a pair of Levi's 501 jeans sold for $27, management might decide on a price point of $20 for J. Riggings jeans and then contract overseas to have them manufactured at $5 per pair. Slow-moving merchandise was discounted until it was sold; about 70 percent was sold at less than its original price.

Five sons of an immigrant Latvian merchant founded the company in 1922. In the 1980s, the Edison family owned one-third of the company's stock directly or through trusts. At that time, Edison Brothers had a staid image appealing to over-40 consumers. About 60 percent of its stores sold footwear. An attempt to develop a women's wear business had been unsuccessful.

In 1987, Andrew Newman, a grandson of one of the founders, succeeded his uncle, Julian Edison, as CEO. Newman and Martin Sneider, a Harvard Business School classmate, engineered a turnaround over the next several years. Following a restructuring charge and a resulting loss of $12 million in 1987, the company earned $36 million in 1988 and $57 million in 1989. Between 1988 and 1991, management invested $310 million in store expansion, 50 percent more than capital expenditures for the previous four years. It targeted menswear for growth, particularly the fashion-conscious teenage and young-adult segment of that market.

But the company also diversified into other types of mall-based retailing. In 1989, Edison Brothers bought an 80 percent interest in a mall-based, upscale restaurant and entertainment chain called Dave & Buster's, which featured a combination of restaurants, bars, and a variety of video and other games under one roof. Units were 30,000 to 70,000 square feet and cost an average of $11 million to build.

By the early 1990s, Edison Brothers had become the nation's largest mall-based retailer. It had 2,600 stores in all 50 states, Puerto Rico, the Virgin Islands, Canada, and Mexico. It operated seven apparel chains, three footwear chains, and 100 family entertainment centers in both upscale and moderate-price malls.

Earnings began to decline in 1993. Edison Brothers started to have trouble moving its merchandise, even after markdowns. One of the problems was that as the economy improved in the mid-1990s, consumers moved to higher-priced name brands such as Levi's and Nautica. Anchor stores in malls continued to do well, but smaller ancillary stores with lesser-known banners had problems.

In early 1995, Alan Miller, who had been responsible for the footwear business, succeeded Newman. Miller was the first nonfamily member to become CEO. Miller hired a new CFO, David Cooper, who had worked as a financial officer for David Murdock.

In April 1995, Edison Brothers filed a shelf registration with the SEC for up to $250 million in possible future debt or stock offerings. Standard & Poor's (S&P) assigned a BB+ senior-unsecured, and a BB—subordinated-debt rating to the filing and downgraded the company's commercial-paper rating from A—2 to B. S&P cited a high level of business risk related to the company's focus on apparel for young adults, an unpredictable consumer group. S&P also was concerned that the company's recent decline in earnings might not be reversed in the near term. Moody's took similar rating actions but noted that Edison Brothers' cash flow remained solid, most likely allowing the company to finance future capital expenditures with internally generated funds.

Edison Brothers started to lose money during 1995. Losses put the company in violation of its loan covenants. As a result, its $225 million of long-term debt was reclassified as short term, raising total short-term debt from $131 million to $356 million. Because of the covenant violations, factors stopped financing new shipments of merchandise. In May 1995, Edison Brothers cut its quarterly dividend from 31 cents to 11 cents per share, reducing the annual payout by $18 million. In August, the dividend was omitted altogether. In June 1995, Edison Brothers spun off Dave & Buster's to its shareholders. The chain had earned $2.4 million on sales of $49 million in 1994, but the high cost of new units had become a drain on the parent company's resources.

Miller and Cooper approached their bank lenders and institutional note holders for default waivers on $300 million existing debt and commitments for an additional $300 million to order inventory for the 1995 Christmas selling season and attempt an out-of-court restructuring. The existing lenders were not willing to extend new loans. Instead, they allowed Edison Brothers to enter into a new $75 million senior-secured facility with Bank of America Business Credit in exchange for an interest-rate increase on $356 million total debt from about 7.5 to 9.5 percent, a one-time forbearance fee of $5 million, and agreement to make a $25 million amortization payment after Christmas.

Miller planned to get rid of about 250 stores. However, according to an October 1995 *Forbes* article, retailing analyst Philip Abbenhaus of Stifel, Nicolaus & Co., the St. Louis-based brokerage firm, claimed that Edison Brothers needed to close as many as 750 stores to regain its financial footing.

Bankruptcy Filing
In November 1995, Edison Brothers filed for protection under Chapter 11 for several reasons: the pre-Christmas selling season up to that point had lower-than-expected results; management anticipated having difficulty making the forthcoming $25 million loan amortization payment; some vendors were not extending trade credit; and, finally, bankruptcy protection would help the company terminate store leases.

Corporate and Liability Structure
At the time of filing, Edison Brothers' corporate and liability structures were both complex. There were 80 legal entities. Liabilities of $548 million consisted of $22 million senior-secured revolving-credit-facility loans, $150 million unsecured senior notes, a $125 million unsecured revolving-credit facility, $105 million liability under letters of credit opened to import merchandise, $81 million unsecured short-term demand notes, and $65 million trade debt.

Creditors' Committee
Early in 1996, the Creditors' Committee was formed. Its members were representatives from three banks, a representative from one insurance company, two trade creditors, and one landlord. The appointment of a landlord to the committee was considered unusual at this time because landlords have different types of claims that are usually difficult to quantify in comparison with other creditors. Given the diversity of the committee, its members were uncertain as to how well they could function as a unit. They wondered whether the group could agree on a relatively simple capital structure in which all creditors would be unsecured and *pari passu*. (Credit claims that are *pari passu* have equal financial footing.)

Import Letters of Credit

One St. Louis bank represented on the committee had issued all of Edison Brothers' import letters of credit. An import letter of credit is a direct extension of credit to the importer. Once shipping and other documents required by the letter of credit have been sent by the overseas exporter's bank to the importer's bank, examined, and found to be in compliance with the terms of the letter of credit, the importer is obligated to pay. There were issues related to perfection of security interests and presentment of letter-of-credit documents between Edison Brothers and the St. Louis bank. If Edison Brothers filed for bankruptcy while goods were on the high seas, there was some question about who owned the goods—the overseas exporter's bank would have already examined the letter-of-credit documents and charged the U.S. bank that opened the import letter of credit on Edison Brothers' behalf.

Also, there was some question whether Edison Brothers' bank had a security interest in the goods or the goods belonged to the general creditors. If there was a discrepancy in the documents, meaning that they did not comply with the letter of credit, the importer was not obligated to pay. If a bank, when examining the documents, overlooked a discrepancy and paid the foreign exporter's bank, the importer might not have been liable to reimburse the bank. A discrepancy could even have worked to the advantage of an importer such as Edison Brothers, short of cash and having difficulty moving its inventory.

Debtor-in-Possession Financing

Bank of America Business Credit provided a $200 million debtor-in-possession (DIP) facility. The company used $22 million of the facility to repay the $22 million senior-secured revolving-credit facility listed above. A $150 million subfacility was available for opening letters of credit. Because almost all the company's merchandise was imported, it needed the ability to open import letters of credit to keep operating.

Reclamation Program

In early 1996, the company agreed with the Creditors' Committee on a global reclamation program for dividing available proceeds among trade creditors. Vendors were granted the option of a 100 percent administrative claim or immediate cash payment of 80 percent of their claims. Thus, they had to evaluate both their chances of receiving a full

100 percent and, if they did, how long they would have to wait. Of $6 million total reclamation claims, $4.5 million were paid under the discounted cash option.

David S. Kurtz, a partner of Skadden, Arps, Slate, Meagher & Flom, notes that trade vendors have become more sophisticated in withholding postpetition trade credit until reclamation claims are settled. This encourages a company to settle reclamation claims as soon as possible.

Store Closings
By spring 1996, Edison Brothers had closed 468 stores and raised $150 million in cash from liquidating inventory. This was at least evidence that management was acknowledging its problem, according to Richard Peterson, first vice president of Bank One. By summer 1996, the company closed the entire 138-store Zeidler & Zeidler chain, all stores in Mexico, and an additional 120 underperforming stores. In fall 1996, management closed an additional 142 stores, bringing total stores closed to about 900. An additional 23 stores were closed in early 1997.

Board of Directors
At the time Edison Brothers filed for Chapter 11 protection, its board consisted mostly of inside directors who were either Edison family members, large equity holders, or division managers. The board was mainly aligned with current equity holders. The Creditors' Committee tried to make the board members aware of how their fiduciary responsibilities had broadened to include all stakeholders when the company filed for bankruptcy. Following suggestions of the Creditors' Committee, the board appointed two new independent directors, and four existing board members did not stand for reelection at the spring 1996 shareholders' meeting.

Exclusivity
Bankruptcy law gives a company a six-month period of exclusivity to file a plan for reorganization with the court. Like many other companies, Edison Brothers sought a six-month extension. The Creditors' Committee supported the extension subject to the company's commitment to provide a 1996 operating plan by March 1996. The committee indicated its contingent support in a written motion to sensitize the

court to its insistence that the company emerge from Chapter 11 as soon as possible.

Sometimes companies try to extend their periods of exclusivity and bankruptcy to build up maximum value while under protection of bankruptcy law. Creditors may support or oppose those efforts, depending on how they expect a longer bankruptcy period to affect their claims. A company with good prospects for turnaround becomes more able to repay its creditors as it gains financial strength. On the other hand, creditors want their claims to be resolved as soon as possible before a company with poor prospects deteriorates even further.

In fall 1996, Edison Brothers sought an additional five-month extension—through February 1997—of its exclusive period. The Creditors' Committee objected for several reasons: The company by then had built up a cash reserve of $150 million. The Chapter 11 process is always expensive, eroding the assets available to creditors. There appeared to be nothing left to accomplish in this Chapter 11 reorganization. Finally, it seemed clear that the creditors would own the equity of the reorganized debtors. The court granted a "final" extension that required the company to deliver a long-term business plan by November 1, 1996.

Claims Trading
One of the major trends in the past five or six years has been the selling of impaired-credit claims by banks. Securities analysts who do not like to see nonperforming loans on their balance sheets have driven banks in this direction. At the same time, investors in distressed securities are becoming more prominent. Often these investors take simultaneous positions in a troubled company's equity, subordinated debt, and senior debt.

By fall 1996, many of Edison Brothers' original creditors had sold their claims to distressed-security investors. Bank members of the Creditors' Committee who sold their claims resigned. Three secondary buyers became *ad hoc* committee members. In time, secondary buyers became the primary economic force among the creditors.

Equity Committee
In spring 1996, the equity holders, who at that point were out of the money, tried to form an Equity Committee to act as a countervailing force to the Creditors' Committee. The bankruptcy court initially

denied the equity holders' motion to form a committee but indicated that it would reconsider such a motion later if warranted by Edison Brothers' financial performance. The shareholders unsuccessfully appealed the bankruptcy court's decision in the district court. In December 1996, the U.S. Trustee appointed the Equity Committee. Other parties did not object because by this time the company's equity potentially was moving into the money based on increased cash and improving projections. In early 1997, the Equity Committee challenged the security valuations of both the company and the Creditors' Committee. The Equity Committee claimed that the enterprise was being undervalued and that at proper values the equity holders would be entitled to distributions. Otherwise, the Equity Committee contended that the creditors would be paid more than in full.

Reorganization Plan

After filing its business plan, Edison Brothers' management began to negotiate a reorganization plan with the Creditors' Committee. There was a conflict between creditors, who benefited from lower valuations, and stockholders, who benefited from higher valuations. Creditors proposed terminating an overfunded pension plan to augment distributions, but there was a possibility of litigation from employees who stood to lose their coverage under the plan.

The Disclosure Statement was approved on June 30, 1997. The Reorganization Plan, effective September 26, 1997, contained a number of complex provisions to maximize value for the creditors and to garner support from all constituencies. The Creditors' Committee and the Equity Committee reached agreement on valuation of security and distribution of warrants and rights—offering protection to the equity holders. Ten million transferable rights were issued, one right per share of new common stock. The exercise price of $16.40 per right was designed to achieve an equity value of $164 million, which was considered the amount necessary to provide creditors with a 100 percent recovery. A right entitled its holder to one share of new common stock and an interest in D&B LLC (limited liability corporation), the spun-off corporate entity that owned Dave & Buster's. The exercise date for the rights was 30 days after the effective date of the Reorganization Plan.

The pension plan, which was overfunded by $48 million, was terminated at the request of the creditors, but termination approval procedures could not be concluded until after the company emerged from bankruptcy. The right to receive the overfunded amount was transferred to an LLC owned by the creditors. The distribution was made in early 1998.

The bankruptcy settlement placed Edison Brothers' real estate into two categories: property kept by Edison and property given to creditors as part of the settlement. The property kept by Edison included warehouses and rights to about 1,700 stores leased and operated by the company. The property given to creditors consisted of Edison Brothers' 434,000-square-foot corporate headquarters building in downtown St. Louis. The Creditors' Committee considered the headquarters building a valuable asset that should be monetized if possible to enhance recoveries; it feared, however, that the value of the building would not be maximized during a bankruptcy. It therefore created an LLC owned by the creditors. The building was transferred to the LLC on the effective date of the Reorganization Plan. The plan provided for Edison to enter into a lease with the LLC. According to a February 1999 article in the *St. Louis Business Journal,* EBS Building LLC, which originally was owned by about 1,500 Edison Brothers creditors, planned to put the building on the market during the first half of 1999. The expected selling price was about $30 million.

Dave & Buster's Spin-Off
Edison Brothers spun off its Dave & Buster's subsidiary to shareholders three months before filing for bankruptcy. Management had concluded that such a spin-off would help it concentrate on the company's core business and would not be considered a fraudulent conveyance (a transfer of assets that works to the detriment of creditors). As part of its due diligence, the Creditors' Committee reevaluated potential fraudulent conveyance issues. The company's board of directors appointed an independent board committee to review the spin-off. Ultimately, the Creditors' Committee and Edison Brothers' management agreed that claims related to Dave & Buster's should be transferred to Edison Brothers' creditors and pursued. The Creditors' Committee thus initiated a cause of action against those who had received Dave & Buster's

shares, the defendants, in the spin-off. The cause of action was transferred to an LLC owned by Edison Brothers' creditors and exercising rights as of the effective date of the Reorganization Plan. A public settlement was offered calling for the defendants to surrender $5.66 per Dave & Buster's share received. As of June 1998, $12 million had been collected with minimal litigation efforts. An LLC was established pursuant to the Reorganization Plan to prosecute a lawsuit and distribute future recoveries to Edison Brothers' creditors. In August 1998, Dave & Buster's, Inc., announced that it had agreed to pay $2.125 million to the LLC in full and final settlement of its claims.

Reexamination of the Business

While Edison Brothers was in bankruptcy, Miller reexamined the business, replacing part of the company's management team and retaining outside consultants. Customer surveys were taken in the stores. Store associates helped redesign their own jobs with more time on the sales floor and less in the back room. In some chains, the merchandise mix was narrowed and the quality level upgraded. The relatively successful Repp Big & Tall stores were upgraded with a wider selection of merchandise. But a large part of the company's focus continued to be the youth market, which management thought had significant growth potential. Management even opened a new chain during the bankruptcy period.

Information Systems

At the time Edison Brothers filed for Chapter 11 protection, it had aging and inconsistent information systems. The Y2K issue had not been addressed, and the company's merchandising and inventory system consisted of incompatible in-house developed applications running in different store chains. While in bankruptcy, the company received permission from the court and creditors to install new information systems. The first step was to install new merchandising, decision-support, and financial systems. The second step, planned for 1998–99, was to install distribution, payroll, and human resource systems. The new merchandising and inventory management systems were expected to show where the inventory of each stock-keeping unit (SKU) was and how fast it was selling. Management expected to use this information to improve the allocation of inventory and reduce markdowns. A chain could tailor its merchandise mix to each region so an item could be marked down just where it was not selling rather than across the chain. The merchandising and finance functions could share data on gross margins and chain performance.

New Management
In January 1998, Lawrence E. Honig was named Edison Brothers' chairman and CEO. He had been a senior executive with Federated Department Stores, May Department Stores Company, and Alliant Foodservice, Inc., one of the nation's largest wholesale food distributors. Under Honig, Edison Brothers started to include more brand names in its merchandise line, to broaden the appeal of its niche-market stores to more mainstream traffic, and to centralize some of the chains' marketing and merchandising decisions at company headquarters. The company tried to strengthen its relationships with vendors by better explaining to them what it was trying to accomplish in each chain. Strategic partnerships were formed with three companies: one that provides import services, a second that specializes in trend merchandising, and a third that works on store design and construction.

In 1998, 62 stores were closed, and the St. Louis headquarters staff was reduced from 700 to 450. In its third-quarter filing with the SEC, dated October 31, Edison Brothers warned that its continuation as a going concern depended on three factors: major improvement in profitability; no significant lessening of trade credit; and securing additional sources of liquidity, such as an increase in the advance rate under the company's credit facilities.

In December 1998, Edison Brothers announced its intention to sell the Repp By Mail Big and Tall Men's Catalog because it did not fit the company's overall strategy. Presumably, another reason was that this relatively strong operation could bring a good price. In January 1999, management announced that same-store sales had increased in December for the fifth straight month. Then financial results turned down again. Same-store sales declined 3.5 percent in January and 6.5 percent in February, when many other retailers reported gains.

Second Bankruptcy Filing

Citing severe competition and disappointing operating results, Edison Brothers filed for bankruptcy a second time on March 9, 1999. The company was having difficulty receiving shipments from its vendors. This in turn caused an inventory shortage, hurt sales, and led to a decline in gross margins. As a result, it was more difficult for Edison Brothers to hit financial targets, and fewer vendors were willing to ship goods.

From the outset, there were signs that the company might be liquidated rather than reorganized this time. Congress Financial Corporation and CIT Group Business credit provided $100 million DIP financing. It was mainly a refinancing of facilities they already had extended, but the new financing was only for a short term; it was scheduled to mature at the end of 1999. Only $1 million was "carved out" for professional and legal fees, far less than the amount that a reorganization would require.

With approval from the bankruptcy court, Edison Brothers entered into a plan to sell its clothing store chains either together or separately. Later in March, the company announced that it had retained two investment banking firms to solicit and evaluate offers to buy all or part of its store chains.

In April, Edison Brothers agreed to sell its Repp Big & Tall stores and its Repp By Mail catalog business for approximately $31.7 million to J. Baker, Inc., which operates a chain of 454 Casual Male Big & Tall Stores. Having received no acceptable offers for the purchase of J. Riggings, JW/Jeans West, and Wild Pair, the company sought bankruptcy court approval to close 664 stores in these chains and conduct merchandise liquidation sales. In late April, it solicited competitive bids from asset redeployment firms. The winner, Boston-based Gordon Brothers, agreed to purchase approximately $167 million worth of merchandise. That liquidation plan was partly amended in May when 285 JW/Jeans West, Coda, and J. Riggings stores were sold for $10.3 million to the Coda Acquisition Group, a private company.

Also in May, Edison Brothers agreed to sell its footwear operations in Puerto Rico to Novus Inc., for $7.2 million and to sell 200 of the 250 stores in its 5-7-9 junior apparel chain for $13.7 million to the owner of Brooklyn-based Rainbow Apparel. Edison Brothers also sold a distribution center in Princeton, Indiana, for $6.1 million. The company sought court approval to hire a realty firm to coordinate the sale of lease rights on 500 retail locations that it did not expect to sell to the buyers of its store chains.

Key Findings

The Edison Brothers case study illustrates two strategic problems:

- First, in the early 1990s, the company expanded too fast in too many formats. This was a time when the overall number of stores in the United States was outgrowing consumer demand.

- Second, because Edison Brothers was a lower-end, private-brand, price-point retailer, its stores and merchandise did not have a strong national brand identity and high-quality image. In the early 1990s, consumers were moving from lower-priced private brands to higher-priced name brands.

The study also illustrates some good tactical management decisions once the company ran into financial difficulty. The fast store closings helped bring the company through the first bankruptcy process. Improving financial performance during bankruptcy both strengthened the equity holders' claims and allowed debt holders almost complete recovery.

The Forzani Group, Ltd.

Background

The Forzani Group, Ltd., based in Calgary, Alberta, is the largest retailer of sporting goods in Canada, with about a 10 percent share of a C$5 billion market. John Forzani, an offensive lineman for the Canadian Football League's Calgary Stampeders in the late 1960s, started the company in 1974 with a C$9,000 investment and remains chairman and CEO today. When the company began, the sporting goods industry was run largely by athletes and had an informal, collegial atmosphere. By 1994 the Forzani Group operated 90 stores in western Canada under four banners: Sport Chek, Forzani's Locker Room, Jersey City, and RnR (Relaxed and Rugged). Despite its size, it retained a family-run, regional structure. That year, it earned C$2 million on sales of C$73 million.

Also that year, two U.S. "category-killer" sporting goods retailers, Sportmart and The Sports Authority, each announced plans to open 25 "big box," 50,000-square-foot stores in Canada. (A category killer is a large store that presents formidable competition because of its selection of merchandise in a particular category, such as sporting goods. A big box is a store in a very large, open space.)

Forzani responded to the competition with an expansion program to protect its territory. The company aggressively rolled out its own Sport Chek category-killer banner. At the same time, it continued to lease desirable real estate and planned to open 40 new stores.

Causes of Financial Difficulty

The Forzani Group reported a C$5 million loss on sales of C$345 million in fiscal 1995 (year ended February 28, 1995) and a C$33 million loss on sales of C$344 million in fiscal 1996. The losses were caused by the failure of the company's management infrastructure to keep up with Forzani's rapid growth.

The company had grown opportunistically without a strategic plan. As a result, it was trying to operate too many retailing concepts under too many banners. Also, some of the acquired companies had their own computer systems, making companywide purchasing and inventory management difficult. These problems were not life threatening, but they impaired earnings.

The biggest problems began in 1994, when John Forzani and his management team realized that the company could either remain a small regional player or become a major national player. To become a national retailer, the company had to increase its critical mass and improve its technology and business processes. Management decided to become a national player and tried to juggle all these issues simultaneously.

John Forzani sought outside professional advice on whether the company's homegrown management had the talent to take the company to the next level. He was told the existing management team could run a national retail chain and did not need to be augmented. In hindsight, he would realize that the essential retailing skill set was not there.

A consulting firm helped the company update its merchandising and retailing methods and its information and control systems. Working with the consultants, Forzani installed a new information system, providing management with decision-making capability on a par with the best retailers. While the new technology was excellent, the company did a poor job in training, parallel testing, and conversion. In particular, the conversion process from the old to the new inventory system was not properly mapped out. As a result, merchandise managers had no confidence in reports from the new system and overbought to protect themselves. Inventories, already a little heavy, increased by another 50 percent. The trade, however, still expected to be paid on time. Because inventory was not turning, a cash crunch developed.

In addition, Forzani's David-and-Goliath-like acquisition of Sports Experts tripled the number of its stores overnight, from about 90 to 270. Management could not run the company as it had in the past. Revenues and costs skyrocketed, but the savings from synergy had yet to be realized.

When Sportmart and The Sports Authority each announced plans to open 25 big-box stores in Canada, Forzani accelerated its strategic store-expansion program. As a result, store-opening costs and new store overhead costs were added to the already heavy new technology costs and the acquisition costs related to Sports Experts. Forzani did not secure long-term financing or equity to fund this expansion; it relied on working capital and cash flow.

Looking back, Robert Sartor, then executive vice president and CFO,* believes there were two clear warning signs of financial difficulty. First, inventory increased sharply, mainly because merchandisers were not confident in the information they had. Second, margins declined as inventory was liquidated to generate cash.

In February 1996, John Forzani sensed trouble, but management persuaded him to wait while things straightened themselves out. By August, he concluded that management was not going to turn the company around. He therefore hired a team from Deloitte & Touche to assess the situation.

---

*Since the time of the interviews for this case, Robert Sartor has been promoted to President, Business Support and Chief Financial Officer, and William Gregson has been promoted to President, Retail and Chief Operating Officer.

The Company Turnaround

The new CFO and head of retailing and merchandising turned the Forzani Group around through astutely managing cash flow; negotiating more favorable terms with suppliers, landlords, and other key constituents; consolidating store banners; reengineering the merchandise mix and store design; establishing incentive compensation for salespeople; improving information systems; reducing overhead; and paying close attention to KPIs.

New Top Management

The Deloitte team advised that both the retailing operations and financial management sides needed a higher level of talent. The team interviewed both Sartor and William D. Gregson, then executive vice president and chief operating officer—corporate retailing. The chairman let Sartor and Gregson review the company's books in detail and talk to each other privately before each decided whether to take on the challenge. They agreed that Forzani was fundamentally sound, with no irreparable structural problems.

Structural Issues

The most important structural issues were real estate, supplier relationships, and overhead. When Sartor and Gregson examined the company's real estate, they found that the stores were well located, with long-term leases at good rates. They saw that Forzani had favorable, 20-year relationships with key merchandise suppliers. Because of those long-standing relationships created by the previous management working directly with suppliers rather than using intermediaries, the largest suppliers were likely to offer some flexibility as Forzani worked through its financial difficulties. Finally, Sartor and Gregson estimated that the company could stem about half of its losses by chopping redundant overhead, most of which was caused by the company's failure to streamline, standardize, and integrate the operations of the retailers it acquired.

Cash-Flow Management

The Deloitte team saw that the business was consuming too much cash. It systematically set out to stop the bleeding, maximizing cash inflows and delaying every possible outflow. Sartor and Gregson assumed disbursement authority. Gregson was responsible for merchandise purchases and Sartor for everything else. Together, they squeezed expenses down in every way they could. They constantly prioritized. For example, Nike was paid to keep running shoes in stock before newspapers were paid for advertising. Sartor observes, "You can't tell managers in an organization to cut costs but still have 500 people with disbursement authority. We had to work seven days a week to manage the payments ourselves, but that's life. We learned what was going on around the company very quickly." He concedes that concentrating disbursement authority in this way would have been more difficult in a larger company.

Inventory and Product Mix

The first step to solve the inventory problem was to write down existing inventory, liquidate it, and convert it to cash as quickly as possible. But before trying to improve inventory management over the longer term, Sartor and Gregson realized they had to change the product mix.

The Forzani stores carried basically three types of merchandise: clothing, footwear, and hard goods, such as weights and exercise equipment. Before the turnaround, they carried too many slow-moving hard goods and their clothing and footwear assortment was too broad and shallow. The stores were trying unsuccessfully to be all things to all people. Management decided to narrow the product line. Instead of 25 squash racquets, for instance, the stores would carry 6, but those 6 always would be in stock, and the salespeople would know brand features exceedingly well. For the shoes, shorts, and warm-up suits they decided to carry, they would stock a full assortment of sizes and colors. Some categories of exercise equipment were dropped because of low margins and high competition from other stores. Equipment for fringe sports such as curling was discontinued; other offerings were narrowed.

Selling, General, and Administrative Expenses

In 1996, the year Sartor joined the company, SG&A expenses were 11 percent of sales. Based on his knowledge of other retailers' operating figures, Sartor believed no company could survive with that level of overhead. SG&A costs were reduced to 7 percent over the next year. Sartor expects they will reach a target of 5 percent of sales by fiscal 2001, a level that should put the company in the first quartile among top retailers.

The Board's Role

Sartor and Gregson worked closely with each other and held weekly teleconferences with the board of directors. The board was made up mainly of outsiders who had relevant skills to help the company—two had business turnaround experience and two were retailers. The critical decision the board faced was whether to help John Forzani bring in a new team and engineer a turnaround or to resign. To help it decide, the board hired an independent legal firm. Sartor believes members of a U.S. board would have been more likely to resign because of personal liability issues.

Cooperation from Key Constituents

Sartor, Gregson, and Forzani agreed and convinced the board that the company could be turned around without filing for court protection only if it could get its key constituents to believe in the new management team and its approach. The four key constituents were identified as suppliers, landlords, GE Capital, and middle managers.

The suppliers had to understand that Forzani needed their support to reengineer its balance sheet and product mix. Forzani needed to defer accounts payable currently due, and it needed suppliers to reopen their lines for new purchases. In return, Forzani's management promised to tell the suppliers when they would be paid for each new shipment. By establishing and adhering to payment schedules, the company slowly regained supplier confidence.

While the real estate portfolio was excellent, some stores were poor performers. Management met with the company's major landlords and made three requests. It asked for rent reductions on certain sites where sales could not sustain rental costs. To conserve cash, it asked for rent deferrals for six months, with all amounts to be repaid within three years. And it asked the landlords to let Forzani out of some sites where continued operations would constrain the turnaround. These difficult and complex negotiations illustrated the importance of both sides sharing the pain to make the restructuring work.

Six major landlords owned about two-thirds of the sites. All wanted to see Forzani remain a viable tenant. None wanted to see 150 sites go dark at once. Each landlord wanted to make sure it received as fair a settlement as the others. The interest-free, voluntary financial support suppliers and landlords provided amounted to about C$20 million.

Before Forzani ran into financial difficulty, GE Capital had committed to make available a three-year, C$75 million revolving credit facility secured by inventory and receivables. By 1996, however, Forzani was in violation of most of its covenants. Management explained to GE Capital how it had reduced operating costs and negotiated concessions from its trade creditors and suppliers. It requested that the covenants temporarily be relaxed and credit facilities extended through an over-advance, a credit extension beyond the maximum borrowing base defined by the lender's inventory- and receivable-based formula. Forzani received a C$8 million over-advance at an effective rate of prime plus 4 percent. Sartor describes GE Capital as tough but fair. He believes the flexibility GE Capital showed was critical to the turnaround and that Canadian banks would not have been as understanding.

Sartor and Gregson soon realized they could not achieve the turnaround by themselves. Furthermore, signs of difficulty might encourage excellent managers to leave. Sartor and Gregson were as frank as possible in outlining the turnaround plan, explaining to managers what they were trying to do and conveying their confidence that the turnaround would succeed. As a result, a great majority of managers stayed.

Concessions from trade creditors, landlords, and GE Capital gave Forzani five months to think about how to reengineer the balance sheet and merchandise mix and how to set new performance standards for store employees.

Reengineering the Merchandise Mix
Management redefined performance criteria. It evaluated what inventory turns might be expected for each product type and category and sought to define minimum acceptable margins. During this process, management could see (1) which products would and would not earn the required hurdle rate, (2) which were underinventoried, and (3) which were overinventoried.

The criteria for evaluating suppliers and their products changed. Three factors drive P&L and balance sheet liquidity in this business: the cost of merchandise, the real margin achieved after markdowns, and the length of time the merchandise stays on the shelf. Management would continue to buy at good prices, but it believed Forzani could earn more by achieving good margins and inventory turns than by squeezing every last dollar from its suppliers.

Reengineering the Stores

Management examined store performance, considering factors such as location, layout, and staffing. As it thought about store design, management realized Forzani was competing not just with other sporting-goods retailers but also with other leading retailers. To an increasing degree, consumers were going to stores such as The Gap rather than to sporting-goods stores to buy sweatsuits and other sportswear. Sartor and Gregson asked themselves why Forzani stores were becoming less relevant. They concluded that if Forzani remained just a sporting-goods supplier, it always would be a small company struggling with cyclicality. They decided that Forzani's product mix was inappropriate for more affluent consumers and that the stores appeared too "macho." The stores' look and merchandise mix had to be reengineered to be more "soft and rounded" to appeal more to women, who did more than 50 percent and influenced more than 80 percent of purchasing. Sartor says, "We realized we had stores built for teenagers, but it was Mom who was buying." Based on their new vision, Sartor and Gregson developed a template for the kind of employees it needed to run the stores.

Employees: Store Level

Seven months into the turnaround, Gregson changed the job descriptions and compensation scheme for store employees. He thought there were not enough people in the stores who knew the products and had a passion to sell them. Therefore, the time and budget devoted to ongoing training increased substantially. A new compensation scheme made each of the 4,000-plus commissioned salespeople entrepreneurs by paying them a modest hourly wage plus a commission for everything they sell. Store supervisors and managers are compensated partly on how well their store has performed compared to its plan. They also can see how all the store plans roll up into the company plan.

Consolidating Banners

By the close of fiscal 1999, Forzani had consolidated from 11 to 5 banners—two for company-owed stores and three for franchised stores. The company-owned store banners are Sport Chek—the 20,000- to 25,000-square-foot big-box stores—and Forzani's—the 4,000- to 7,000-square-foot, mall-based stores, primarily in Alberta. The other stores have been sold to independent operators or franchised.

Franchise operations let Forzani sell merchandise without having to manage the real estate and carry the inventory. Going forward, Forzani will have three franchise brands: Sports Experts, 6,000- to 8,000-square-foot, mall-based stores primarily in Ontario; Podium Sports, stores primarily in rural communities and small shopping centers in Quebec that carry a wide selection of sports equipment, footwear, clothing, and team sporting goods; and Zone Athletik, a new banner in Quebec selling athletic clothing and footwear in 2,500- to 3,000-square-foot stores. Forzani offers franchisees a full-service program, including marketing, advertising, buying, accounting, and human resources support. A loss prevention program and a franchise-training academy covering sales, merchandising, and store-level administrative functions are planned.

Key Performance Indicators

Before new management engineered the turnaround, Forzani had no KPIs. Now the company's management truly believes in the adage, "You manage what you measure." The KPIs are well defined and understood by the board and all levels of management. They include sales per square foot in the stores; the progression of sales per square foot in each store; units per transaction sold by each store employee; average size of transaction sold by each employee; sales per hour compared to compensation for each employee; and central costs—SG&A expenses.

Forzani uses top retailers such as The Gap and Eddie Bauer as benchmarks. To perform on the same level, it must continually set targets to improve the productivity of its real estate. Sales per square foot vary from store to store because of the quality of real estate and local competition. This is why progression in sales per square foot is important. But people measures are even more important than real estate measures. Thus, store employees are paid based on their individual sales productivity. On the basis of benchmarking with all publicly owned U.S. retailers, Sartor believes achieving a target of 5 percent for SG&A expenses, which includes all advertising expenses, would put Forzani in the top quartile. That requires running a tight shop regardless of how big the company gets and disposing of every noncore (i.e., nonretailing) asset. Except for a lean corporate headquarters in Calgary and one warehouse, Forzani leases its real estate.

Information Systems

Initially, the sponsor of the new management information system was the consulting firm that designed and sold it. When the consultants left, Gregson and his merchandising team assumed responsibility for the system and began an ultimately successful retraining effort. In retrospect, the process would have been smoother had management identified sooner who within the company would be responsible for system implementation and training, and when. Now that the computer system and software have been implemented companywide and people are trained to use it, Sartor believes Forzani has one of the best category-management information systems in the business. Management can monitor profitability and gross margins every day. SKUs can be moved around when there is excess inventory in one location and a shortage in another. Having been responsible for information technology as part of the finance function in other companies, Sartor observes that technology most often fails to fulfill expectations because of poor execution or sponsorship. There must be a champion who has a passion and a commitment to the new technology so that it can be implemented properly.

Equity Infusion

To strengthen its balance sheet, Forzani issued new equity in two tranches. The company raised C$17 million in an August 1997 special warrants issue to repair the balance sheet. It raised another C$17 million in a February 1998 special warrants issue to repay its secured-term credit facility and to reduce the balance on its revolving-credit facility. This financing improved its working capital position and provided capital for store renovation and expansion. The securities were sold mainly to a relatively small group of large institutional investors. The second offering was accomplished in just two days, including the "road show" presentations to the investors.

Capital Structure and Dividends

Sartor believes the optimal capital structure for a company such as Forzani is a 28 to 32 percent ratio of debt to total capitalization. This ratio is low enough as a target to allow for the cyclicality of the industry, seasonal inventory peaks, and financing provided by the trade. A lower leverage ratio means too much high-cost equity financing. Higher leverage puts the company at risk in the event of a competitive squeeze or market downturn. If Forzani had public debt, Sartor believes it would aim for a single-A credit rating. He would not want to drive up the company's leverage even for an opportune acquisition.

Forzani pays no dividends and has no plans to do so in the near future. Every penny earned is still used to reduce debt, solidify the balance sheet, or open new stores.

Acquisitions and Investments
Forzani has stringent rate-of-return criteria for acquisitions and investments and has recently rejected most proposals to purchase real estate or other sporting-goods retailers. Having consolidated and improved the management of its existing store network, Forzani's management does not feel compelled to expand through other large acquisitions, particularly if it has to pay premiums. Of the U.S. big-box retailers, both Sportmart and The Sports Authority have withdrawn from the Canadian market. Recently, many small, independent stores have failed. The site of a failed independent store provides Forzani an ideal opportunity to build and operate a new store according to its own carefully formulated store-design and staffing template.

Most Helpful Parties
Among the parties most helpful in the turnaround, Sartor cites John Forzani, the chairman; GE Capital; and the turnaround consulting firm. John Forzani was willing to recognize trouble at key points and take responsibility for remedies. He knew when he needed help. When he brought in a new management team, that developed a sensible recovery plan, he endorsed the plan and made sure no one interfered with its implementation. The lender, GE Capital, exhibited more flexibility than Canadian banks probably would have at the time. It did what it said it would every step of the way.

Conflicts Between Shareholders and Management
The principal conflicts between shareholders and management arose when the new management faced institutional shareholders that were holding Forzani stock at a substantial loss. Management presented those shareholders with its strategy for the turnaround, a well-thought-out business plan that capitalized on the company's strengths, which

gained the investors' confidence that management could fix the business and generate positive cash flow.

Taxation
The primary tax issue related to Forzani's turnaround is a tax-loss carry-forward that will extend through 2001.

Corporate Valuation
Sartor believes an astute investor looks primarily at cash flow and that earnings per share is a flawed number. Management looks at the value of Forzani in much the same way a buy-side analyst would. Free cash flow can be projected for two or three years, after which a growing perpetuity is used, and cash flows are discounted at the weighted average cost of capital. Sartor warns that the unexpected entry of new U.S. competitors could create a price war and undermine those projections.

In building shareholder value, Sartor believes a company such as Forzani must balance growth with profitability. Too often he has seen retailers focus mainly on growth. They do not appreciate that sustaining rapid sales growth requires heavy ongoing capital expenditures, which penalize the ongoing profitability of the business. Sometimes they would do better trying to increase returns on their existing assets.

Sartor believes Forzani's stock can achieve a multiple premium in the market by generating high-quality free cash flow compared with alternative investment opportunities and by taking advantage of market consolidation to build market share. He is not opposed to sales growth, but has clear investment parameters concerning cash invested, cash return, and payback, which govern how that sales growth will be achieved. He believes internal investment measures such as economic value added can be useful, but outside investors must understand how management uses them.

Reasons Not to File for Court Protection
Forzani's motives in avoiding the bankruptcy process in Canada are fundamentally the same as they would have been in the United States. First, the bankruptcy process is hugely expensive; tens of millions of dollars must be paid to accountants, lawyers, and consultants. Second, management loses control of the process; it is no longer able to make its

own decisions, put its own reputation on the line, and implement the turnaround. Third, there are too many constituents at the table, and not all are on an equal footing. Investors in distressed securities and other claims enter the picture looking for short-term gains but having little interest in seeing the company turn around. Finally, there is no guarantee that the process will succeed; on the contrary, the success rate is poor.

If Forzani had needed to break large numbers of leases, management might have thought differently. However, under those circumstances, Sartor and Gregson probably would not have joined the company. They would not have left good jobs to go through a court-protected reorganization, spending weekends arguing fine points with lawyers and accountants.

Key Findings

- It is important to manage for cash in the short term.

- In a turnaround, the finance function plays a critical role, but the business cannot stand still while the balance sheet is repaired. Operating management has to think right away about running the business over the next two or three years. A strategic recovery plan must be prepared and ready to be implemented as soon as the funds are available.

- During the crisis stage of a turnaround when a company is bleeding cash, management must act quickly and decisively. There is no time for debating, pontificating, or politics.

- When a company makes an acquisition, senior management must lead the consolidation. The need to change must be recognized; the company cannot run the way it did.

- Information technology most often fails to fulfill expectations because of poor execution or sponsorship. If there is no champion of the new technology, it will not be implemented properly.

Musicland Stores Corporation

Musicland is the largest specialty retailer of prerecorded music in the United States. Between 1993 and 1996, the company substantially increased its leverage to finance continuing expansion of its store network. In 1994, cash flow available to service debt obligations declined because of competition from discount stores and flattened industry sales. Through store closings and negotiation with vendors, landlords, and lenders, the company narrowly avoided bankruptcy. Its financial performance rebounded sharply in 1997 with a pickup in overall music sales. In 2000 Musicland was acquired by Best Buy Co.

Background

Musicland operates mall-based music and video stores under the nationwide trade names Sam Goody and Suncoast Motion Picture Company and stand-alone full-media stores under the nationwide trade names Media Play and On Cue. To simplify brand identity, the company recently changed the trade name of most Musicland stores to Sam Goody. The full-media stores offer magazines, books, video games, educational toys, greeting cards, apparel, CDs, and videotapes. These stores compete in their markets with Best Buy, Borders Books, Circuit City, Barnes & Noble, and mass merchants. Media Play stores, averaging 48,000 square feet, are in large metropolitan areas. On Cue stores, averaging 6,200 square feet, are in smaller cities. The mall-based stores are considerably smaller than the full-media stores. The average sizes of the Sam Goody and Suncoast stores are 4,300 square feet and 2,400 square feet, respectively. At the end of 1997, Musicland operated 1,363 stores in 49 states, the District of Columbia, Puerto Rico, and the United Kingdom.

Business Performance Indicators

Management's principal measures of store performance are sales per store, sales per square foot, return on net assets, and store contribution on a pre- and postallocation basis. It receives daily reports of sales numbers—yesterday's sales, month-to-date sales, and year-to-date sales—compared with prior periods. Store managers are paid a salary plus a bonus based on store performance. The primary factor in store performance is sales, but shortages and payroll are also factors. A mall store typically has about 11 employees, including a manager, an assistant manager, a third key person, and part-time employees. To help with the chronic retailing problem of employee turnover, Musicland recently implemented an award program based on store and individual performance.

Musicland's CEO, Jack Eugster, was hired in 1980 to run a money-losing record-store chain owned by Primerica. In 1988, with the backing of the investment banking firm, Donaldson, Lufkin & Jenrette, he led a group that bought Musicland in an LBO for $410 million. During the next three years, Musicland added 200 stores, increased sales from $600 million to $1 billion, and reduced debt from $300 to $230 million. In 1992, Musicland was taken public, raising $130 million and reducing debt to $103 million. Then leverage started to increase again. The company did both a debt and a stock offering in 1993 to finance continuing store expansion. Over the next three years, it opened 100 Media Play stores and 168 On Cue stores.

Causes of Financial Difficulty

Starting in 1995, Musicland's financial results began to deteriorate because of four principal factors: aggressive store expansion by other music, book, and video retailers; loss-leader discounting by big-box, category-killer consumer-electronics and music stores such as Best Buy and Circuit City; a lack of strong selling hits in the music industry, which affected all retailers; and overexpansion of the company's own Media Play stores in response to initial encouraging results.

The Company Turnaround

Musicland was turned around through negotiation with banks and vendors, store closings, improvement in working-capital management, reduction in overhead and capital expenditures, and a fortuitous upturn in music-industry sales.

Bank and Vendor Negotiations

In 1994, Musicland began to see cash-flow problems and negotiated an easing of bank-loan covenants relating to tangible net worth, debt to total capital, and the fixed charge coverage ratio. The banks in turn reduced Musicland's credit lines from $350 to $325 million. In 1995, cash flow decreased again, leading to a further easing of covenants and a cutback of bank lines to $275 million. As both operating cash flow and bank lines were reduced, the company began to lose financial flexibility.

Because of the reduction in bank lines, Musicland needed $50 million in financing at the beginning of 1997. It turned to its vendors, first asking whether amounts due could be converted to interest-bearing loans. The vendors refused. Then the company started to pay current balances but leave old balances unpaid, a practice known as a standstill.

In the event of bankruptcy, a vendor may, with the approval of the bankruptcy judge, be allowed to reclaim goods shipped to the customer during the 10 days prior to the bankruptcy filing. Musicland therefore paid its vendors by wire for current purchases every 10th day, and the vendors in turn shipped another 10 days' worth of merchandise. Smaller vendors, who at first refused to go along, relented after the larger vendors agreed to ship under this procedure. As a result, the company received 98 percent of the merchandise it would have under normal circumstances.

When a new, $50 million bank term loan agreement was reached in June 1997, Musicland was able to arrange a 20-week repayment schedule for amounts past due to vendors. However, as a condition for receiving payment according to the company's schedule, vendors were required to reinstate their regular terms for new shipments. The company's 10 largest vendors agreed to this arrangement as a group. The vendor group already had worked together on the bankruptcies of some of Musicland's competitors, such as Camelot, Strawberries, and The Well. Virtually all past-due accounts were paid at the end of December 1997, relieving Musicland's vendors of the burden of negotiating with their auditors over how to classify past-due receivables.

Keith Benson, CFO, points out that a standstill often does not work because vendors do not trust that they are being treated as fairly as their peers. He believes the success of Musicland's standstill arrangements was largely the result of the relationships Eugster had built with the vendors over 15 years, always being frank and always paying bills. Jim Nermyr, treasurer, also notes the importance of treating vendors equally. The company took a strong stand against special payments or terms for any vendor during this period.

Nermyr recalls that no vendor negotiations were easy, but the music and video vendors were less difficult to deal with than the book and software vendors. Musicland had long-standing relationships with the former but had only started buying from the latter for the Media Play and On Cue stores in 1993 and 1994. Those vendors were less understanding when they started getting increased returns and slow payments late in 1995. In the final analysis, Musicland lost a few discounts during the turnaround period, but vendor cooperation allowed it to buy almost all of its merchandise at a reasonable price.

Store Closings

When the signs of financial difficulty became clear in 1994, Musicland began an aggressive store-closing program. It closed 236 stores: 65 in 1995, 65 in 1996, and 106 in 1997. With a consultant's help, management immediately identified stores that were not producing target returns and mall stores with high-cost leases as candidates for closing. It faced harder decisions with some of its newly opened Media Play stores. Some were in locations with good long-term potential, but closing them could help Musicland's cash flow. A large Media Play store had about $1.5 million in inventory that had already been paid for and could be returned for credit toward purchases made for other stores. If the company could negotiate a lease termination with the landlord for a cost of $750,000, then the remaining $750,000 worth of inventory would help its cash flow.

A normal cash payment to terminate a lease would be about one year's rent, but some landlords accepted lower payments, such as a half-year's rent. They were persuaded that it was better to receive 50 cents on the dollar immediately than to receive no more than that in the event of a prolonged bankruptcy proceeding. Some mall owners were willing to reduce rents because they recognized the benefit of keeping viable stores operating. In the nonmall stores, the company had the right to sublease. It closed about 20 superstores and continued to pay rent until a new tenant was found. Mall operators, however, do not allow this practice—known as "going dark"—because vacant stores hurt a mall's image.

The level of supply and demand for retail space between 1995 and 1997 did not help the company's negotiations with its landlords. Other retailers, including some of Musicland's competitors, were filing for bankruptcy. At that time, even successful retailers such as The Gap and The Limited were closing stores and looking for smaller spaces.

Distribution Center Closing

Musicland had two distribution centers. The newer center had more advanced sorting and other automated systems and was not unionized. The older, unionized center was closed in January 1996.

Working Capital

The company improved inventory turnover and reduced working capital by such methods as eliminating slow-selling merchandise and shortening the cycle time for inventory being returned to vendors. A just-in-time purchasing system allowed the distribution center to receive from vendors boxes of merchandise packed with the inventory each store needed. The distribution center could reship the boxes to the stores without further handling. At Musicland, a one-tenth improvement in the inventory turnover ratio decreases working capital requirements by $20 million. The 13-month rolling average of inventory turnover increased from 1.8 at the beginning of 1996 to 2.3 by the end of 1998, freeing about $100 million in working capital.

Capital Spending

Capital spending was reduced to bare essentials. Store openings and remodelings were almost completely curtailed. Capital expenditures were $18 million in 1996 and $11 million in 1997, compared with a peak of $110 million in 1994.

Gross Margins

Price pressure from Best Buy and Circuit City, most severe in 1995 and 1996, eased in 1997. Both competitors had their own financial difficulties in 1996 and early 1997, causing them to raise prices to improve profitability. As a result, Musicland was able to raise prices to improve its own gross margins, from 33.6 percent in 1996 to 34.8 percent in 1997 and 35.5 percent in 1998.

Overhead

General and administrative expenses were reduced in the stores and the company headquarters. A consulting firm with retailing expertise helped the company implement best practices in its large Media Play stores. The headquarters staff was reorganized from four divisions into a more centralized structure and reduced.

Music Sales

Music sales, which flattened in 1996, began to accelerate in the middle of 1997. Nermyr says, "It was like somebody turned the light on." The turnaround in sales was accentuated by the closing of competitors' stores. For example, when one competitor's store in a mall in Laredo, Texas, closed, Musicland's sales there increased by 40 percent.

Avoiding Bankruptcy

Musicland avoided bankruptcy through sheer determination and the conviction that everyone would lose if it filed for Chapter 11 protection. Members of management who had been involved with the LBO held 15 percent of the stock, which would be worthless in the event of bankruptcy but could rise significantly if the company turned around. Virtually every outside party suggested filing at some point, but no individual party wanted to be responsible for pushing the company over the brink. Despite the possibility of a deal being voided in certain instances by the bankruptcy court, some negotiations succeeded because the creditor thought bankruptcy was inevitable and preferred to cut a deal. At several critical points in the creditor negotiations, Musicland's financial and legal advisors leaned toward filing for bankruptcy, but Eugster insisted that none of the interested parties would benefit. Shareholders would get nothing, and bondholders and bank lenders would get only half to two-thirds of their claims. It was better to keep negotiating.

Who Was Most Helpful

Both outside financial advisors and the board of directors supported Musicland's management during the turnaround.

Financial Advisors

Musicland's banks required it to engage a financial advisor. It hired a consultant from a national accounting firm. The consultant and his group were helpful in supporting the decision to close stores and accelerate lease terminations. It was particularly difficult for management to contemplate closing the Minneapolis-area Media Play stores right in its home territory, but the lead financial advisor said, "You always have another shot at it. This time you need to close the stores and get your cash. You're talking about saving the company. Some day you can come back and do it again."

The advisors also provided good financial modeling support by helping to identify which stores should be closed and the expected savings. If a landlord reduced the rent on a store by 10 percent, Musicland could immediately evaluate whether that would be sufficient. CFO Keith Benson adds, however, that the company's engagement with the financial advisors confirmed that its financial reporting, inventory management, and other operating systems were sound. The advisors were comfortable with all the data they requested for their analysis.

While they were very helpful in those areas, the financial and legal advisors sometimes created the impression that they were there more to help the company through an orderly bankruptcy filing process than to help it avoid filing. Legal and consulting fees are, of course, one of the factors that make bankruptcy expensive. In retrospect, Eugster would have preferred to hire the advisors with the understanding that they would be terminated if the company filed for bankruptcy.

Benson and Nermyr agree that financial advisors are needed for negotiation support, that they bring focus to the necessary analysis, and that they provide useful second opinions and outside perspectives even if their opinions are not followed, but they must be managed. Musicland probably paid more in advisory fees than it had to. The advisors were paid to analyze which stores were losing money, but management could have survived with fewer iterations. More than necessary was spent in preparation for a Chapter 11 filing when Eugster was determined not to file. Also, the well-paid, young advisory team members seemed brash and arrogant to the company staffers.

Board of Directors

The board of directors consisted of five businesspeople from outside the company and two members of management. The board relied on management's initiative in the turnaround process, but it was supportive. A bankruptcy attorney attended all board meetings during the turnaround period. In discussions about the company's liability, Eugster made his recommendations and then left decisions to the board. He was willing to leave the room so board members could talk to the bankruptcy attorney because the board had to reach its own fiduciary conclusion whether the company should file for bankruptcy. Nermyr believes that if the board had said, "Jack [Eugster], we think you should file," Eugster probably would have done so.

Cost of Financial Difficulty

Musicland's costs directly related to financial difficulty were fees paid to financial and legal advisors, payments to terminate leases, and write-offs of fixtures and equipment and other store-opening costs that could not be recovered. The company's ability to redeploy inventory substantially lessened the financial impact of a store closing.

Interests of Shareholders and Management

The interests of shareholders and management were largely aligned because most of top management had been shareholders since the LBO.

Investor Relations

When Musicland's financial performance declined and its stock price dropped from $22.00 to $0.68, most institutional shareholders sold their stock. Management continued to participate in quarterly conference calls with investors and analysts but discouraged company visits and tried to keep a low profile to avoid the possibility of providing misleading information.

Retail investors had bought most of the institutional shares. Unlike institutional investors, who in a large-portfolio context are used to taking losses and moving on, some retail investors who feel misled are prone to sue. It is particularly difficult for management to communicate with investors when earnings are declining, but Musicland's management was able to provide straightforward information and avoid any threat of litigation.

Investors specializing in distressed companies bought some of the stock and most of the bonds. Because three of those investors acquired most of the bonds, communications on matters such as bond waivers were relatively easy. The new bondholders generally supported management's efforts to avoid bankruptcy because such an outcome would allow them to make substantial gains on bonds they purchased at deep discounts.

Managing the Risk of Financial Difficulty

Before Musicland ran into financial difficulty, management did not think high leverage posed substantial risks. Because the company's LBO succeeded when many others failed between 1988 and 1992, management was willing to use debt to finance store expansion between 1993 and 1995. Now, after narrowly averting bankruptcy, management is more prone to maintain a conservative debt-equity ratio. In Nermyr's opinion, Musicland's ideal capital structure would entail 40 to 50 percent debt to total capital and about a triple-B credit rating.

Tax Issues

Prior to its financial difficulty, Musicland had deferred taxes, which then disappeared from the balance sheet. Those deferred taxes have now reappeared, increasing the company's tax rate. Musicland's tax rate was zero in 1997, 30 percent in 1998 and 1999, and will stabilize at a more normal 40 percent in 2000.

Observations on Bankruptcy Law

Management feels fortunate not to have learned more than it did about bankruptcy law. However, Tim Scully, assistant treasurer, believes current laws provide an incentive to file. For example, some retailers file for Chapter 11 because it helps them cancel leases. None of Musicland's advisors, lenders, or vendors ever introduced the possibility of a Chapter 7 filing, but they often suggested that a Chapter 11 filing would help give the company a fresh start. During its financial difficulty, the company could not get any new financing, but banks were lining up to provide DIP financing in the event it filed for bankruptcy. Scully finds this ironic.

While Musicland's management is glad it averted bankruptcy, it now competes for retail space with other music retailers that eliminated their debt through bankruptcy. Landlords need to understand why those retailers' balance sheets look stronger and why it is to the landlords' advantage to deal with a company that avoided bankruptcy.

Surviving the Turnaround

Benson, Nermyr, and Scully had the advantage of going through the turnaround as a coherent team, but the experience still was stressful. Over time, fatigue builds from long days, sleepless nights, weekends that become part of the workweek, and no vacations. Because of the complexity and tension inherent in a turnaround, it is difficult not to think about it all the time.

Key Findings

The company took on too much debt, overexpanded, and then was too weak to weather a downturn. During the expansion period, the new Media Play and On Cue locations looked like opportunities to generate substantial sales and profits. But business runs in cycles. Good times never last forever, and unanticipated negative factors come out of left field.

■ Going forward, Musicland inevitably will see competitors over-paying for retail spaces in highly desirable locations, and it will be difficult to avoid the temptation to do the same. However, Benson says the company already has passed up some deals that were too expensive. In the past, management was not willing to lose a deal.

■ Scully emphasizes the importance of good, long-term vendor relations.

■ A strong CEO with determination helped keep the company out of bankruptcy.

■ Once financial difficulties became apparent, a strong accounting and reporting system helped management determine what actions to take. Before deciding to reduce costs in a particular category, management "drilled down" to analyze subcomponents and find out which costs were necessary and which were not. Doing so helped it estimate how the business would be hurt and what risks would be incurred if certain costs were reduced.

Red Rooster Auto Stores

This privately owned auto parts wholesaler and retailer ran into financial difficulty after decades of steady growth because of overconfidence, inadequate attention to profit margins, employee compensation above industry standards, and weak financial controls. Management turned the company around by basing performance measures and employee compensation on gross profit rather than sales, reducing the employee count through job redesign and attrition, improving information- and inventory-management systems, and sharing information among employees.

Background

Red Rooster Auto Stores, with 1999 revenues of $10 million, operates five auto-parts stores in the greater Minneapolis area. The business was founded in 1934 as Motor Parts Service, Inc., which is still the name of the parent company. It started as a machine shop with a supplementary business in auto parts. Now 95 percent of the business is auto parts and 5 percent is in machine shops, whose work consists of repairing blocks, resurfacing heads, pressing bearings, and turning drums and rotors.

Red Rooster's business is 60 percent wholesale and 40 percent retail. Wholesale customers are auto-repair shops, garages, and dealers. The two largest stores, which are 18,000 square feet each, generate approximately 80 percent of total sales. The three smaller stores, which average 3,000 square feet each, generate the remaining 20 percent. Most customers are located within an eight-mile radius of a given store.

Red Rooster stays competitive through its reputation for stocking or finding needed parts, its sales and counter personnel's product knowledge and problem-solving capability, and its fast service. A repair shop often does not know what part it needs until a car is on the hoist. The hoist is tied up until the part is delivered, creating downtime for both the customer and the shop. A fleet of 33 Red Rooster trucks is on the road all day long, delivering parts to customers.

Causes of Financial Difficulty

Red Rooster's financial difficulty stemmed from a combination of over-confidence after decades of prosperity, an emphasis on sales rather than gross profit, inappropriate employee compensation, and weak financial controls.

Sales Culture

In the early 1980s, decisions by Red Rooster's five-member management team were strongly influenced by the bottom-line focus of Dewey Johnson, the company's CEO, and his son, Roger, the company's CFO. After Dewey retired in 1984 and Roger moved to Texas in 1987, the focus shifted toward sales. The new CEO was primarily sales driven, and the new CFO followed his lead. Whenever there was a slump in profits, sales efforts were stepped up, particularly to wholesale accounts. Because these efforts always seemed successful, management became overconfident.

Employee Compensation
Red Rooster had a leading market position in the Minneapolis area and strong cash flow. Management helped maintain morale with total compensation of up to 63 percent of gross profit. The level of pay, however, was not based on any formula or tied to any performance measure such as sales. An industry consultant described the company's employee compensation as "benevolent." A bank lender found it to be substantially above industry averages.

Profit Margins
In the late 1980s, Red Rooster's gross profit margins eroded from 42 to 37 percent of sales as the company lowered prices to remain competitive. Other wholesalers were also cutting prices, and new competitors, both local and national, were opening stores. Despite declining margins, employee compensation was not reduced. As a result, the company lost money for three consecutive years from 1988 to 1990.

Buyout Financing
While Red Rooster was losing money, it incurred the additional burden of buying out several retiring owners, with cash payments spread over 15 years. The number of owners declined from eight in the early 1980s to three in 1990. The buyouts reduced book equity and increased liabilities, resulting in a negative book net worth. (Red Rooster's real estate, with a market value of close to $2 million, was almost fully depreciated.)

Job Design
The company's managers and employees lacked job descriptions and clearly defined objectives. During slack times, in-store salespeople were idle while others were hired to clean and stock inventory. What employees actually did was based largely on the interests of senior managers and owners. For example, a store in Faribault, a rural Minnesota town, was purchased with little market analysis because one manager convinced the management team that owning another store would be good for the company.

Financial Controls
Financial controls were lax. As a result, some unnecessary expenditures were buried, unnoticed. While Red Rooster was losing money, it always paid within suppliers' net terms; however, it missed many of its discounts.

Information Sharing
The former top management team shared little financial information. As a result, other managers and employees had little sense of ownership or understanding of how the company's financial performance affected their personal compensation.

The Company Turnaround
Red Rooster Auto Stores was turned around by new management, profit-related performance measures and compensation, improved expense control, sharing information with employees, and allowing capable young managers to earn an ownership interest in the company.

New Management
Between 1987 and 1990, Roger Johnson, although living in Texas, remained available for consultation but made only occasional visits to the company. He grew uncomfortable with the way things were going, returned on a part-time basis, and did some auditing. Seeing evidence of poor expense control, declining profit margins, and a liquidity squeeze, Johnson and his partners decided to retain an industry consultant. The consultant's recommendations included making changes to the management team. As a result, the company's president resigned, and the partners elected Tomm Johnson, a fellow partner, to be president and CEO. Roger Johnson returned full time as CFO.

Role of Outside Professionals
The industry consultant helped with a reorganization, a job-design plan, and operating ratios for other auto-supply stores against which Red Rooster could benchmark. As a first priority, he recommended reining in the company's employee compensation. Management also enlisted the help of Red Rooster's banker and its accountant. The banker granted a one-year moratorium on principal payments. The accountant worked with management to develop a five-year financial plan.

Employee Compensation

When the turnaround effort began, employee compensation was about 63 percent of gross profit, compared with an industry average of 52 percent. During the first year, Roger Johnson proposed and the management team adopted a target of 55 percent. After that target was met, the management team hired another industry consultant who helped develop a new target plan of 45 percent before bonuses. Base pay was cut by about 30 percent for managers and 8 percent for other employees. A new incentive compensation plan provided for bonuses based on individual store performance. The plan was not well received by employees because it required immediate pay cuts. Some employees left, but despite initial misgivings, most concluded that they would be better off in five years if both they and the company performed well.

There also was a new bonus plan for the in-store sales team. Each store allocated 18.5 percent of its gross profit for inside sales payroll. The portion not used for base salaries was awarded to the store as a bonus, so payroll expense was always 18.5 percent of gross profit. If a store spent more, the excess was applied against the 18.5 percent for the next month. That plan is still in effect. Store managers and employees understand that bonuses are the result of increasing gross profit or reducing payroll expense. Outside sales commissions are set at 11.6 percent of gross profits.

Partners are compensated based on their job descriptions and responsibilities rather than the size of their investments. Base compensation is determined from industry data. Bonuses are tied to overall company performance and meeting objectives.

Expense Control

Other expenses were reduced and capital expenditures limited during the five-year recovery period. The company kept delivery trucks longer. Drop shipments delivered parts from manufacturers directly to Red Rooster, rather than through a cooperatively owned warehouse. The warehouse still handled the paperwork but earned a smaller administrative fee.

Communication

Virtually all of the company's financial information, except for individual employee compensation, was opened to company members. Although management is not opposed to providing corporate financial information such as income statements, balance sheets, cash-flow statements, budgets, and budget-variance analysis to employees, most are more interested in information related directly to their jobs and compensation, such as sales, gross profits, and store payrolls. Employees can voice concerns and ask questions in monthly "pizza meetings" and participate in annual off-site strategic planning meetings. Management publishes a weekly store performance report.

New Performance Measures

The company implemented across-the-board, easy-to-understand performance measures. Because gross profit is particularly important, it is measured in several ways: by store, by week, and by current versus previous year. The inventory department is measured based on the inventory turn and the gross-margin return on inventory. Accounts-receivable managers receive days-sales-outstanding targets. Minimum gross profit margins were defined for the outside sales force; this required a culture change because it involved forfeiting business that did not meet the required margins.

Roger Johnson set 18.5 percent of gross profit as a target for in-store sales payrolls, 29 percent for total store payrolls, including stockroom and other support staff, and 45 percent for the total company payroll. Now, store managers must keep their total store payrolls within the target. On the basis of projected employee work schedules, the CFO helps store managers estimate their monthly payrolls. Together, they determine how much gross profit is required to cover base pay and build the bonus pool. At any time, a manager can retrieve a month-to-date or year-to-date store performance report. A store's inside sales team can track performance and project the store's bonus pool for the month, and for the full year. Salespeople can also access a report to track individual performance during the day.

Training related to the new performance measures was geared toward helping employees understand the numbers and how improved performance in each aspect of store operations could affect their bonuses. Employees learned that keeping base salaries in line was a storewide responsibility. The training created a culture change in which stores began policing themselves.

The inside sales force has learned that related sales, also known as cross sales, translate into increased gross profit and larger bonuses.

Management can measure related sales for each salesperson by dividing the number of line items by the number of invoices. A line item corresponds to a part number. If, for example, a customer buys four spark plugs and a pair of wiper blades, there are two line items on the invoice. Employees who consistently have multiple line items per invoice tend to do the most related selling. An employee who averages just over one line item per invoice is likely filling orders without suggesting other purchases.

Management deems the company's financial performance acceptable if the gross profit per man-hour is above $28; employees know that they probably will not get bonuses if it drops below $28. The dollar amount increases as payroll expense increases.

Job Design
Jobs were redesigned and job descriptions were based on what needed to be done. Some employees took on expanded responsibilities. During slack times, store salespeople helped with functions such as stocking and counting inventory, processing returns, cleaning, and administrative work.

Workforce Reduction
Redesigning the company's job structure enabled management to reduce the workforce from about 100 to 80. Aside from the president and director of human resources, who resigned, the reduction was accomplished entirely through attrition.

Computer System
The company's computer system, installed in 1995, is a package specifically designed for the auto-parts business. People at all levels were involved in the decision to purchase the system and therefore had a sense of ownership when it was installed. Red Rooster's criteria, in order of importance, were (1) the ability to connect with customers, (2) point-of-sale features, (3) inventory-management features, and (4) the accounting system. Accounting was the lowest priority because management already had decided to purchase another PC-based system for the general ledger and accounts payable. That system allows people who are not at the certified public accountant level to do a large part of financial statement preparation. Because employees were

trained on the system before it was delivered, the implementation and parallel runs went smoothly.

Armed with information from the industry-specific system, the PC-based accounting system, and the payroll service, CFO Roger Johnson tracks numerous measures daily, including the wholesale-retail sales mix and store payrolls, against the company target. He can determine for each pay period the number of hours worked, the gross profit per man-hour, and the percentage of gross profit for each department.

Inventory Management

Balancing customer satisfaction and an acceptable inventory turn is increasingly difficult because of parts proliferation. Whereas one muffler might have fit Chevrolets from the 1957 through 1963 model years, now there might be four mufflers for a model year. Using the industry-specific computer system and industry reference books, Red Rooster's inventory manager analyzes data such as vehicle registrations and the sales history, failure rate, and replacement rate for each part number. The manager can determine stock levels that will provide optimum coverage but remain within departmental targets for inventory turn and gross margin return on investment.

Store Rationalization

Sales and gross profits for the store in Faribault, Minnesota, while moving in the right direction, were insufficient to justify keeping the store open when the lease was terminated in 1992. Red Rooster bought a store in Rogers, Minnesota, in 1995. Management did a feasibility study based on the business it already had in the area serviced by its nearest store, existing business under the previous owners, and potential new business. The new store started with one person at the counter and an outside salesperson calling in the area twice a week. Then account activity started to take off. Within a few months, the Rogers store was selling five times as much as under the previous owners. In early 1998, the company bought another store, in Apple Valley, Minnesota. By the end of the year, the store was doing double the volume with a higher gross margin than under the previous owners. A store in Lexington, Minnesota, was added in 1999.

Corporate Reorganization

In 1990, Motor Parts Service, Inc., the original company, was the sole corporate entity. It was a C corporation that carried the company-owned real estate on its balance sheet. Motor Parts Service was split into two parts. It was converted into a Subchapter S corporation, whose income is taxed at the individual-owner level rather than the corporate level. Motor Parts owns the real estate that Red Rooster Auto Stores, a limited-liability company, leases to conduct the active business. Because Motor Parts loses its Subchapter S status if passive income, such as rent, exceeds 25 percent of total income for three consecutive years, Motor Parts also owns equity in Red Rooster Auto Stores. Employees own the rest of Red Rooster Auto Stores' equity.

New Partners

Splitting the company in two made interests in Red Rooster Auto Stores affordable for younger partners. By the mid-1990s, there were only three owners: the CEO, the CFO, and a retired partner. The CEO and CFO wanted more partners in the firm and did not want to buy back any more stock. They realized that if they wanted new, younger owners to succeed them, they would have to pave the way through either higher compensation or financing. They implemented a buy-sell agreement that defined buyout terms and set the price at book value. In early 1998, four managers in their thirties bought an interest in Red Rooster Auto Stores, financed by Motor Parts Service. Roger Johnson says, "Psychologically, it was important for us to realize that now some other guys were just as interested as we were in making the company succeed."

Key Findings

Roger Johnson shared the following lessons from his experience with Red Rooster's turnaround:

- Gross profits, not sales, pay the bills. Measure financial performance as a percentage of gross profit.

- Management should be open with employees about performance measures and financials.

- Management should allow employees to participate when the company does well.

■ A company needs to use industry operating data for benchmarking.

■ Management positions should not be designed to fit the people available. The positions should be designed first; then people should be recruited.

■ Management must have the courage and conviction to stick to its plan.

■ CEO Tomm Johnson adds that the company's financial problems between 1987 and 1990 cannot be blamed completely on the former management. Rather, the three owners at the time should have been more vigilant.

9

High-Technology Sector

Parametric Technology Corporation and Computervision

Computervision, a market leader in CAD/CAM (computer-aided design/computer-aided manufacturing) products in the early 1980s, ran into financial difficulty for two reasons: Its competition overtook it technologically, and it was overleveraged after a hostile takeover and LBO. The solution was a purchase by Parametric Technology Corporation, a younger, more nimble competitor.

Background of Computervision

Computervision, founded in 1972, was a pioneer in CAD/CAM. At first it sold hardware and software bundled as a turnkey package. In 1982 it had a leading 25 percent market share and earned $45 million on $435 million in sales. It had a 15.8 percent operating margin after depreciation and a 10.3 percent after-tax return on sales. Sales grew to $960 million in 1987, but the operating margin slipped to 8.5 percent and the return on sales to 6.7 percent. By that time, while Computervision remained strong among the largest industrial users such as airframe and automobile manufacturers, its overall market share had declined to 12 percent. IBM led with a 25 percent market share. Smaller rivals had gained a share of the higher-volume, low end of the market with less expensive software that could run on a variety of hardware platforms.

In February 1988, Computervision succumbed to a hostile takeover by Prime Computer, a player in the declining minicomputer market. Prime Computer saw the CAD/CAM market, where it had a 3.6 percent share, as a growth opportunity. In November 1988, MAI Basic Four, a minicomputer manufacturer controlled by arbitrageur Bennet LeBow, made a hostile bid for Prime Computer with the secret financial support of Drexel Burnham Lambert. (Drexel's role later was revealed in a court proceeding.) Prime Computer's management responded by cutting costs severely and reducing postsales support, which impaired customer service. Fiscal 1988 financial results showed declines in the company's operating margin to 7.2 percent and in its return on sales to 1.2 percent.

J.H. Whitney, a New York investment firm, emerged as a white knight, taking control of Prime Computer in January 1990 in the largest LBO of a computer company as of that time. As a result, Prime Computer was left with $925 million in debt, including a $500 million bridge loan from Shearson Lehman Brothers, Inc., at 4 percent over prime with an interest-rate increase every 120 days as an incentive to refinance. The company intended to refinance the bridge loan through Shearson in the high-yield bond market, but that market collapsed shortly after the LBO.

Between 1990 and 1993, Prime Computer's minicomputer sales declined from more than $1 billion to less than $200 million. Earnings from CAD/CAM defrayed losses on minicomputers. Employee count was reduced from 12,000 to 6,000. In 1992, the company changed its name to Computervision to reflect what by then was its core product.

Recapitalization

Computervision's heavy debt load created pressure for an initial public offering (IPO). In August 1992, despite poor market conditions for technology stocks, Computervision went public again, selling 52 percent of its stock for $300 million. It also raised $300 million in a bond issue. In addition, the owners of $313 million in debt, which was primarily held by Shearson, traded their debt for common stock in the company. As a result, Computervision's debt dropped from $925 million to $358 million, and its annual interest payments were cut from $122 million to $54 million. The initial offering price of the stock originally was estimated to be $19 but dropped to $12. Six weeks after the IPO, the company warned of a disappointing third quarter; the stock price plunged to $6. Several class-action lawsuits were filed, alleging that Shearson had a conflict of interest in underwriting stock to repay the debt it held and that the firm knew bad news was coming at the time of the offering. While some analysts believed Computervision was continuing to lose market share, the company's management argued that sales tend to be booked toward the end of the quarter and that European customers, who accounted for 60 percent of sales, had delayed purchases because of the European currency crisis that began in early September.

Kemper Financial Services and Putnam Management Company, together purchased about half the Whitney debt on the open market at low prices. Later, after the recapitalization, they sued Computervision. They alleged that Whitney's reduced ownership, from 100 percent of Prime Computer at the time of the LBO to 33 percent of Computervision after the public offering, diminished chances for repayment. A settlement gave each a 1 percent equity stake in Computervision and required DR Holdings (the subsidiary set up by J.H. Whitney as the parent of Prime Computer) to declare bankruptcy to ensure an equitable distribution of its 33 percent holding of Computervision. DR's debt consisted of $124 million owed to Whitney and Shearson insiders, $334 million owed on bonds distributed to Prime Computer shareholders in lieu of cash at the time of the LBO, and $104 million to bondholders in a separate issue.

Shearson wrote off $245 million of its $500 million bridge loan and gave up $80 million in interest payments. It received $250 million in cash and a 10 percent equity stake in Computervision as a result of the IPO. Following the IPO, Shearson increased its equity interest to 22 percent to maintain a market in the shares. Prudential Life Insurance Co., had underwritten $70 million in zero-coupon bonds for the Whitney takeover, and Bank of Boston and Chemical Bank, which together lent $355 million to Whitney to fund the takeover, basically broke even as a result of the recapitalization.

Computervision became profitable again from 1994 to 1996 as it exited the computer hardware business and focused on CAD/CAM software that could run on various platforms. One promising product was electronic product definition (EPD) software, which provided access through the Internet to all the mechanical design, configuration, workflow, and technical data needed for complex products such as airplanes. Computervision maintained relationships with large customers such as Airbus, Rolls Royce, and Peugeot, focusing on complete solutions, including hardware, software, and service. Because Computervision no longer had the market's leading CAD/CAM products, it concentrated on service and discounted its prices to survive. Its results from quarter to quarter often were uncertain as it anticipated closing relatively few large deals, some as high as $25 million to $50 million, that locked customers in for four of five years with discounts for up-front payment. Although the revenues for those deals were deferred over the life of the contracts for accounting purposes, the cash—received either directly from customers or as a result of discounting customer promissory notes—financed the company's operations. Management hoped to survive in this way long enough to allow development of its new EPD products. Computervision was losing business from customers concerned about its ability to provide software support over the life of a product such as an airplane. Newer solid modeling technologies of competitors such as Parametric were eclipsing Computervision's approach to three-dimensional modeling, a "wire frame" adaptation of its surface-modeling software.

In hindsight, Parametric executives who worked at Computervision before the merger of the two companies see other problems, too. Computervision's management and decision-making process seemed cumbersome and bureaucratic. Its management took a long time to analyze things; its style was not as tough and direct as Parametric's. There were unnecessary layers of management. People came to meetings to deal with political agendas rather than to make decisions. As a result of management indecisiveness, when Computervision encountered financial difficulty in the mid-1990s, it did not downsize quickly enough.

Background of Parametric

In 1974 Samuel Geisberg, a former geometry professor at the University of Leningrad, left Russia and found a job at Computervision. In 1980, his brother Vladimir, who had a similar background, also left Russia to join Computervision. While at Computervision, Samuel Geisberg proposed a new CAD/CAM product but was turned down. As Computervision's installed base of legacy products grew, it became difficult to propose disruptive technology innovations to its customers. (A disruptive technology is one that has long-range potential, such as the personal computer in the 1970s, but no initial appeal to mainstream customers.)

Samuel Geisberg's response was to leave Computervision. In 1985 he founded Parametric and began to offer CAD/CAM software with enhanced capabilities. Parametric announced earnings of $2.2 million on revenues of $11 million for its fiscal year ending in September 1989 and raised $19 million in its first public offering shortly thereafter. As Parametric grew, Vladimir Geisberg became head of CAD/CAM product development at Computervision and a real competitor.

Parametric's Acquisition of Computervision

In November 1997, Parametric announced its acquisition of Computervision as a wholly owned subsidiary. Some industry experts were surprised that a successful, growing, financially strong software company would want to acquire another company with diminished market share and a heavy debt load. But Computervision had valuable technologies, a good marketing organization, and a strong position in CAD/CAM software with large aerospace and automobile manufacturers, where it competed with Parametric and Dassault Systems SA, a spin-off of the French aerospace concern. Computervision's main problem was heavy debt, which restricted it from reinvesting in new technologies and created doubt in the marketplace about its ability to remain a viable competitor.

Parametric and Computervision had held informal discussions about a possible merger but had not seen a fit. Given Parametric's own innovative CAD/CAM technologies, Computervision seemed too expensive. The discussions became more serious when Computervision anticipated difficulty meeting large balloon debt payments due in February 1998. The company appeared to be headed toward either a restructuring, with debt holders taking over, or bankruptcy. M.D. Sass, a turnaround investment firm, held a board seat and a substantial position in the company's equity and debt, which indicated that bankruptcy was a possible outcome.

In the beginning of the merger discussions, Computervision proposed selling just its legacy CAD/CAM product and keeping the EPD product that provided more opportunity for growth. But Parametric saw other aspects that made buying the whole company appealing. First, despite its technologies and strong growth, Parametric had not been able to win over the largest aerospace and automotive customers, where Computervision was strong. The only alternative to Computervision's software customers in those industries were willing to consider was a competing product made by Dassault Systems. Second, Parametric had developed some work-group products and process life-cycle management products and wanted to build an enterprise data management product. Computervision's EPD product line looked like a good fit and an attractive opportunity. Finally, Parametric saw an advantage in pooling-of-interests rather than purchase accounting for the merger: Parametric's large cash reserve could be used to retire Computervision's debt; Parametric already had become a cash generator and was repurchasing its own stock; and most of Computervision's value was in its debt.

Because most of the purchase price was for the retirement of debt, Parametric made the acquisition with relatively little dilution. Parametric paid Computervision about $4 per share, substantially higher than the range of $2 to $2.50 when merger discussions began but far below the range of $12 to $16 several years before. Distressed-security investors who bought Computervision's debt at a deep discount made a handsome profit. The company's debt traded at 40 percent of par before the merger announcement, rising to 101 percent when the announcement was made. An additional $100 million in value went to arbitrageurs who held Computervision's stock as a speculative investment.

Unexpected Benefits

Two of Computervision's development projects turned out to be more valuable to Parametric than they appeared during the due diligence process. The first was a low-end, Windows-based modeling software package called Designwave (later renamed Pro/DESKTOP by Parametric) that competed with another successful Dassault Systems product. The second was a joint venture with a Minneapolis-based start-up called Windchill that was developing enterprise information management software architecture. Metaphase, a joint venture between Control Data and Structural Dynamics Research Corporation, had a successful enterprise data management product in use in client-server networks. Windchill's founders set out to develop a Web-based enterprise data management product. Computervision was not financially able to create a similar product itself but provided seed money in the form of an investment for certain rights to market Windchill's products with its own. After the acquisition, Parametric learned more about Windchill's technology and purchased the remainder of the company. Now Windchill's data management products are among Parametric's main strategic thrusts. Because they are Web-based, Windchill products can run on a greater variety of computer hardware in more locations than software based on a client-server system. Parametric refers to leveraging the Internet in this way as collaborative product commerce.

The Merger

Parametric's purchase of Computervision was, in effect, the final step in Computervision's turnaround. The Parametric finance function spearheaded the integration process. To realize the benefits of the merger, it was important to get the two companies working together as quickly as possible, so Computervision immediately was integrated into Parametric. Decisions on whom to keep and whom to let go also were made right away. The day the acquisition was finalized, signs were changed and new business cards issued. There was a welcome meeting for remaining Computervision employees and exit interviews for those leaving. The former Computervision staff was downsized by about 500 people; the resulting head count was at a level Parametric could support.

Key Findings

- High leverage, particularly an LBO, is inappropriate for a growth company with technological risk.

- Disruptive technologies may become crucial market opportunities.

- Indecision and delay, such as Computervision's failure to reduce its staff quickly enough, can hamper or destroy a turnaround.

GenRad, Inc.

GenRad, Inc., a Boston-area high-technology company, was driven more by an engineering culture than a business culture. It diversified away from its core strengths and lost its leadership position in test equipment. After a period of losses, a new CEO spearheaded a turnaround by delayering management, listening to the customer, defining core businesses, selling unproductive assets, and shifting the business paradigm from test equipment to diagnostic services.

Background

GenRad is a leading worldwide supplier of integrated test, measurement, and diagnostic solutions for manufacturing and maintaining electronic products. It was founded in 1915 in Cambridge, Massachusetts, as the General Radio Company. In its early days, the company was a market leader with the introduction of electronic test equipment such as oscilloscopes, stroboscopes, and vacuum tube voltmeters. GenRad pioneered the automated test equipment industry in the early 1980s but ceded leadership to Hewlett-Packard later in the decade. GenRad maintained a market niche between California-based Hewlett-Packard at the high end and Boston-based Teradyne at the low end, partly because of customers' reluctance to rely on single suppliers. Poor management and ill-fated attempts to diversify away from core businesses caused the company to lose money every year from 1984 to 1993—longer than any surviving New York Stock Exchange company. Cumulative losses totaled $200 million, creating negative book net worth.

At the same time, the company had the obligation to service $57 million in convertible debentures issued in 1986 to fund research and development (R&D). By the early 1990s, SG&A expenses were more than 50 percent of revenues and growing faster than revenues. Customers were defecting to GenRad's competitors because they were concerned about the company's survival and ability to service their equipment, and the New York Stock Exchange threatened to delist GenRad.

James F. Lyons, the current chairman and CEO, says the company was technically bankrupt in 1993 because of difficulty borrowing and getting insurance. GenRad's directors' and officers' liability insurance carrier considered not renewing its policy because of the threat of a lawsuit from the company's largest shareholder. Its asset-based lenders considered not renewing their lines of credit because they lacked confidence in its management strategy and business prospects.

The lawsuit threat forced the board of directors to begin a search for a new CEO in late 1992. Lyons was hired in July 1993 to turn the company around. He had been president of Carrier Corporation and American Medical International (AMI) and a senior executive at United Technologies and Xerox Corporation. Lyons decided to join GenRad because he had never faced the challenge of a turnaround before. In his previous positions, he had run divisions or companies that were solid but needed more leadership, better strategic vision, and, in the case of AMI, the financial skills to carry out an LBO.

Causes of Financial Difficulty

The eight CEOs prior to Lyons were engineers. GenRad's management had more of an engineering than a business mentality. There were no formal business or product-marketing strategies. There were few links between product development plans and financial projections. What the company called strategic planning was actually short-term operational planning. Rather than product and systems marketing, the company had marketing communications. Engineers thought they understood the technology better than the customers did and therefore didn't need to listen to them.

An entrenched board of directors consisted of an attorney, a commercial banker, an electrical engineering and computer science professor at MIT, and a retired insurance company CEO. There was little turnover. Board members liked to believe they were influencing the company, but they did not know how to run a business. Lyons recalls that they asked questions about minor details but not about fundamental business strategy and how the company could become profitable again.

The organization was top-heavy. Lyons says the organization chart seemed to list managers for everything. There were six layers of management between the CEO and hourly workers on the manufacturing floor. There was little evidence, however, of management development or role models. Employees, described by Lyons as dedicated survivors, were cynical about senior management and skeptical of its commitments. The staff had no passion or enthusiasm and no motivating vision other than survival.

When the test equipment business started to lose money in the mid-1980s, management reduced expenses by curtailing R&D and closing sales offices. As a result, GenRad's market share declined from 55 percent to 35 percent, and Hewlett-Packard became the market leader. Hewlett-Packard considered buying GenRad in 1990 but concluded it was not viable. Despite losses, the board continued to compensate senior management with bonuses and stock options, which were repriced at $.01 per share, because it thought keeping the management team would help attract an acquirer.

The Company Turnaround

Lyons describes three turnarounds at GenRad: a financial turnaround in 1994 and 1995, in which the company was rescued from the brink of bankruptcy; a strategic turnaround in 1996 and 1997, when new product and marketing strategies were developed and sales growth resumed after a nine-year hiatus; and an organizational turnaround in 1998 and 1999, when the company's engineering, manufacturing, marketing, and finance functions were reorganized to fit its new strategies. When Lyons joined the company in mid-1993, he had to stabilize a crisis. He also had to generate confidence among employees, customers, vendors, lenders, and investors. He resolved to listen before acting and to make no strategic moves in the first six months. No matter how bad the situation, it was essential that he emphasize the positive.

Financial Targets

In July 1993, Lyons met with the New York Stock Exchange Compliance Committee to prevent GenRad from being delisted. He said the company would earn $.25 per share in 1994, $.50 in 1995, and $1.00 in 1996. He felt that setting these targets was essential both for the stock exchange and for the company's management. The 1994 and 1995 targets appeared to be attainable through divestitures, restructuring, organizational delayering, and manufacturing-cost reductions. To reach the 1996 target, the company would have to increase revenues by 15 to 20 percent. That would require reinvestment, although no clear business or product strategy had been developed. Lyons, however, never wavered from his original earnings-per-share targets. All employees knew that if the company did not make its target, they would not get bonuses; and several managers resigned over the issue. In fact, GenRad met its 1994, 1995, and 1996 earnings targets by a comfortable margin. By April 1995, Lyons could stop meeting with the New York Stock Exchange Compliance Committee.

Lyons continues to set simple, overall targets for revenue, expense, and earnings per share. He participates in business strategy discussions and major decisions such as laying off employees but gives operating managers most of the responsibility for achieving the targets. Lyons does not try to outguess his technicians but rather tries to ensure that technical decisions make sense in the context of business objectives. He wants to avoid having a technically superior product that is unsuited to the market or that cannot be sold profitably. In his experience, estimated revenues and the ROI for new products usually are fictitious. Most products either significantly beat ROI projections or fail to achieve them.

Changes in the Board of Directors and Management

Gradually, the board of directors Lyons inherited resigned. The new directors he appointed were primarily CEOs of high-technology businesses. Most of GenRad's senior and middle managers were terminated and new managers recruited. In Lyons' words, the managers who were terminated "didn't get it." They did not understand that their knowledge was out of date and they needed to change their perceptions of themselves and the business. Lyons sees the same problem today with GenRad's sales organization. Its members do not sufficiently understand the significance of e-business or see the Internet as a sales and distribution channel.

Sale of Real Estate

GenRad's new management found substantial cash-generating opportunities by selling real estate, subletting, and terminating leases on facilities that were underutilized or idle. In 1996, the company sold its 400,000-square-foot headquarters in Concord, Massachusetts, near Boston, for $6 million cash, and booked a $3.8 million gain. Operations were moved to more economical build-to-suit facilities in Westford, about 30 miles from Boston. New facilities helped GenRad break with its old culture and establish a new, more business-oriented outlook.

Identification of Core Businesses

GenRad hired McKinsey & Company, Inc. to help determine which businesses merited salvage and reinvestment and which should be sold or closed. It later hired the head of the McKinsey team as chief strategic officer. GenRad took a $43 million restructuring charge in 1993 to account for the elimination of "performance overhangs," such as unproductive real estate and businesses that did not fit management's strategic vision.

The two core businesses with growth potential appeared to be electronic manufacturing systems (EMS), which are functional and in-circuit board testers for personal computer and telecommunications equipment manufacturers, and advanced diagnostic solutions (ADS), which are automotive-service testers for automobile manufacturers and repair shops. However, management believed these businesses would have to adopt a new business paradigm.

To round out its product line, GenRad made both acquisitions and divestitures. One acquisition was a company that sells fixtures and test programs customers use along with GenRad's test equipment. It sold two product lines—design automation tools and structured test products. In both cases, GenRad served only a small niche of the market and did not have sufficient product development or marketing infrastructure for a broad customer franchise. To make either of these businesses profitable, the company would have had to make substantial R&D and marketing investments in areas that did not play to its core strengths in manufacturing operations.

Skunkworks

To help redefine business strategies and shift the strategic paradigm, Lyons invested $15 million in a "skunkworks" program. (The term "skunkworks" originated with teams that developed advanced reconnaissance planes such as the U2 at the Boeing Company.) Lyons selected a team of 13 engineers and two salespeople who had a combination of technical competence, intellectual curiosity, and enthusiasm; provided space for them in a separate building; and asked them to talk to customers and then recommend how GenRad should redefine its business strategy. The skunkworks helped GenRad determine that it was primarily in the software business rather than the test-equipment business. GenRad could add customer value by providing diagnostic tools to improve quality and productivity in customers' manufacturing processes and thereby reduce or eliminate the need for tests. Customers told the skunkworks engineers that if their manufacturing processes were in control, they would not need end-of-line tests and circuit tests. Several years ago, GenRad's software orders typically amounted to a few thousand dollars. Recently, several customers placed software orders in the millions. Because GenRad's software business has substantial growth potential, it invests a disproportionately large percentage of that segment's earnings in R&D. Lyons warns that such an investment strategy must be managed carefully so other businesses that generate steady cash do not lose motivation because they are perceived as cash cows.

New Business Paradigm

GenRad has evolved from a test-equipment and automotive-diagnostic equipment manufacturer to a software company. Now, virtually all its engineers are software engineers.

Lyons says using test equipment at the end of the process only allows a manufacturer to identify defective finished products. But a manufacturer wants to identify where its processes are drifting and what causes defects so it can make real-time changes or, if need be, shut down those processes. To gain such control, a manufacturer needs sensors and software. GenRad provides both model-based and case-based reasoning software to meet those needs.

GenRad is gaining a competitive advantage because competing test-equipment manufacturers do not offer a similar breadth of products. Lyons concedes, however, that GenRad still needs to develop internal delivery systems, such as product development and marketing, and the outside appearance of a software company. The company is developing a franchise with manufacturing operations and information technology (IT) departments, where software decisions are made for the manufacturing floor. Whereas manufacturing operations focus on measures such as time to market, time to volume, throughput, and quality, IT focuses on the ability of software to work within a total enterprise system. Through its acquisitions of Mitron and Industrial Computer Corporation, GenRad developed software products, expertise, and market position far faster than it could have internally.

Customer Relationships

Close customer relationships are essential to GenRad's product development strategy. Customers are the principal source of information for product development and strategic planning. Major customers fund projects that result in generic products GenRad can sell to others. For example, Ford has funded a fuel-injection software program, Jaguar a vibration-control program, and Rolls Royce a vehicle-test system to be used in the manufacturing process. General Motors is interested in the fuel injection software project; Ford has no objections because it expects the product cost to decline when GenRad has another customer. Major customers also provide leads for acquisitions. In the past three years, the company has acquired five companies, three of which it learned about through its clientele. Typically, the customer was more interested in using the small company's niche product if it was part of GenRad's broader package of services.

Market Share

Through heavy spending on R&D, pricing, and cultivating customer relationships, GenRad has regained its lead in the test equipment market over its two larger rivals, Hewlett-Packard and Teradyne. GenRad also has enlarged and redefined its market, moving into diagnostic solutions and software for manufacturers where those rivals do not compete.

Test equipment and diagnostic software is GenRad's core business, whereas it is but one of many businesses for Hewlett-Packard and Teradyne. (Hewlett-Packard spun off test equipment and related businesses as Agilent Technologies in 1999.) Ford picked GenRad over Hewlett-Packard for a $400 million car-factory contract in England because GenRad appeared to be more focused on the test-equipment business. Lyons has tried to leverage GenRad's relatively small size through fast decision making, a short chain of command, and empowerment and delegation at all levels.

Approval of Capital Expenditures

Lyons holds operations reviews every quarter but no product reviews. Discussion focuses on business strategies and marketing plans. Lyons is concerned about how competitors respond to GenRad's initiatives. He questions whether new products represent extrapolations of previously known customer needs or whether they are bolder steps in new territory to serve future customer needs, known as "discontinuous change." Most capital expenditures are approved at the division level. Engineering projects are approved on the basis of strategic and competitive logic, not on net-present-value or ROI calculations.

Engineers and salespeople are asked to do what is in GenRad's and the customer's long-term best interest. In the first quarter of 1997, development began for a new product called a high-density tester. At the operations review meeting, Lyons told the engineers, "Don't ask for permission; tell me the decisions you have taken." They had decided to spend $2 million to develop a new tester they planned to bring to the market in the fall. The product generated $15 million incremental revenues in 1997 and $30 million in 1998, far more than forecast. Lyons emphasizes that he did not approve the project; the engineers took the initiative.

In a fast-changing world, Lyons wants to avoid committees and "gates" that could make GenRad unresponsive. Competing with larger corporations whose decision-making process appears to be more cumbersome, GenRad tries to gain a competitive advantage by moving quickly.

Reorganizing to Realize the Vision

GenRad's organizational turnaround in 1998 and 1999 entailed global account management, in which one account manager is responsible for a corporate customer worldwide; global manufacturing, in which a product is manufactured in one place for the worldwide market; and centralized software development in several locations so knowledge gained in a given customer-sponsored project can be shared throughout the company.

Enterprise Resource Planning Software

Many of GenRad's basic business processes, such as order entry, order fulfillment, and customer service and support, are manual and have been in place for as long as 25 years. The company is working with an enterprise resource planning (ERP) vendor to update and automate those processes. Lyons says, "Since we are now a software company, we understand the implementation of an ERP system better than if we were a hardware company at the mercy of an ERP vendor." Once the ERP system is installed, Lyons expects several generic business processes to apply to all of GenRad's businesses. He believes the ERP system already is positively affecting quality and cost.

Management Style and Corporate Culture

Lyons has replaced GenRad's matrix organization with a flatter structure. He has endeavored to create a new corporate culture based on teams and empowerment and to instill values such as candor, mutual trust and respect, and listening. His top three criteria for recruiting people, in order of priority, are passion, integrity, and competence.

People who have worked in command-and-control organizations are sometimes too rigid to survive in GenRad's more informal culture.

Most of Lyons' business insight comes from listening to employees. He believes GenRad's employees collectively know the answers to most of the company's business problems. They are encouraged to send e-mail messages to him directly. As a result, not many things happen at GenRad without Lyons hearing about them. Recently, he learned from an e-mail about a deep discount offered on a sale to a large customer. When he questioned it, he found that it enabled GenRad to establish an entrée with the customer, from which it recently leveraged an $11 million order.

Lyons observes that creating a new corporate culture has been difficult because GenRad is an 85-year-old company whose worldwide average employee tenure is 15 to 20 years. He has eliminated the cynicism and skepticism that permeated the company after nine years of operating losses. However, the company still needs a lot of work; new management talent will be hired from the outside.

The Role of the CFO

Lyons wants a CFO whose skills match the company's foreseeable future needs. He also looks for character, which he considers more important than competence. In Lyons' view, character includes both integrity and the ability to lead and make tough decisions. He believes companies need different types of CFOs, in terms of background and skill mix, at different stages of their evolution, just as they need different CEOs. The CFO skills required for the divestitures and financial turnaround in 1994 and 1995 differ from the operations leadership skills needed today. That is why there has been a recent change. The CFO must participate in most aspects of the CEO's decision making, understand the company's strategic vision, and articulate that vision to employees and the public. Lyons says, "A well-informed, articulate, confident CFO carries great weight with investors and bankers as we develop and implement our strategy. The relationship between the CFO and CEO is central. When they are complementary and in lockstep, it is a win-win situation."

GenRad's CFO, in Lyons' words, "owns the operating plan." The CFO is responsible for the order-entry process, from which flow the backlog and the sales forecast. Therefore, the CFO is responsible for the quarterly earnings outlook. The industry tends to be rear-loaded in its sales patterns; between 30 and 60 percent of sales for a given quarter are booked in the third month. Predicting quarterly earnings is thus a challenge, and the CFO must work closely with sales and operating management and know how to communicate earnings expectations to Wall Street.

During Lyons' tenure, four CFOs have left. The first was a long-term GenRad employee who was disappointed that Lyons, not he, was appointed CEO. The second and third were competent, Lyons believes, but burned out because of pressure. Lyons found the fourth CFO to be too introverted—he said little in meetings between Gen-Rad's management and major customers, and he did not interact enough with line managers to discuss the financial implications of their operating performance.

Capital Structure

Starting in 1994, GenRad's EBITDA grew rapidly. Today it earns gross margins of about 70 percent and operating margins of 15 to 20 percent in its core businesses. In 1997, the company forced conversion of its $50 million outstanding debentures into common stock, thereby becoming debt free, and started a stock-repurchase program. As is typical for a growing technology company with significant opportunities to reinvest its cash, GenRad pays no dividends. GenRad bought $8 million in stock in 1998. It expected to generate $25 million to $50 million in cash in 1999 and to buy a substantial amount of stock in a Dutch auction. (A Dutch auction is one in which the price of an item is gradually reduced until it elicits a responsive bid. In this case, the organization conducting the Dutch auction would distribute stock to all bidders at the highest successful bid price.)

Financial Performance Measures

GenRad's management incentive structure is based on the performance of its stock. The company uses basic performance measures such as return on assets, return on sales, and return on equity. After implementing comprehensive new information systems, Lyons expects to use more sophisticated metrics.

Taxes

GenRad will benefit from net operating loss tax carryforwards until 2001. Earnings-per-share targets will have to be managed carefully so investors do not perceive a decline in performance when the company starts to pay taxes again.

Key Findings

It is unusual for a technology company to incur debt to fund R&D expenses; however, debt was not the main cause of GenRad's trouble. Rather, it was the accumulation of operating losses and management's inability or unwillingness to reduce the company's break-even point. For Lyons, turning the company around did not require rocket science, but rather leadership and business basics. Lyons, who is not an engineer and does not consider himself good at detail, concentrates on strategy and knows when to delegate and trust his managers. He summarizes his personal management strategy as follows:

- Keep it simple: Set simple, straightforward targets and objectives.

- Never panic: In crises, the CEO and other senior managers cannot appear worried.

- Listening is the essence of communications: Listen to customers, lenders, shareholders, and employees. Lyons thinks most of his good decisions have come from listening to people and getting the "data points." In uncertain situations, even when managers cannot provide solutions, they help people feel better by hearing them out.

- Be humble: Humility is as important as confidence.

- Be prepared to respond to surprises, good or bad: Communicate the former quickly and hold the latter until a specific, credible solution has been developed.

- Work assiduously to know what you don't know, even if you don't understand it: That will give you humility, insight, and a compelling need to listen.

- Walk the talk: Talking the talk is easy; walking the talk is what makes people believe and commit. Behavior is determinant. Words are not.

- See every problem as an opportunity: Every opportunity, if not exploited, is a challenge to fail.

- Don't micromanage: The CEO can never know enough details to micromanage effectively. His or her job is to create the vision, articulate the strategy, and let others make it happen.

- Selectively create chaos: Do this where there is no organizational change or where people are resting on their laurels.

- Create ambiguity: Do this in job descriptions, business charters, and personal business objectives. Encourage creative responses to nontraditional opportunities.

- Stimulate paradigm shifts and risk taking: Encourage and reward people for thinking outside the box. Describe the box and its impediments to innovation.

- Be a cheerleader: Give credit, don't take it.

- Mentor: Impart unselfishly what you know and the lessons you have learned from your mistakes.

- Be humane in terminating employees: They may become customers.

Kollmorgen Corporation

Kollmorgen Corporation, a producer of motion-control and electro-optical equipment for industrial and military applications, lost money for several years and depleted a substantial portion of its equity as a result of overdiversification, a decline in government defense spending, and the expense of fending off a hostile takeover attempt. A new management team turned the company around by selling off businesses that did not fit within its core competencies, using the proceeds to rebuild its balance sheet, and investing in new businesses to strengthen its core business segments. The company was acquired by Danaher Corporation in 2000.

Background

Named for the inventor of the submarine periscope, Kollmorgen began in 1916 as a small, Brooklyn-based optical company that was contracted to design, build, and install the first workable periscope aboard the first U.S. submarine. Since then, the company has remained the sole U.S. designer and leading worldwide supplier of periscopes.

Kollmorgen's Industrial and Commercial Group accounted for about 55 percent of its 1999 sales and 50 percent of net profit; its Aerospace and Defense Group accounted for 45 percent of sales and 50 percent of net profit. The Industrial and Commercial Group provides top-of-the-line servomotors and electronic drives and controls primarily to original equipment manufacturers (OEMs) that require reliable, repeatable, and precise control of speed and position. The current market for electric motors is about $60 billion worldwide.

Kollmorgen competes in the high end of the market, which accounts for about $4 billion in sales. Within this segment, no company has more than an 11 percent market share. A major competitive advantage is the sheer depth and breadth of Kollmorgen's product line. Its motors, drives, and controls are available in virtually any size and power rating. The Industrial and Commercial Group also includes an engineering services business that provides specialized engineering, design, software development, and project management services for the electric utility industry.

Causes of Financial Difficulty

Kollmorgen's financial difficulty was caused by diversification outside its core businesses, a decline in government defense spending, and the expense of fighting off a hostile takeover attempt.

Diversification

In the 1980s, Kollmorgen's management saw a compression of margins in its core businesses and decided to diversify. It developed an electronic interconnections business consisting of printed circuit boards and discrete wire circuit boards. It set up a venture capital division and bought partial interests in several semiconductor-equipment manufacturers. In 1988, Kollmorgen was a decentralized business with 14 divisions and $345 million in sales, having doubled in size over the previous 10 years.

Defense Business

A significant proportion of Kollmorgen's motion control and electro-optical equipment sales during the 1980s came from the aerospace and defense industries, which benefited from increased defense spending during the Reagan administration. The company's backlog dropped by 10 percent in both 1990 and 1991 as defense spending declined. As a result, Kollmorgen's workforce of 2,500 was too large. At the same time, the company was losing money on several fixed-price defense contracts.

Unsolicited Takeover Attempt

In late 1988, Vernitron Corporation sent an unsolicited merger proposal to Kollmorgen's CEO, invested in Kollmorgen's shares, and engaged two investment banking firms for financial advice and high-yield takeover financing. Vernitron was an industrial-electronics company with about $100 million in sales. It was principally engaged in the design, manufacture, distribution, and sale of electro-mechanical components for the aerospace, defense, telecommunications, and other industrial OEM markets. Vernitron was privately owned and highly leveraged as a result of a 1987 LBO. In January 1989, following rejection of the merger offer by Kollmorgen's board, Vernitron made a tender offer for all of Kollmorgen's shares and commenced litigation to invalidate a poison pill Kollmorgen recently had adopted.

Kollmorgen responded with a lawsuit seeking to enjoin the Vernitron tender offer based on violations of Federal Reserve margin rules and misleading information in the offering materials concerning financing arrangements. In a press release, Kollmorgen's CEO said Vernitron's offer was highly conditional based on questionable financing through a firm having its own legal and financial difficulty; that a reportedly all-cash offer likely would include PIK preferred stock; and that the buyer, one-third the size of Kollmorgen, likely would have to sell off parts of Kollmorgen and reduce essential R&D.

In May 1989, after Vernitron initiated a proxy solicitation, Kollmorgen reluctantly agreed to the merger, conditioned on a favorable vote by Kollmorgen's shareholders and consummation of Vernitron's financing. Vernitron announced in September that it was unwilling to proceed with the merger because of its own deteriorating financial performance and "unspecified other factors," interpreted as difficulty in arranging the financing. Vernitron initiated another unsuccessful proxy contest in early 1990. Later that year, Kollmorgen repurchased all of its shares from Vernitron, settled outstanding litigation, and reached mutual agreement not to pursue any further merger-related activities. Ultimately, fighting the Vernitron takeover attempt cost Kollmorgen about $7 million, plus an unquantifiable diversion of management's attention.

The Company Turnaround

After the distracting, expensive battle with Vernitron, Kollmorgen was in poor financial condition and strategically unfocused. Debt was high. Many business units were performing poorly. Starting in 1991, a new management team turned Kollmorgen around by selling off noncore businesses, rebuilding the balance sheet, acquiring companies to strengthen its core businesses, outsourcing, and manufacturing overseas.

New Management Team

In 1991, the board hired a new CEO and CFO to help rebuild the company. Gideon Argov, the new CEO, had been an Israeli tank commander at age 18, and later president and CEO of High Voltage Engineering Company and a consultant at Bain & Company. Robert J. Cobuzzi, the new CFO, had previously been CFO of High Voltage Engineering Company and Ausimont NV.

Workforce Reduction

One of the new management team's initial steps in 1991 was to downsize the company in response to a reduced backlog and limited sales growth in defense and commercial markets. The workforce was reduced from about 2,500 to 1,700 people.

Divestitures

Kollmorgen divested several businesses that did not fit its strategic plan. In 1989 and 1990, it sold its electronic interconnections business segment, reducing the company to about $200 million per year in sales. In 1996, it sold a French company that makes instruments for electric utilities. In 1997, it sold its Macbeth color-instruments division, which made spectrophotometers, densitometers, and other specialized instruments and materials. The Macbeth division had good products and a good market position but lacked critical mass and was outside Kollmorgen's core competencies. Rather than trying to sell this business directly, management thought it could create more value by first combining it with another business. In January 1997, Kollmorgen combined Macbeth with the color-control systems division of Gretag AG, based in Zurich, Switzerland. Several months later, Kollmorgen sold its 48 percent interest in the combined entity, Gretag Macbeth Holding AG, in a public share offering on the Swiss stock exchange. Kollmorgen received after-tax proceeds of $41 million, which it used for other acquisitions and debt reduction.

Acquisitions

While shrinking Kollmorgen to its core businesses, management started to grow those core businesses internally through timely and strategic acquisitions. To maintain leadership in each of its niche businesses, the company has been selling and sourcing on an increasingly global basis. In 1997, Kollmorgen acquired two foreign companies. First, it purchased Fritz A. Seidel Elektro-Automatik GmbH—now Kollmorgen Seidel—a family-owned, Dusseldorf-based manufacturer of digital-servo drives, high-voltage drives, and other motion-control equipment. Kollmorgen needed a larger European presence for its industrial/commercial products division and benefited from Seidel's knowledge of the European marketplace. Seidel, despite strong products and a good marketing and sales organization, needed to become part of a larger multinational organization to stay competitive as its customers and competitors consolidated. The merger was accomplished after prolonged negotiations to ensure a cultural fit.

In the second quarter of 1997, Kollmorgen completed its acquisition of Servotronix, a motion-control software firm based near Tel Aviv, by purchasing 90 percent of the firm's shares. Several years earlier, after deciding to seek a partner rather than develop these capabilities in house, Kollmorgen had conducted a worldwide search and bought a 10 percent interest in Servotronix for several hundred thousand dollars to demonstrate serious interest in working with Servotronix. The two companies formed a design team of American power-electronics engineers and Israeli software experts and introduced a new line of digital servo-drives in 1996. Cultural adjustments in the course of this project paved the way for the merger.

Also in 1997, Kollmorgen made an unsuccessful attempt to acquire Pacific Scientific Company to further strengthen its high-performance motion-control group. Another company acquired Pacific Scientific for a price substantially above Kollmorgen's offer.

In 1998, Kollmorgen acquired Magnedyne, a California company that designs and produces high-performance direct current motors. In 1999, the company made three acquisitions to solidify its position in the motion-control business: Calzoni S.p.A., an Italian manufacturer of hydraulic masts used in the latest generation of periscopes; Semicom, a Czech manufacturer of servomotors that will provide a new low-cost manufacturing capability in Eastern Europe; and New England Affiliated Technologies, a designer and assembler of systems that incorporate multiple motion-control components for precise positioning.

Outsourcing

Outsourcing and overseas manufacturing helped Kollmorgen reduce its manufacturing costs. Outsourcing helps the company focus on its core competency of technical design. For example, Kollmorgen Artus, a French division selling integrated motion-control systems to the aerospace and defense industries, outsources machining and metal bending. This allows the division to concentrate on designing, assembling, and supporting complex packages of software, power electronics, mechanical systems, and motors. Kollmorgen recently established two low-cost manufacturing facilities in Asia: A facility in Vietnam produces motors and sensors for Artus at about half the European cost. A facility in India now produces brushless motors at a competitive cost, although it took a year of training and plant configuration to meet Kollmorgen's capacity and quality standards.

Leverage Reduction

Severance pay, charge-offs, and other downsizing moves eliminated most of Kollmorgen's book equity in the early 1990s. By the end of 1992, book equity had declined to $7 million; total debt was more than $70 million. Since then, the company has rebuilt its balance sheet through spin-offs, divestitures, a reduction in cash dividends, and curtailing its stock buyback program. In 1998, a combination of improved earnings, modest dividends, and divestitures enabled the company to increase book equity to $55 million and reduce its debt to about $38 million, representing about 40 percent of market capitalization. In 1999, debt rose to about 60 percent of market capitalization as a result of a poor earnings year and three acquisitions. Cobuzzi would like debt to be about 35 percent of capitalization, but the company has to be flexible to increase leverage temporarily for acquisitions.

Corporate Staff

Kollmorgen has a lean corporate staff, reduced from 20 when Argov and Cobuzzi joined the company in 1991 to 10 today. Management teams in the field run their own businesses. Each division has a controller who works with the corporate controller on detailed quarterly budgets and plan-versus-actual reviews. Financial results for all business units are produced about four days after the end of each month. Cobuzzi says, "Our job is to provide the business units with financing and to help them view their businesses strategically on an ongoing basis."

Key Findings

Cobuzzi believes it is most important for a company to maintain its focus. While some companies still argue for diversifying into counter-cyclical businesses, he believes there is a stronger case for a company such as Kollmorgen to concentrate on being very competitive in a few lines of business. In his opinion, companies that do not concentrate on specific products risk losing their markets to more focused competitors. He believes companies, like people, get in trouble when they try to do too many things. Although the total motion control market is about $5 billion per year, Kollmorgen leads in certain segments, such as servomotors. In addition to technical product features, the company tries to differentiate itself through low-cost manufacturing, on-time delivery, and good service.

Another lesson is that even if a merger fills an important gap in a company's capabilities, cultural issues ultimately are a key to making the merger work. These issues are easy to underestimate even in domestic acquisitions and particularly difficult in international acquisitions.

Real-Estate Sector

Cadillac Fairview

adillac Fairview, based in Toronto, is one of North America's largest fully integrated commercial real-estate operating companies. At the end of 1999, it had C$4.6 billion in assets and 102 properties totaling 51 million square feet, including 49 shopping centers and 42 office properties in Canada and 11 shopping centers in the United States. It was taken private through an LBO in 1987. To succeed, the LBO required continued growth in cash flow and property values, but a depressed Canadian real estate market between 1989 and 1995 kept that from happening. Since reorganizing under the Canadian Companies' Creditors Arrangement Act (CCAA) in 1995, Cadillac Fairview has pursued a growth strategy within the constraints of capital-structure policies that acknowledge the risks of the business.

Background

Cadillac Contracting and Developments Ltd. started in 1953 as a real-estate development company. It originally built apartments for steady income and houses for profits. Real estate was a growth business in the 1950s because of the baby boom, business expansion, and the resulting enlargement of Canadian cities. In 1974, the company merged with two other developers, Fairview Corporation of Canada and Canadian Equity and Development Company, to form Cadillac Fairview. From 1974 to 1986, Cadillac Fairview, operating as a Canadian public company, expanded by developing office buildings, mixed-use properties, and shopping centers in prime locations in major metropolitan markets in Canada and the United States.

By 1986, Cadillac Fairview was Canada's 27th largest company. That year, management retained two investment banking firms to solicit offers for all the company's outstanding shares. The reason, according to its president, Bernard Ghert, was management's belief that the value of the common shares substantially exceeded their market price.

Business Characteristics

Commercial real estate is a highly competitive, cyclical industry. The requirement for capital is the only barrier to entry. The supply and demand for office and retail space is subject to many interrelated factors, including general and local economic conditions; competition among properties; fluctuations in market rents; trends in the retail industry; tenant bankruptcy and insolvency of tenants; changes in employment levels; household disposable income; consumer spending; and changing consumer shopping habits, such as use of the Internet. A portfolio of real-estate assets is relatively illiquid and thus cannot be adjusted easily in response to changing economic and investment conditions. A commercial real-estate investment and operating company is subject to risks such as a reliance on anchor tenants, the potential failure or abandonment of leases, the ability of tenants to renew leases upon expiration, the ability to refinance debt at maturity, and interest-rate fluctuations.

Causes of Financial Difficulty

Cadillac Fairview's leveraged buyout increased the company's debt service when the real-estate market was in a prolonged slump, evidenced by a decline in both cash flow and property values.

The LBO

Cadillac Fairview was purchased in a 1987 LBO by about 40 U.S. pension funds for C$2 billion, consisting of C$500 million common and preferred stock and C$1.5 billion subordinated debentures that accrued interest at 13 percent. The purpose of the subordinated debentures was to provide a tax shield to Cadillac Fairview. The investment also provided for the issuance of Series B Subordinated Debentures, which under certain circumstances the institutional investors were required to buy. Finally, the company assumed C$2 billion mortgage debt and arranged a C$2 billion bank facility consisting of a C$400 million working-capital line of credit and 10-year term loan with aggregate availability of C$1.6 billion. The initial availability of the loan was C$950 million, but it provided for the accrual of interest to bring the balance up to C$1.6 billion in five years. If cash flow from operations and the sale of assets was insufficient, Cadillac Fairview had the right to exercise the Series B puts, requiring the institutional investors to invest an additional C$600 million, which would pay the outstanding amount under the term loan down to C$900 million. Interest then would continue to accrue, bringing the outstanding amount back to C$1.6 billion by the time of the bullet maturity at the end of 10 years. There were no specific plans to deal with this bullet maturity other than a general notion of asset sales or refinancing.

The purchase of the company closed and the banks funded the loan in November 1987. Because of the complexity of the transaction, however, all parties agreed they would have to redocument the loan. As a result, there was a second closing in March 1988 with an amended and restated loan agreement.

The investors bought the company for a capitalization rate of less than 6 percent and financed it with debt at interest rates ranging from about 9 to 12 percent. (The capitalization rate, a measure of yield, is calculated based on net operating income and purchase price.) Their willingness to pay such a high price was based on an estimated internal rate of return of more than 14 percent, justified by projections of steadily increasing cash flow and property values. Real-estate values were climbing in the United States, encouraging investors to seek out new opportunities. Cadillac Fairview had strong operating cash flow and a strong franchise in high-end Canadian office and retail properties. Investors saw no way they could assemble another comparable portfolio of Canadian real estate.

JMB Realty Corporation, a Chicago-based real-estate firm, arranged the deal. JMB had a lucrative advisory agreement under which it was paid fees, initially about C$32 million per year, based on Cadillac Fairview's asset value.

The transaction was structured to minimize Cadillac Fairview's cash obligations in the first few years. It paid interest only to the extent cash was available for distribution. That determination of available cash was left largely to JMB's discretion. It is hard to believe today that a transaction could be structured in this way, but there are at least two explanations.

First, the institutional investors were concerned primarily with total return over the long term, not with short-term cash flow. Second, LBOs at that time were increasingly aggressive in using instruments such as pay-in-kind securities, debt instruments in which interest was paid by issuing more debt instruments to minimize cash requirements in the early years.

The accrued interest on the debentures caused Cadillac Fairview to report a loss each year for tax purposes and accumulate a tax-loss carryforward. Under Canadian tax law, benefits from a tax-loss carryforward begin to expire in seven years. Therefore, projections underlying the LBO transaction assumed that some assets would have to be sold before the end of the seventh year to absorb those tax benefits. However, there were no specific plans as to which assets would be affected.

Decline in Real-Estate Values
Starting in 1989, the Canadian real-estate market turned down, reducing property rents, prices, and liquidity. A North-American recession that began in 1989 and lasted until 1995 in Canada was one cause; another was competition after Wal-Mart and other large U.S. chains opened stores in Canada. In addition, the combination of a 7 percent Canadian Goods and Services Tax and a favorable exchange rate encouraged cross-border shopping.

Despite the unfavorable market environment, Cadillac Fairview had more of a balance-sheet mismatch problem than an asset-performance problem. The cash-flow performance of most of the company's properties was within 10 percent of projections. Only a few properties completed between 1987 and 1991 missed their targets. However, the investors were left with a negative spread between asset returns and financing cost. High leverage worked against them. They had to hold their investments until either the real-estate market improved or a restructuring was possible. The real-estate market, though, remained depressed until 1995, far longer than expected.

The pension-fund investors received C$225 million interest payments on their debentures before those payments ceased in 1990. By 1991, they began to realize that the problem was more than temporary and to consider whether they could press for an overall financial reorganization.

Although JMB continued to charge its full advisory fees, its primary responsibility had become reporting to institutional investors. Cadillac Fairview's management had been delegated responsibility for day-to-day operations and even long-term strategy. This built management's credibility with the investors so that management ultimately was dealing directly with the institutional investors. Subsequently, JMB agreed to a reduction in its advisory fees.

In 1992, Cadillac Fairview exercised the Series B puts, requiring the pension-fund investors to invest an additional C$600 million in subordinated debt. The puts were a contractual obligation, but some of the pension-fund investors recalled that when the deal was put together, Cadillac Fairview's exercise of those puts was explained as a remote contingency. Nonetheless, the pension-fund investors generally thought they had no choice but to advance the funds.

This surprised some commercial bankers in the senior-credit syndicate, who did not expect the pension funds to invest an additional C$600 million without requiring some type of restructuring of the credit line. The banks conveyed their surprise to H. Stephen Grace, president of H. S. Grace & Company, Inc., who was advising several of the pension funds on their Cadillac Fairview investment and was working with several of the senior-credit lenders (banks) on other restructurings.

Looking back, Grace believes the pension-fund investors had the opportunity to join with Cadillac Fairview management and JMB in requiring the bank group to negotiate a comprehensive restructuring of the company's debt as a condition for the additional investment. The pension funds had considerable leverage in the form of the sizable investment they were being asked to make—and given their blue-ribbon status. Furthermore, Grace's analysis revealed that the C$600 million would not address all of Cadillac Fairview's short-term cash-flow problems—only a restructuring of the debt would do that. The banks had a strong inducement to cooperate: They wanted the new C$600 million; many of them had strong lending relationships with the major corporations whose pension funds had invested in Cadillac Fairview; and they were motivated to keep additional troubled real estate off their own balance sheets.

The pension funds were hampered by the fact that the chairman of the lead bank in the senior-credit syndicate was a director of Cadillac Fairview, and he pushed for them to make the additional investment.

Certainly his independence to represent the shareholders was questionable. He possibly should have recused himself. A further hindrance was the pension funds' inexperience in addressing troubled investments and their failure to recognize the need to unite, agree on common positions, and to present a united front in the contentious workout negotiations.

As Grace had projected, the simple contribution of C$600 million without a comprehensive restructuring was inadequate to address Cadillac Fairview's financial requirements. Therefore, he was not surprised when Cadillac Fairview's management, in summer 1993, proposed a plan to recapitalize the company. The plan called for the institutional investors to invest an additional C$1 billion to pay down the bank debt, but they were under no obligation to do so. Management explained that the company would have difficulty paying the steadily accruing interest on the bank loan because its cash flow was not growing and its property values were either stable or decreasing. It said the institutional investors did not have much choice because the banks were protected. The banks had security in specific real-estate assets as well as a form of security under Canadian law known as a "floating charge" over all the company's assets. The floating charge is sometimes described as a net that can be dropped over the company that provides a fixed charge over all the company's assets.

Under the terms of the proposed recapitalization, the interests of institutional investors that chose not to participate would be diluted. Many of the pension fund investors did not want to participate in the recapitalization if it would hurt some of their fellow investors. As a result, they asked Cadillac Fairview's board of directors to retain J.P. Morgan & Co. to review the plan, provide a fairness opinion, and propose alternatives.

Drafts of the J.P. Morgan report began to appear in fall 1993 in preparation for final presentation at the Cadillac Fairview board meeting in February 1994. One of the report's prescient recommendations was that banks settle for less than 100 cents on the dollar. Based on various assumptions, J.P. Morgan estimated that the company had C$450 million positive net worth after covering its mortgage debt, about 17 percent of the pension funds' $2.7 billion investment to date. (All but 7 of the original 40 pension-fund investors had by then sold out to distressed-security investors, who bought about 80 percent of the debentures for C$350 million, representing 18 cents to 22 cents on the dollar.)

Managing in Default

The covenants in the syndicated bank-loan agreement included a cash-flow test and an overall loan-to-value test. Graeme Eadie, president, and John Macdonald, senior vice president, finance, and treasurer at the time of the restructuring, delivered a default notice with respect to the loan valuation to the bank syndicate shortly after the board meeting on February 7, 1994. The banks thus stopped funding the C$400 million working-capital line of credit. Given the company's bank account structure and cash-management system, management foresaw a cash squeeze. Management was advised to ensure that a segregated pool of cash was available and to set aside $50 million to cover the company's normal monthly cash swing.

Among the overriding issues throughout the whole restructuring were whether management had the credibility to run the business, whether creditors would allow management to run the company's day-to-day affairs while it was in default, and who would be in charge of the restructuring effort. In the beginning, the bank syndicate seemed to pressure the company as much as possible to gain whatever benefit it could in terms of enhanced cash reserves, increased security, or better control over information and company business affairs. But under Canadian insolvency law, Cadillac Fairview management was obligated to act in the best interests of all stakeholders.

By the end of February 1994, it was obvious to Macdonald that Cadillac Fairview would need a new cash-management system and a new way to operate. The solution was a cash-conservation program he developed and implemented in March 1994. It provided for no further payments to JMB, no payments of any kind to shareholders or subordinated debenture holders, and no interest payments under the bank syndicated credit facility. In addition, all debt maturing was deemed to be extended on the same terms and conditions on a month-to-month basis pending completion of the reorganization.

Finally, the cash-conservation program segregated the company into "core" and "noncore" assets to deal with approximately C$2 billion of mortgages on various properties, some wholly owned and others held as partial interests in limited companies and partnerships. The core assets were expected to generate positive cash flow and value. Lenders on the core assets would become general creditors of the company. Noncore assets, however, were not considered to have strategic value; in fact, many had a negative cash flow. Lenders on the noncore assets had recourse only to the properties in which they had security interests.

Three Creditor Groups

Cadillac Fairview's management encouraged the formation of three creditor groups: the syndicated bank lenders, the mortgage lenders, and the institutional investors. Both the creditors and the company thought it was beneficial for members of those groups to coordinate their negotiating positions. The bank syndicate was organized from the time the loan was negotiated and disbursed. The mortgage-creditor group formed quickly because its members recently had worked together on problems with other Canadian real-estate groups. But management could not persuade the institutional investors to unite or retain professional experts in a timely manner.

After the notice of default was delivered to the banks in February 1994, Macdonald recalls, "The calm lasted approximately 24 hours." Lenders first called to ask questions about the payment of interest on the current basis, and then meetings began. Their tone was far from courteous. In the most difficult meeting, J.P. Morgan and the O'Connor Group, a New York-based real-estate advisory firm, presented to the bank syndicate their assessment of the company's value and a likely restructuring that would require the banks to accept a discount on the face value of their debt.

When Macdonald presented the cash-conservation program to the bank syndicate and the mortgage creditor group in March 1994, individual lenders might not have been satisfied with their positions, but at least they had a definitive plan. Operating results were to be reported to all lenders on a monthly basis so they could assess their positions.

By this time, management had achieved the credibility to continue running the company without formal court protection and to move the restructuring to the next phase. Management's position was helped by creditors' recognition that most of Cadillac Fairview's assets were still generating positive cash flow and that the company's capital structure was the root of the problem.

Finding a Strategic Investor

By June 1994, with the company operating under a known cash-conservation program and creditor groups receiving regular information, management could focus on a restructuring plan. An initial public offering (IPO) was rejected as too time-consuming and too risky. Asset sales were rejected for the same reasons and because they would not have generated enough cash in the short run. Furthermore, asset sales would destroy Cadillac Fairview's franchise value. Management therefore concluded that the best approach was to find a strategic investor interested in making a long-term investment in a significant real-estate portfolio.

Canadian Banks' Role

Management and its advisors had assumed that, given the size of Cadillac Fairview and its stature in the Canadian business community, the four Canadian banks that had been lead lenders in the syndicate would take charge and direct the ultimate restructuring. But it became clear that many of the banks had endured too many troubled episodes with well-known real-estate names to want to work through another long restructuring. Management would later see this as fortuitous because it could find new investors who were motivated to see the company survive.

Distressed-Security Investors' Role

Based on the valuation estimates in the J.P. Morgan report, an active market developed for the debentures held by the institutional investors. In retrospect, the distressed-security investors might have been better advised to buy Cadillac Fairview's senior debt than its subordinated debentures. Part of the debentures' appeal, however, was that they carried substantial equity voting rights, enabling the distressed-security investors to win a majority of seats on Cadillac Fairview's board in September 1994. Initially, the distressed-security investors appeared to have landed a bargain by purchasing an 80 percent controlling interest in the company for C$350 million, about one-fifth of what the pension-fund investors had paid.

Property values, however, continued to drop after the distressed-security investors bought in. A study in late 1994 by KPMG Peat Marwick, commissioned by Cadillac Fairview, estimated the median liquidation value of the company to be C$890 million above the property debt. In this liquidation scenario, senior lenders would have received 85 cents on the dollar; debenture holders would have received nothing.

Whitehall Street Real Estate Partnership V, controlled by Goldman Sachs & Company, had accumulated 28 percent of Cadillac Fairview's senior debt. After unsuccessfully proposing a restructuring, in December 1994 it forced the company to apply for protection under the CCAA, an unprecedented move in Canadian experience. Whitehall claimed to be acting to create a sense of urgency in turning Cadillac Fairview around, a motive that other investors questioned.

Restructuring Proposals
During the first half of 1995, management continued to seek strategic investors. It developed numerous restructuring proposals that tried to reconcile the interests of potential new investors and holders of senior debt, debentures, and mortgages. Alliances continually were made and broken. Finally, when every party seemed equally uncomfortable, management sensed that a final compromise was close.

The Company Turnaround
Agreement on a reorganization and financial restructuring plan was reached in April 1995 and approved by the courts in July. Starting later that year, a new management team was formed. Since then, operating performance has improved and a new capital-structure policy has been implemented.

Reorganization
On August 3, 1995, Cadillac Fairview completed a financial restructuring that raised C$832 million in new capital. The Ontario Teachers' Pension Plan Board and its affiliates were the major new equity investors, along with Blackstone Realty Advisors. The Whitehall Street Real Estate Partnership V was the third major shareholder. Banks and other lenders provided a new $C360 million credit facility that capitalized the company at a rate of 10 percent. The average interest rate for the company's long-term debt was 11 percent.

New Management Team

Bruce W. Duncan, a former JBM executive, was recruited as CEO late in 1995. He brought in a new management team in early 1996, including Jon N. Hagan as executive vice president and CFO. During 1996, the Canadian economy began to improve. The new management team moved the company beyond the restructuring phase and began to implement a growth strategy.

Corporate Strategy

Cadillac Fairview's overall strategy today is to continue to solidify its position as the dominant Canadian retail and office franchise. Under that strategy, the company manages the value of existing properties and its capital structure and undertakes strategic acquisitions and development. It maintains a competitive advantage by controlling properties in key locations where it would be uneconomical for competitors to construct comparable properties. It owns and manages 30 percent of Canada's super-regional shopping malls and 20 percent of the downtown class-A office space in Toronto. Joint venture partners are part owners of some of those properties, with Cadillac Fairview as the controlling investor and manager.

Capital Structure

In November 1997, Cadillac Fairview raised C$350 million in an IPO for 13 percent of its shares. The offering was eight times oversubscribed. Management had three strategic reasons for the IPO:

- It foresaw an increase in pension and other institutional investors buying shares of public real-estate companies and wanted to establish a track record for its stock.

- It foresaw continuing consolidation in the real-estate sector and wanted to have funds available for continued acquisition of new properties (publicly traded stock could be used to acquire new assets, and some asset sellers could benefit by receiving stock rather than cash because they would avoid immediate capital gains for tax purposes).

- It wanted to provide an exit strategy for some of the company's stockholders, so it used IPO proceeds to repay debt incurred for recent acquisitions and to add to working capital.

Since the restructuring, Cadillac Fairview's cash flow has grown significantly, and the average cost of debt has been reduced to about 7.5 percent. Every 1 percent reduction in the company's average cost of borrowing increases its annual cash flow by about C$17 million. Hagan and his team have reduced the cost of borrowing by replacing high-rate, restrictive covenant debt issued at the time of restructuring with more normal credit facilities. For example, in June 1998, the company paid off a C$101 million participating loan from Ontario Teachers with proceeds of a second mortgage on its interest in the Toronto Eaton Centre. It incurred a C$16 million one-time charge in connection with repayment by replacing 12 percent debt with 6 percent debt, which generated interest savings that increased the company's annual cash flow by C$4 million.

Unlike most real-estate investment trusts in the United States, Cadillac Fairview is a C corporation. Management chooses to pay no dividends but rather to reinvest cash flow in the company's growth. Investors thus realize their returns as capital gains rather than dividends and are taxed at the capital gains rather than the ordinary income tax rate.

Cadillac Fairview has several criteria in managing its capital structure. The company uses a reasonable amount of leverage for tax shelter but maintains a debt-service coverage ratio of more than 1.5 times. The ratio is calculated based on EBITDA and interest payments but not principal payments. The company's policy is to maintain a level of debt between 50 and 65 percent of total enterprise value (defined as the sum of the corporation's debt and the market value of its shareholders' equity). Floating-rate debt is limited to 25 percent of total debt and is sometimes hedged with interest-rate cap contracts. Finally, debt maturing in a given year is limited to what can be repaid from free cash flow in case the markets do not favor refinancing. Most of the Cadillac Fairview's debt is secured and has 10-year bullet maturities.

Later Performance and Sale

Between early 1996 and early 1999, the new management group acquired C$1.5 billion in assets. Funds from operations (FFO), the most widely used real-estate industry cash-flow measure, grew at an average rate of more than 22 percent on a per-share basis and 40 percent on an absolute basis. FFO is net income from operating activities before the impact of depreciation and amortization of assets that are unique to real estate, which exclude items such as office equipment and cars.

Some of the properties completed in the late 1980s were handed back to the lenders, but most began to perform as originally projected. Hagan looks at the difficult period between 1989 and 1995 as a big six-year gap, after which business began to grow again as it had in the 1980s.

In 1999, retail sales in Cadillac Fairview's malls were C\$474 per square foot, compared with C\$410 for its closest competitor. But while the company's performance continued to improve, its stock price lagged below its 1997 IPO price of C\$32. Other Canadian real-estate stocks also performed poorly at this time. One possible explanation was that, after a stock market correction in 1998, investors remembered real-estate problems in the early 1990s and were unwilling to bid real-estate stock prices back to their previous levels. Investors may have considered large landlords such as Cadillac Fairview, with its exposure to both the retail and office-space markets, vulnerable to an inevitable economic slowdown. The lagging share price was a particular problem for Whitehall, which owned 19.8 percent of the company, and Blackstone, which owned 10.3 percent. These investors had acquired their stock at C\$16 per share in 1995, as part of the restructuring under Canadian bankruptcy law, expecting annual returns above 20 percent within a short time. The Ontario Teachers' Pension Plan Board, on the other hand, thought Cadillac Fairview's real-estate portfolio had good potential returns over the longer term. In January 1999, Ontario Teachers' increased its stake to 21 percent.

In March 1999, Cadillac Fairview's management announced a shareholder rights plan to ensure that all shareholders would be treated fairly in any transaction potentially involving a change of control of the company. The plan also was designed to prevent a "creeping takeover" in which partial purchases could be used to circumvent the shareholder rights plan. For example, an investor could first purchase 51 percent, then another 10 percent, and still another small percentage, and eventually leave the remaining investors with a stub of illiquid and therefore worthless stock. The plan addressed a concern that Canadian securities law does not give the board of directors sufficient time to explore takeover bids and develop alternatives. Management also wanted to prevent an outside party from splitting up the company.

In September, management announced that it was considering strategic alternatives to increase shareholder value, including the sale of assets or the entire company. Because of its high market capitalization, some investors expected Cadillac Fairview to be sold off in parts to real-estate investment trusts and other major real-estate investors rather than to be sold to one investor. But in December 1999, Ontario Teachers' agreed to buy the 78 percent of Cadillac Fairview it did not own at C$34 per share, providing Whitehall and Blackstone with significant returns on their C$16 per share investments and enabling all other shareholders to realize reasonable value for their investment.

Key Findings

- The LBO was based on optimistic projections that did not materialize. Whether the arrangers of the LBO were in error or the world turned against them is a matter of opinion. The company has subsequently developed a capital-structure policy that reflects interest rate risk and the riskiness of its asset base and earnings stream.

- Although the pension-fund investors had a weak credit position vis-à-vis the senior lenders, they had strong negotiating leverage because of their institutional relationships with the bank lenders. Had they become more of a team, they might have recognized their leverage and forced all parties to consider a comprehensive restructuring of Cadillac Fairview's debt when the company exercised the Series B puts in 1992. They also might have recognized their weak position and considered the proposed recapitalization plan in 1993 more seriously. At both junctures, they could have avoided losing as much as they did.

- Management needs to surround itself with good professional help experienced in restructuring, according to John Macdonald. Cadillac Fairview retained lawyers, investment bankers, and financial advisors. Each was essential at various stages. Macdonald acknowledges that the appearance of consultants, who are paid top dollar and often seem to have a cavalier attitude, is unsettling for employees who are worried about their jobs, working extended hours, and receiving level or reduced compensation. But he believes the company could not have survived without the consultants. They provided advice and credibility to management in its efforts to salvage the company.

■ Information is crucial. Management needs to meet with creditor groups regularly, provide clear and consistent information to all constituents, and avoid surprises.

■ Working through a restructuring as a continuing member of management presents particular challenges. Management has to try to remain objective about allegations by creditors while attempting to reestablish the credibility it needs to continue running the company. In Macdonald's view, often it is easier for the "new guy" to deal with a restructuring.

■ In Macdonald's view, a successful company sits on a three-legged stool made up of the company's assets and operations, its management group, and its capital structure. A successful restructuring is difficult if there are problems in two, let alone all three, areas. Cadillac Fairview's real-estate assets were arguably second to none in Canada. Macdonald admits his bias but points out that management was able to run the company through the restructuring. The real problem, he says, was the flaws in the capital structure of the LBO.

■ Hagan emphasizes the key role of the finance function. When a company emerges from CCAA or restructuring, financial credibility is an issue. The finance function plays a critical role in telling the company's story and explaining why a similar situation will not recur. It takes the lead in gaining access to the capital markets, without which a real-estate business cannot survive and grow.

Service Sector

Burlington Motor Carriers, Inc.

Burlington Motor Carriers, Inc., filed for Chapter 11 protection six years after its LBO because of high overhead and over investment. New owners who purchased the company from bankruptcy right-sized its overhead, invested in state-of-the-art information systems, and strengthened relationships with high-volume customers.

Background

Burlington Motor Carriers was divested by Burlington Northern Railroad and taken private through an LBO in 1989. It filed for bankruptcy in December 1995 and was purchased out of bankruptcy by its current owners in December 1996.

Business Characteristics

Trucking is a highly competitive, cyclical, capital-intensive, low-margin business with few barriers to entry. Although there is an industry trend toward consolidation of truckers by the largest shippers, the business is still relatively unconcentrated. The top 20 companies account for about 5 to 6 percent of total business. Competition is based on service, price, and capacity.

In down cycles, large carriers tend to suffer less than small carriers, partly because of established customer relationships. Operating leverage, a function of fixed and variable equipment and labor costs, varies within the industry. To keep fixed costs down, some trucking companies subcontract part of their business to independent owner-operators during peak demand periods.

Drivers must be managed carefully because they are the most critical resource in the truckload business. Their work environment is arduous. They are away from home for long periods, endure long waits at customers' docks, and sometimes must help load or unload. The pay is modest, particularly considering the number of hours away from home. Although few injuries occur, there are many accidents on the road, which result in poor morale and high turnover. The supply of drivers, particularly those with safe driving records, is therefore tight. Even with insurance, an unsafe driver can cost a trucking company millions of dollars. A driver with a good safety record who quits today will have numerous job offers tomorrow.

Causes of Financial Difficulty

In 1989, Burlington Motor Carriers was purchased from the Burlington Northern Railroad through an LBO by a group of managers, who had been running the company, and an investment firm. The managers had a small equity stake, and the investment firm held the rest. The company's operating ratio was about 96 percent for the first several years after the LBO. It barely generated enough cash from operations to service its debt. Dissatisfied with the management group's performance, the majority owners brought in an aggressive new CEO. To accelerate growth, the new CEO raised $100 million in a public bond issue and an additional $100 million in equipment financing. Burlington had always carried just dry freight with no temperature control, and now it planned to offer more specialized services, such as refrigerated, blanket-wrap, and container hauling.

But the company purchased trucks and equipment to offer these new services before it had additional customers and drivers, so its overall equipment utilization diminished. That problem was exacerbated by a decision to buy cabover trucks. A cabover looks like the front of a bus: The driver sits on top of the engine and must climb a foot or two higher than in a standard truck, where the driver sits behind the engine. This unpopular cab configuration made it much harder to recruit drivers.

As a result of the expansion program, Burlington's sales increased from $200 to $390 million in a year and a half, but the company's operating margin was insufficient to service its high level of debt. Management responded by trying harder to generate revenues. To keep the trucks rolling, it let driver-hiring standards diminish. Losses from accidents consequently increased to $20–$30 million per year. The combination of accident losses, poor operating margins, and high leverage drove the company into bankruptcy in December 1995.

The Company Turnaround

Bankruptcy Process
Burlington spent one year in bankruptcy, and its prebankruptcy management continued to run it as debtors in possession with the objective of finding a buyer or liquidating the company. All parties concerned wanted to finish the process as soon as possible before the company lost its business momentum. It was running out of cash and soon would not be able to pay for new licenses. Recruiting drivers while in bankruptcy was difficult, especially because customers could direct their business to other trucking companies. In the end, however, this bankruptcy took less time than many others, largely because the principal creditors—about 10 equipment lenders—were a relatively small, concentrated group.

Purchase from Bankruptcy
Thomas F. Grojean and the Philadelphia investment firm of Dimeling, Schreiber & Park purchased Burlington in December 1996. Grojean, the current chairman and CEO, was an experienced trucking company owner and manager who made a convincing case to the judge on the basis of his industry experience. Dimeling, Schreiber & Park, the majority owner, specializes in taking companies out of bankruptcy. Brian Gast, the current CFO, joined the company when the new owners took control. He had been CFO of another trucking company and previously had worked in turnaround consulting and investment banking. He had become familiar with Burlington's situation when he visited to perform due diligence for one of the unsuccessful bidders.

Some thought Grojean was underestimating the risks in turning Burlington around, but he was aided in his due diligence by new management in operations, by marketing, and by sales managers from his other trucking companies. Despite its problems, Burlington still had a good service reputation with large, Fortune 500 shippers. Grojean concluded that the company could be profitable if his management team could reduce its costs and increase its yield. He was able to win the judge's approval to buy the company by offering a higher price and demonstrating a successful track record in the business. Grojean and his group invested about $23 million, some of which was used to pay off creditors, and took on about $90 million in debt.

A business can be purchased out of bankruptcy in several ways. Sometimes a new owner buys a company's assets but not its liabilities, thereby taking over a business that has been cleansed of the bankruptcy process. Burlington's new owners instead took selected liabilities as well as assets out of bankruptcy. By assuming these liabilities, they were able to buy the company sooner for a better price than if they had insisted on a complete cleansing, but taking care of those liabilities was time consuming for the company's new management.

Issues with Unliquidated Administrative Claims

Brian Gast and his finance staff had to spend far more hours than expected dealing with residual issues related to the bankruptcy, such as settling trade liabilities (unliquidated administrative claims). Each item had to be analyzed to determine its value, which was a difficult distraction for an already lean finance staff and kept Gast from spending more time on new business and cost analysis.

Cost Reduction

Burlington's business had contracted substantially during its year in bankruptcy. Sales declined from $450 to $220 million. About 1,600 cabs and 3,000 trailers were returned to creditors, reducing the fleet by about 40 percent. The new management team right-sized the overhead to the company's diminished size. It reduced the office staff by almost 200 people, eliminated several terminals (maintenance facilities and driver bases), renegotiated office leases and service and supply contracts, and negotiated lower premiums and risk-retention amounts on its insurance contracts.

Product and Customer Focus

Burlington today specializes in substantial relationships with large, Fortune 500 companies. The company's strategy is to continue to grow and strengthen its "core carrier" relationships with the largest shippers as they consolidate their carriers. To do this, Burlington must maintain capabilities at various levels throughout the contiguous 48 states. The company must also demonstrate financial viability. Therefore, an important part of Gast's job as CFO is to ensure that as Burlington grows, it can service its debt and that each new piece of business has the right cost-price relationship. Working with the marketing and sales staff, he constantly tries to weed out unprofitable business and bring in more profitable business.

Information Systems

Information systems technology, satellite communication, and software designed specifically for the trucking industry are essential competitive tools. They help the company manage its fleet and control costs. A satellite tracking system allows shippers to determine where trucks are and monitor the performance and miles per gallon of each truck. Burlington's truck dispatchers use "optimization" software to optimize truckloads and select the best and the next-best equipment to carry a particular load. Smaller competitors are generally less able to afford such systems and capabilities.

Financial Targets

Burlington's leverage remains about four-to-one. Most of the company's debt is held by equipment-financing companies, some of which are banks. When the owners bought the company, they negotiated some flexibility in debt-repayment terms with the equipment lenders in case performance during the first few postbankruptcy years did not meet expectations. Burlington does have working-capital lines of credit; however, it has limited ability to borrow in the event of a cash shortfall. It completed a sale and leaseback of its headquarters building and has begun to explore diversifying its sources of debt. Management is also considering taking Burlington public in the next several years, which would provide funds for future acquisitions and reduce leverage.

Management receives daily reports of revenue and truck utilization and monthly reports with detailed costs broken down by terminal, business unit, region of the country, and dedicated fleet (trucks dedicated to one customer). In this low-margin industry, cost control and generous cash reserves are crucial. All costs are measured on a per-mile basis. In a company whose trucks run 20 million miles per month, a saving of even a half penny per mile can make a big difference.

Key Findings

The two management teams that ran Burlington after the LBO grew the business by borrowing and investing in new capital equipment, but they bought the equipment before they had the business to justify it. In Grojean's opinion, the trucking business does not have high enough operating margins or capital turnover to justify such a risky strategy. It is better to have too much business and use subcontractors for the overflow.

High leverage added to the normal perils of business cycles. Having to run the business with minimal cash diverted management's time from business development and cost management. Grojean points out that if a trucking company makes a mistake today, it goes right to the bottom line. Like the airline industry, trucking companies do not have an inventory of products that they can sell tomorrow if they do not sell today.

Management spent far more time than it had anticipated in dealing with the liabilities that came with the company. Because the new owners were willing to assume these liabilities, they were able to purchase the company sooner for a better price than if they had insisted on complete cleansing. Nevertheless, Grojean and the investment firm concur that they would be reluctant to buy another company in this way because they had to spend $4–$5 million per year on repairing equipment that was not well maintained while the company was failing and in bankruptcy.

Fairmont Hotels & Resorts

Prior to its turnaround between 1991 and 1994, the Fairmont Hotel Management Company, the predecessor of Fairmont Hotels & Resorts, was reluctant to discount its top-tier prices for fear of compromising its market image. Recognizing the need to increase occupancy, a new management team allowed average daily rates (ADRs) for hotel rooms to drop while increasing occupancy and revenue per available room (REVPAR), thereby restoring profitability. This case study illustrates the importance of customer- and product-profitability analysis as well as understanding the key performance indicators that drive a business.

Background

Fairmont Hotels & Resorts is the largest luxury hotel management company in North America, with 34 city and resort hotels in the United States, Canada, Bermuda, Barbados, and Mexico. Fairmont hotels are full-service properties with 500 to 750 rooms, large public areas, restaurants, and meeting facilities. They compete in an upper tier with chains such as Four Seasons and Ritz Carlton. Some Fairmont hotels are company owned; others are managed under contract with outside property owners.

The Fairmont, on the top of Nob Hill in San Francisco, is the chain's flagship. Since it opened in 1907, it has been one of the best-known luxury hotels in the city. Benjamin H. Swig purchased the property in 1945. In 1965, the Swig family bought the Roosevelt Hotel in New Orleans, creating the second Fairmont. The family opened new hotels in Dallas in 1969 and in Chicago and San Jose (in California's Silicon Valley region) in 1987. Through his company, Kingdom Hotels, Prince al Waleed bin Talal bin Abdulaziz al Saud became a major shareholder and chairman of the company in 1994. The Plaza Hotel in New York City was added to the chain in 1996 and the Copley Plaza in Boston in 1997. In 1998, the Swig family sold its remaining interest to Maritz, Wolff & Company, a hotel-investment partnership that owns several hotels under various brands. Fairmont's 1998 revenues were $420 million.

In May 1999, Fairmont Hotel Management agreed to a partnership with Canadian Pacific Ltd. and its wholly owned subsidiary, Canadian Pacific Hotels & Resorts. Canadian Pacific acquired a 67 percent interest in the new company, called Fairmont Hotels & Resorts, and Maritz, Wolff and Kingdom Hotels each retained a 16.5 percent interest. Canadian Pacific, with 1998 revenues of C$690 million, is Canada's largest owner and operator of full-service hotels. Its 28 properties include Chateau Frontenac in Quebec City, the Royal York in Toronto, and the Banff Springs and Chateau Lake Louise in the Canadian Rockies. The Canadian Pacific name, which has strong equity in Canada, will continue to be used as part of the Fairmont Hotels & Resorts brand. In 1998, as its first step outside Canada, Canadian Pacific purchased Princess Hotels, with properties in Acapulco, Barbados, Bermuda, and Scottsdale, Arizona. They were renamed Fairmont Hotels.

Business Characteristics

The hotel business has two components—ownership and management—that often are considered separate businesses. The hotel owner generally finances the property with high leverage and realizes a return in the form of operating cash flow and capital appreciation in real estate. The owner pays the hotel manager a fee to run the property. Usually the fee covers costs and a small profit margin. There is an incentive structure so that the management fee increases, both in dollars and as a percentage of revenues, as the hotel's profit margin increases. The ownership business is riskier than the management business because the owner's earnings are more volatile and the owner has the added burden of an asset, often financed by heavy debt, that could lose value.

Marriott Corporation decided to separate its ownership and management businesses in 1993. The hotel real-estate ownership business was spun off to create Host Marriott Corporation; the hotel-management company that remained was renamed Marriott International Corporation. (This transaction is described in the authors' 1998 study, *Building Value with Capital-Structure Strategies.*) Fairmont was both an ownership and a management company until it started to sell ownership interests in its properties to outside investors in the 1990s.

Causes of Financial Difficulty

Between 1986 and 1991, the U.S. lodging industry incurred significant losses because of overbuilding, excessive debt, declining real-estate values, and declining travel during the Gulf War and the subsequent recession. In 1991, the Fairmont Hotel Management Company, which both owned and managed its hotels, approached insolvency because of competitive pressure and heavy debt related to its Chicago and San Jose properties. Room rates could not be raised to keep pace with inflation and therefore did not provide sufficient cash flow to pay for renovation and enhancements.

The Company Turnaround

The most important elements in Fairmont's turnaround included new management, separation of hotel ownership and management, a more professional approach to marketing and labor-cost management, and the skillful use of key performance indicators.

New Management

Robert I. Small was hired as Fairmont's new CEO in 1991. He had gained a strong reputation with the resorts division of Walt Disney World, Marriott Corporation, and other hotel management companies. According to W. Terry Umbreit in "Fairmont Hotels' Turnaround Strategy" (*Cornell Hotel & Restaurant Administration Quarterly,* August 1996), Small began by setting two objectives: to increase occupancy and to attract new capital from outside investors. To achieve these objectives, he analyzed each hotel's operations and financial performance and trained managers to operate the company in a more businesslike way, including taking a more professional approach to marketing. Hotels were renovated and information systems updated to help bring the quality of the Fairmont brand, which had been slipping, back in line with its historic reputation. A new CFO, director of accounting, controller, and management information systems (MIS) supervisor were hired. The accounting staff, which previously focused primarily on expense control, was reduced.

A new vice president of human resources was hired. She oversaw the development of a comprehensive safety and supervisory training program, an improved worker compensation insurance program, and employee recognition programs. Service standards and operating procedures were established and documented for all hotel service positions and explained regularly to the employees. Management focused on the characteristics of successful employees, such as self-respect and an interest in helping others, and improved its hiring procedures. A computerized labor-scheduling system determined staffing requirements based on business volume to reduce the employee headcount.

Management also initiated a more professional approach to marketing, including market research, profitability analysis of each service and segment of the hotel's customer base, and sales targeted toward the most important customer groups.

11

Product Profitability

Every conceivable service was defined as a separate product, each with its own P&L. For example, food and beverage products are now divided into categories such as formal restaurants, informal restaurants, room service, parking, local catering, group catering, weddings, and special events. Standard telephones, telephones with modem connections, and fax machines are separate product categories. In this way, management can tell whether each product is profitable. If a service must be offered as a loss leader, management is aware of it. No longer can an additional service feature be justified only because it enhances the hotel's luxury image.

Market Segmentation

Management also analyzed sales and profitability of each product by customer market segment. For example, market segments for hotel rooms included domestic and international transient guests, weekend guests, members of affinity groups, corporations with volume discounts, conventions, and receptions. Market segments for banquets included affinity groups (which also occupy hotels rooms while the banquets take place), social events and meals, corporate meetings, weddings (including rehearsal dinners, ceremonies, and receptions—a huge part of banquet revenue), cultural events (a subsegment of social events that focuses on ethnic groups), and holiday parties.

Market Research

The new management team met individually and conducted focus groups with travel agents, meeting planners, and corporate-travel executives. According to Umbreit, the focus groups perceived the previous management as arrogant, inflexible, unfriendly, and unwilling to listen to customers' needs. The company had been unwilling to negotiate room rates for fear it would compromise its top-tier image.

Sales

On the basis of its market research, management developed sales campaigns to increase both corporate and transient business. The sales staff began to make regular visits to corporate customers and travel agents in the United States and overseas. Reservation offices were opened in major international cities. Marketing partnerships were formed with banks, credit-card companies, airlines, and car-rental agencies.

Pricing

Pricing strategies were developed for each market segment. Corporate volume discounts were negotiated on the basis of the estimated volume and profitability of each corporate account. Special weekend rates were advertised during slow periods.

Key Performance Indicators

Skillful use of two of the hotel industry's key performance indicators (KPIs), REVPAR and ADR, was one of the keys to restoring Fairmont's profitability and increasing its value.

To increase room occupancy, Fairmont had to become flexible in its room rates. In 1991, under Small's direction, the number of occupied rooms, the percentage of occupancy, and REVPAR began to grow. To achieve these improvements, management allowed the ADR to drop for two years before gradually increasing room rates as the market improved. Corporate volume discounts and seasonal rate adjustments helped increase occupancy rates. With yield-management techniques similar to those used by airlines, Fairmont now can adjust pricing to reflect seasonal trends and increase occupancy in slow periods. Logical as they seem, these policies were not easy to implement in 1991. Competitors complained that reduced pricing would hurt the industry; even the Fairmont board of directors resisted the idea in the beginning. Small needed strong convictions in order to succeed.

Operating Margins

The finance function worked with the management of each hotel to measure and improve operating margins. Time clocks replaced manual sign-in and sign-out sheets. According to Charles C. Bond, executive director, accounting and finance, this eliminated false reporting of work hours and enabled the company to track hours by job code and improve its labor standards. With those standards and hotel occupancy forecasts, management could more accurately determine the required number of hours in each job category; for example, the number of turndown attendants per occupied room, the number of front-desk clerks per arrival or departure, or the number of waiters per diner in the hotel's restaurants. In the past, the hotels had set staffing requirements for low, medium, and high occupancy with insufficient gradations between each level. As a result, departments often were either understaffed, affecting service, or overstaffed, affecting profitability.

Operating managers having greater confidence in the new system's labor-hour reports than in the previous reports the accounting department prepared manually, saw the new system as a tool for improving their business performance. With improved labor-hour reporting, the company could compare the number of full-time-equivalent employees per occupied room with other hotel companies and the performance of each hotel in the chain by department and job code.

The comparison of periodic results for each profit center in each hotel created internal competition. Ideas on how to improve profitability were shared in quarterly business-review meetings that included each hotel's general manager, sales director, and food and beverage director. Henry Bose, vice president—finance, planning and business development, reports that the result was an overall improvement in measures such as food cost as a percentage of food revenue, beverage cost as a percentage of beverage revenue, and controllable expenses as a percentage of total revenues. As a result, the hotels reduced their overall payroll expenses between 12 and 18 percent.

Valuing the Business

One of the most important performance indicators is the continuing internal valuation of the business. Fairmont Hotels & Resorts is valued using standard real-estate industry cash-flow models. A procedure unique to the hotel industry is subtracting a capital-expenditure reserve from EBITDA to calculate net operating income or net cash flow, which is discounted at the weighted average cost of capital to determine corporate value. The capital-expenditure reserve, ranging from about 3 to 7 percent of revenues, is separate from depreciation. It represents actual hard dollars set aside for periodic renovations. A hotel property can be valued based on current performance, but it also can be valued on potential improved performance, assuming changes in factors such as room rates, expenses, and customer mix.

Key Findings

The finance function needs to work with line management on designing and continually monitoring key performance indicators such as product quality, product profitability, customer-segment profitability, and—specific to the hotel industry—REVPAR and ADR. These measures must be incorporated into a company's overall financial and operational review systems.

St. Luke's Hospital—San Francisco

The staff of this independent*, not-for-profit hospital is challenged by both its mission to help the needy in a low-income neighborhood and by the constantly changing health-care industry environment. The hospital has had to make continuous cost reductions during the past decade while maintaining its quality of service. It also has had to increase its income by developing new products and services.

Background

San Francisco has nine hospitals serving the higher-income neighborhoods north of Market Street. Two hospitals serve the mostly lower-income neighborhoods south of Market Street, where 40 percent of the population lives. All the hospitals north of Market Street belong to health-care systems. The two south of Market Street are the county hospital and St. Luke's.

Thomas Brotherton, an Episcopal minister and physician, founded St. Luke's in 1871 to serve the poor. Today, St. Luke's is one of 78 institutions in the Episcopal Diocese of Northern California. The bishop of Northern California sits on the hospital's board. Other institutions in the diocese include churches, schools, homeless shelters, drug rehabilitation centers, and community halfway houses.

St. Luke's is known as a disproportionate-share hospital because it receives more than 25 percent of its revenue from charity care and Medicaid. (There is a limited amount of federal and state funding for disproportionate-share hospitals.) St. Luke's has 260 beds and 1,000 employees, including 375 doctors. The hospital provides 52,000 days of patient care per year. Its emergency room, the busiest in the city, cares

---

* St. Luke's recently became the 29th hospital to join Sutter Health Systems, a not-for-profit network. The hospital will receive a capital contribution of approximately $65 million, one-third in the first year and two-thirds over a 10-year period. Sutter will select new board members, but only from a list nominated by the existing board and approved by the Episcopal Diocese. The capital contribution will help its finanical stability, St. Luke's will continue to pursue its community mission—to provide charity care.

for 100 patients per day. Reflecting the diversity of its neighborhood, 36 percent of St. Luke's patients are Hispanic, 27 percent white, 17 percent African American, 14 percent Filipino, and 4 percent from other ethnic groups.

Causes of Financial Difficulty

From the beginning, 10 percent of the St. Luke's beds were reserved as charity beds. Today, about 7 percent of its health-care services are free. More than one-third of its revenue comes from Medi-Cal, California's Medicaid program for low-income people, which reimburses at lower rates than most other health insurance providers.

The financial challenges St. Luke's Hospital faces can be understood only in the context of changes in the $1 trillion per year health-care industry. Until recently, the great majority of hospitals were independent, not-for-profit institutions established by the communities they served. Building a hospital was often the event that defined a community's existence. But now, many community hospitals are relinquishing their independent status as they are sold to commercial health-care systems or merged with not-for-profit systems. During the past five years, the percentage of U.S. hospitals belonging to health-care systems has increased from 16 to 50 percent. Two-thirds of CEOs in independent hospitals believe their institutions will become part of larger systems within the next five years.

The Clinton administration's proposed health-care legislation in 1993 and 1994 precipitated this rapid change. Integrated-delivery health-care systems were built on the assumption that everyone would belong to a health maintenance organization (HMO), which would subcontract all health care to integrated health systems. Those integrated systems would provide all hospital, outpatient, and long-term care. Through contracts with independent practice organizations, they also would provide all physician services.

The proposed legislation did not pass. As a result, while HMOs have grown substantially in the past few years, not everyone belongs to one; those who do insist on a wide choice of physician and hospital providers. Smaller operations such as St. Luke's, running a fee-for-service business, can pull business away from large HMOs.

The growth of managed care has substantially reduced hospital utilization and per-diem rates. Before managed care, insurance companies were unlikely to question a doctor's decision to hospitalize a patient and generally paid whatever the hospital charged. Now a doctor must convince a utilization reviewer of the patient's need to be in the hospital. Nurses representing HMOs must evaluate daily whether the patient still needs to be hospitalized. Hospitals have had to cut their per-diem rates to get HMO contracts.

An early discharge, necessary in the current cost-cutting environment, may be inconvenient but not usually life threatening. A patient may be allowed less time in the hospital to rest and recuperate after an operation. A mother might be sent home 12 to 24 hours after giving birth. A child with pneumonia may be given an antibiotic at home. As a result of this trend, St. Luke's no longer has a 40-bed pediatric unit. Jack Fries, CEO, says, "The industry has squeezed out all the social reasons for people to be in the hospital."

Fries believes HMO-initiated cost reductions have been, to a large extent, a healthy reality check. In the past, 900,000 doctors nationwide, operating mostly as independent cost centers, controlled an industry in which they had little financial interest except for the success of their own practices. Doctors decided which hospitals, medicines, and equipment to use. Consequently, their decisions largely controlled hospitals, pharmaceutical companies, and medical device makers. Hospitals continually added rooms and equipment to support doctors' needs. In the absence of pressure to reduce cost, they grew inefficient. Insurance companies that paid most of the bills had little control over doctors or hospitals. Because of the inefficiency in the system, there was room to cut costs when HMOs and insurance companies began to exert more control.

Advances in technology, particularly in surgical procedures, also have reduced the length of hospital stays. A patient may go to an outpatient or ambulatory surgery unit instead of to a hospital. In summary, the combination of HMO growth and technology has changed the hospital business by reducing utilization and forcing cost reductions. Because of reductions in government health-care expenditures mandated by the Balanced Budget Act of 1997, pressure to reduce hospital costs is expected to continue.

Addressing the Financial Challenges

This is not a story of a single turnaround, but rather of multiple turn-arounds in a dynamic economic environment. When Fries became CEO of St. Luke's in 1987, the hospital was losing more than $6 million per year. He says, "We have turned ourselves around more times than I can remember in the last 11 years." In his opinion, managing in health care is not like climbing a mountain, but like white-water rafting with occasional calm stretches.

Guiding Principles

Fries runs St. Luke's with three guiding principles: Continually improve quality and cut costs; serve all patients, including the needy; and continually diversify and look for new sources of business. The need to cut costs while simultaneously serving the needy was apparent to Fries at the outset. Strategies to diversify and increase business developed over time.

Cost Reduction

Employee compensation represents two-thirds of St. Luke's' costs. There are few opportunities to reduce costs through outsourcing in the health-care industry. In 1987, St. Luke's had 4.7 full-time-equivalent employees (FTEs) per hospital bed. (An FTE is a frequently used unit of efficiency for delivering service in hospitals.) Today, St. Luke's has 3.5 FTEs, an efficiency level almost unequalled in the industry. In 1987, 86 percent of the nursing staff were registered nurses. Since then, half the registered nurses have been replaced with licensed vocational nurses and clinical nurse assistants, who are paid half as much.

Such reductions are the result of constant restructuring and reengineering, along with efforts to improve service. With the help of outside consultants, management has restructured the hospital's workflow three times. In between restructurings, it has constantly tightened its budget. As a result, St. Luke's has been able to keep costs low enough to serve patients belonging to any HMO or managed-care contract without imposing across-the-board, percentage layoffs. Reductions always have been made by restructuring the work.

Care for the Needy

St. Luke's maintains a clearly stated mission to serve the poor, who account for half its patients. Its benefits are available to all, limited only by its means. Those who choose to work there are committed to its mission.

Diversification

Admissions to acute-care hospitals traditionally have been the largest source of hospital revenue. The daily charge for staying in an acute-care facility, with medicine, x-rays, and nursing care, might be $2,500. By comparison, a patient might be charged $800 per day in a subacute unit, $500 per day in a skilled nursing facility, and $300 for an emergency department visit.

Because of advances in technology and the growth of managed care, acute admissions have declined substantially and continually nationwide. Therefore, St. Luke's must continually develop new sources of revenue to survive.

Ten years ago, St. Luke's received 25 percent of its revenue from outpatient services and had no inpatient psychiatric care, no skilled nursing facility, and no subacute unit. Today the hospital receives 40 percent of its revenue from outpatient services. It operates a 31-bed inpatient psychiatric unit, a 39-bed skilled nursing facility, and a 40-bed subacute unit that are almost always full.

St. Luke's also has expanded its network of neighborhood clinics, founded in 1920; there now are 16 physicians in 10 locations, most of which the hospital acquired by buying out the practices of retiring doctors. As at the main hospital, those unable to pay full fees are charged on a sliding scale. The clinic network feeds the main hospital and is responsible for 15 to 20 percent of its admissions. Because the clinic network is not yet profitable, it brings down overall profitability.

Mission

Fries believes what makes St. Luke's unique is not so much its ability to carry out its three-part business plan as the rationale for its goals and the factors that make their achievement possible. No one actually owns the hospital. It receives only minimal funding from the diocese. What keeps St. Luke's going is its mission to provide care, with dignity, to all regardless of ability to pay. The hospital has been through many crises during Fries' tenure and most likely will endure many more. During these crises, management can get carried away solving problems and setting goals and forget its mission. At monthly board meetings, though, the bishop keeps the mission on track. He observes that at one time or another every institution in his diocese has had problems, yet most of them did survive and are continuing to fulfill their missions. Fries says, "If it weren't for the bishop, we wouldn't be here."

A 25-member community advisory board reminds the surrounding neighborhoods that if St. Luke's does not survive, they will be left with only the county hospital. The advisory board helped St. Luke's renegotiate a health-care contract with the city, which brought it more in line with the rates other hospitals were receiving.

Management Style

Fries' previous experience was with larger health-care organizations. There, he was concerned with longer-term strategic and financial planning. Those institutions raise and invest large sums of money. Managers talk about "optimizing" and "maximizing." They gain leadership experience but not under crisis. Budget cycles and marketing and financial targets are also important at St. Luke's, but the greater concern is day-to-day survival. Because the future in health care is difficult to predict, management focuses more on meeting its budget and moving into the next year without a deficit.

The financial pressure and the mission to survive influence the hospital's management style and the people who work there. St. Luke's attracts graduates of top medical schools who want to serve diverse, urban communities rather than earning more in higher-income communities. Also, because 35 percent of admissions are Latino and 15 percent are Filipino, the hospital attracts doctors from those backgrounds who want to serve their own people.

Every month, Fries participates in an orientation session for new employees. He tells the employees that they did not accept a job, but a mission, and the mission is more important than any employee's career. St. Luke's has no tolerance for lack of teamwork. Management reacts harshly to any department heads who deem their people or their operations the most important. Fries tells managers, "I can't promise you anything but the biggest challenge you have ever had in your professional career. You'll probably burn out in a few years, and when you do, we'll give you a bouquet of roses, thank you for all the wonderful things you have done, and trade you to another team. And you'll be replaced by someone who is new, vigorous, and able to continue this noble task." Rather than forced resignations, there is natural attrition. Leaving is not viewed as letting the team down. Management celebrates both the gifts of a departing employee and the potential of a new employee.

Finance Staff

Whereas the CFO of a publicly held company might derive satisfaction from achieving a certain bond rating or return on capital, the CFO of St. Luke's derives satisfaction from using his professional skills to help the organization survive. The CFO in an HMO is driven primarily by financial targets and has little day-to-day contact with the medical and nursing staff. In contrast, the CFO in a disproportionate share hospital such as St. Luke's has a highly visible role, leading the entire staff in finding ways to maximize revenues and reduce expenses. He works with the purchasing department to make sure the hospital gets maximum discounts. He and the controller work with vendors to keep supplies flowing when cash is tight. Like the rest of St. Luke's staff, the CFO and controller probably could find higher-paying opportunities elsewhere, but the sense of satisfaction would be hard to duplicate.

Key Findings

- Cost reduction is the most effective way a hospital can improve its bottom line. It is one of the few areas under its direct control—it is fast and guaranteed to work. No one knows the possible extent of cost reduction, but benchmarking provides a guide. Out of necessity, St. Luke's made cost reductions that initially seemed impossible. While the CFO was the key to cost control at St. Luke's, operations had to buy in, take the lead, and develop the plan.

- Continuous cost reduction, however, can burn out an organization. When the mission is founded on an external need, those who remain must bear the pain of organizational restructuring. When gains from cost reductions eventually taper off, volume growth is often an effective strategy. Increased volume can make a noticeable contribution when costs have been minimized. Therefore, cost-reduction strategies should go hand-in-hand with new business development.

Microserv Technology Services

Microserv Technology Services, based near Seattle in Kirkland, Washington, was started in 1985 to offer corporate clients a single provider of service for multiple brands of computer equipment. Since then, the information technology business has evolved considerably, as have the requirements for service providers to be competitive. Microserv's founder and original management team were computer repair experts with few financial, marketing, or general management skills. After sorting out cash-flow, capital-spending, and borrowing problems, a new management team reoriented the company's marketing strategy from direct selling to corporate customers toward partnerships with large original equipment manufacturers (OEMs), independent service organizations (ISOs), value-added resellers (VARs), and other information-technology organizations. To spur growth and prepare for the future, the new CEO hired a management team capable of running a much larger organization.

Background

In 1985, Gary Lukowski founded Microserv to provide computer repair services to large corporate users such as Boeing. Big companies at that time faced a growing problem maintaining numerous brands of computer and peripheral equipment because dealing directly with each equipment maker was costly and inefficient. Microserv provided a more economical alternative.

Lukowski had been a midlevel service manager for a large computer manufacturer. He financed Microserv by mortgaging his house and borrowing $25,000 from his brother-in-law, a venture capitalist. Starting with three employees, Microserv earned a good reputation for repairs and parts support. The key to success, Lukowski believed, was flexibility in meeting customers' demands and willingness to service equipment of any type and age, whenever and wherever the customer desired.

By 1989, Microserv had 46 employees, about 100 clients, and annual revenues of more than $3 million. That year, the company won an award for excellence from the Small Business Administration. Most of the employees had backgrounds similar to Lukowski's; they had worked in middle-management or technical positions with high-technology equipment manufacturers or large corporate users. A former banker served as CFO. Under maintenance contracts with the Boeing Company, Microserv supported 15,000 items of equipment. Other customers included financial-service organizations, mail-order retailers, federal and local government agencies, and entertainment and manufacturing companies. To meet customer needs, the company set up four field service offices in different regions of the United States.

By 1993, Microserv had 100 employees and more than 650 corporate customers. The company serviced the products of more than 300 manufacturers, maintaining an inventory of more than 25,000 parts and components. It leased a 30,000-square-foot headquarters building that housed a laboratory, logistics center, a data center, and a clean room, which has filtered air and precise temperature control for maintenance of sensitive equipment. Six outlying regional service centers provided depot repair service and served as headquarters for field engineers. Each center had about five employees and $100,000 in spare-parts inventory.

Industry Characteristics

Microserv offers on-site hardware maintenance support, in which customers may pay for up to seven-day, 24-hour availability and restoration periods ranging from two hours to a day. It offers depot-repair service, in which piece of equipment is taken to one of the company's repair sites and returned in three to five days. Microserv also provides system and peripheral upgrades and installation, disaster-recovery programs, network and software support, customer training, warranty service for hardware manufacturers, and parts management and distribution services.

The company has two types of inventory that it accounts for in different ways. The supplies inventory consists of parts and supplies consumed in making repairs. As items are used, the cost-of-goods-sold account is debited and the inventory account is credited. The repairable-parts inventory is a stock of replacement parts and complete machines available as "loaners" to minimize customer downtime. Because repairable parts never permanently leave inventory, their cost cannot be charged to specific jobs. Therefore the repairable-parts inventory is treated as a fixed asset and depreciated over five years.

When Microserv was founded in 1985, its typical customer was a relatively low-level MIS or data-center manager. The customer merely needed to get the computer fixed; Microserv was well suited to the task. The top service providers at that time were hardware equipment manufacturers and third-party service providers such as Microserv.

Since then, the information technology services market has evolved through four stages: (1) product repair, (2) systems maintenance, (3) systems integration, and (4) business integration. In stage one, from about 1986 to 1988, computer-equipment service had no ties to a company's business strategy. Users viewed service support as part of the vendor's commitment to product performance. The total customer service market was estimated to exceed $42 billion, with more than 81 percent in hardware service revenue. OEMs servicing their own products dominated the market. Third-party maintenance companies were emerging, however, and there was an indication of potential revenue opportunities from nonhardware services. OEMs did not put their best people in the service business and were uninterested in working on even their own equipment much beyond the warranty period. Further, OEMs tended not to be enthusiastic or skilled at servicing other manufacturers' equipment. This provided an opportunity for independents such as Microserv.

In stage two, from about 1988 to 1992, businesses began to depend more on their systems for daily transactions and production. In 1988, the information technology services market was estimated to be $79 billion. Computers were linked through corporate networks. Systems managers looked for a single point of contact for hardware and software services and support. Maintenance became less labor intensive and more tools based. Service providers partnered with their customers to extend, augment, or replace in-house staffs to provide systems design, planning, custom programming, and operations-management services. Leading service providers developed strategic alliances with other market leaders, such as equipment manufacturers, consulting firms, and Big Five accounting firms.

In stage three, from about 1993 to 1998, corporations looked to information technology services to support their overall business strategies. Chief information officers (CIOs) became integral members of top management and focused on concepts beyond the comprehension of the corporate purchasing function, such as uptime and the total cost of equipment ownership. In 1994, the information technology services market was estimated to be $168 billion. Service providers were evaluated based on their ability to understand their customers' business processes. To an increasing degree, corporate customers outsourced noncore competencies such as information systems maintenance, and service providers outsourced parts of their own systems maintenance contracts. The top service providers began to provide true multivendor/multiplatform support and global systems integration. Services they could not provide profitably—for example, specialized equipment maintenance to ISOs—were subcontracted to specialists such as Microserv.

In stage four, which began about 1998 and continues, professional services have become a large part of the market. The corporate customer looks to one vendor for all its information technology needs.

Service providers fall into a hierarchy. The top tier consists of firms such as IBM, Electronic Data Systems, and Arthur Andersen, which can provide full, life-cycle management services, with selective outsourcing, on a global basis. Microserv falls in the second tier, which provides full service in a more limited product area or geographic territory or to a particular industry, using what Microserv calls a "vertical industry approach." By studying a specific industry, understanding its trends and business processes, and aligning itself with other technology specialists, Microserv can become an expert at servicing companies within that industry.

Causes of Financial Difficulty

Microserv's financial difficulty was caused by a lack of managerial capability, which resulted in a failure to manage cash flow, inappropriate capital expenditures, an inability to understand financial statements and performance measures. Another cause was the evolution of the computer service environment, which caused vendors to change their product and marketing strategies.

In 1993, despite Microserv's progress, the venture capitalist who had provided initial debt financing became concerned about the exposure this and other companies in his portfolio had to a decline in defense spending. He arranged Microserv's sale to an English company in the high-technology service business that wanted to develop a global presence. The buyer backed out at the last minute for reasons unrelated to Microserv, but preparation for the sale was both expensive and distracting for a company whose management capabilities and control systems were already stretched by the demands of a growing business.

As Microserv grew, it had devoted insufficient resources to managing the business. Lukowski found being CEO stressful. He told the board he would prefer to concentrate on product and business development rather than administration.

Gerald F. Ryles, Microserv's current chairman and CEO, joined Microserv's board of directors in 1993 and was invited by the venture capitalist and other directors to serve as CEO in 1994. After earning his MBA, Ryles spent six years with two consumer packaged goods companies, worked as a consultant for McKinsey & Co., managed troubled divisions for a forest-products company, served as CEO and COO for a paper-recycling firm, and, as CEO, turned around and sold a troubled check-printing company. When the Microserv offer arrived, he was looking for a new company to invest in and manage. Although his previous experience was with larger companies in low-margin, commodity, cyclical businesses, Ryles thought most of the lessons he had learned would apply to Microserv. For example, when he joined a company, he preferred to start by giving its existing staff a chance to perform rather than bringing in a new management team and creating a "we-they" syndrome.

Sense of Priorities

As he became familiar with Microserv, Ryles observed that employees were technically well qualified and imbued with a serve-the-customer spirit and a can-do culture. The company, however, lacked managerial capability. There were detailed policies on trivial matters but inadequate strategic business and financial plans. While telephone expenses were tracked in detail, customer service contracts appeared to be filled out casually, field-service reports were overdue, and parts were issued to customers without charge or explanation. Because financial information was kept between Lukowski and the CFO, operating managers did not understand how their performance contributed to the company's financial results.

Capital Spending

As Microserv grew in the early 1990s, it moved into a new space with high-end furniture and features such as raised floors and a "clean room" for sensitive equipment maintenance. The justification for some of those expenditures, such as the clean room, had not been sufficiently thought out. As a result, capital expenditures were $1,041,000 in 1992 and $869,000 in 1993, which was one of the reasons operating cash flow was negative in those years.

Cash-Flow Management

At another company, Ryles had seen the CFO warn management that it was looking at the wrong numbers, pointing out that the company's operating cash flow was negative. Since then, Ryles has looked behind the accounting statements to find out how much cash a company generated in its operations and how it used the cash. He found that although Microserv's income statements for 1990 to 1993 reflected positive operating income, the company's operating cash flow after depreciation, capital expenditures, and increases in working capital was negative in three of those four years. The net cash flow after debt service and taxes was strongly negative in all four years.

In early 1994, Microserv had $2 million in term debt, a fully drawn working-capital revolving credit of $500,000—a large amount of debt for a company with $500,000 in working capital and $7.5 million in revenues. The company was violating a covenant in the revolver that required the loan balance to be reduced to zero for 60 days in every 18-month period. Payables were stretched. Some suppliers had the company on credit hold; others required a cash deposit or cash on delivery. Ryles concluded that if the company was not technically in bankruptcy, it was headed there. The bank lender, noting a five-to-one debt-to-equity ratio, considered putting the company into bankruptcy but thought the chances of recovering its loan would improve if the bank helped the company turn around. The bank monitored Microserv's cash balances, salaries, bonuses, and capital expenditures.

11

Ryles believed that by being cooperative, Microserv avoided being assigned to the bank's workout group.

Ryles found that the staff, accustomed to managing small items, had difficulty comprehending larger ones. For example, it was concerned about unauthorized $50 telephone expenses rather than the expense of running the entire telephone system. People did not know how to manage cash receipts and disbursements. Because checks were cut twice per month and mailed immediately, some bills were paid two weeks before they were due.

Vulnerability to Large Customers

In 1995, while Microserv's financial position was improving, a sales-tax dispute illustrated its vulnerability to a large customer. The customer decided unilaterally not to pay a sales tax for certain parts and services purchased from Microserv. But Microserv had already paid the tax on the customer's behalf and expected to be reimbursed. Although the dispute was resolved two years later, Microserv was not reimbursed for more than $300,000 in taxes and consequently moved into a higher bracket for the payment of business and occupancy taxes for the state of Washington.

In another dispute, a large customer decided to pay by event for certain equipment rather than through a monthly maintenance charge. The customer was trying this new approach with several of its vendors. The result for Microserv was a $70,000-per-month, 15 percent reduction in fixed maintenance fees, with no reduction in cost. Earlier, the customer had requested separate maintenance fees for each device rather than more standardized pricing. With standard pricing, Microserv earned a relatively large margin for servicing new equipment that covered the high cost of servicing old equipment. The customer at first agreed that the price would rise for some items and fall for others, but in the end the monthly maintenance fees would be about the same. Then the customer foresaw internal political problems with rising maintenance fees for some older equipment and asked to pay by event for these items. Thus, Microserv learned a lesson in pricing. Previous pricing was based on "seat of the pants" analysis. The company needed to better calculate its costs and contingencies. Armed with more facts and better analysis, it could not be bullied by a large customer.

Changes in Customer Needs

In its first several years, Microserv was able to satisfy customer needs by hiring qualified technicians to repair computer equipment. But during the systems integration stage in the mid-1990s, more corporations wanted total information systems services that were beyond Microserv's capabilities. To survive, Microserv would have to change its product and/or marketing strategy.

The Company Turnaround

Microserv was turned around by improving management of cash flow, changing product and marketing strategy; developing specialized capabilities and internal business-profitability models in areas such as parts and logistics; and hiring a management team capable of running a larger company.

Cash-Flow Management

In his early months as CEO, Ryles' first priority was cash-flow management. He required staff members to prepare a spreadsheet showing expected receipts and disbursements week by week for six months going forward on a rolling basis. He preached the importance of cash at management meetings and tried to explain the rudiments of cash-flow management to staff members.

The company became solvent in a few months after the staff developed a cash-flow mentality. By June 1994, Microserv was not using any bank debt for the first time in its nine-year history. One performance measure became the number of days the company was debt free each month. At the end of 1994, Microserv had a positive cash balance of $233,000. Sales for the year were $7,500,000—representing a $200,000 decline from 1993—but operating income was $613,000 compared to $205,000, and net operating cash flow was $1,000,000 compared to an $88,000 deficit in 1993.

Change in Marketing Strategy

Ryles recognized that direct calling on corporate customers was not working, largely because the information technology services market was in the systems-integration stage. Corporations wanted an integrated solution to their hardware, software, and communications needs. While equipment maintenance still provided 90 percent of Microserv's revenue, the leading providers offered a broader range of hardware, software, network, and integration services. In response, Microserv changed its distribution channel. Rather than continuing to pitch to corporate users, it developed partnerships with top-tier OEMs, VARs, and ISOs.

A timely contract with IBM helped Microserv recognize the benefits of the partnership approach. In early 1995, after founder Gary Lukowski had been calling on IBM for three years, he was offered an opportunity: IBM was competing for a large contract with Boeing and wanted to subcontract the maintenance of some older equipment. This $300,000 subcontract gave Microserv its first experience in subcontracting with IBM. Since then, Microserv's annual business with IBM has grown to $9 million. Through IBM, Microserv now has significant equipment-service relationships with large organizations, such as Airborne Express, Kaiser Permanente, and Washington Mutual Savings Bank, as well as Boeing. Microserv opened field offices in cities such as Miami, Philadelphia, and Wichita primarily to serve those organizations, and then developed additional local business.

Recently Microserv began a similar subcontracting relationship with Dell. Boeing selected Dell as the vendor for all its personal computers and peripheral devices, amounting to more than 80,000 units. IBM is Dell's service contractor for maintenance and warranty fulfillment, subcontracting the bulk of the work to Microserv.

Parts and Logistics

Microserv secured a $2.5-million-per-year maintenance contract from IBM for an additional 60,000 Boeing personal computers because of its parts and logistics expertise. Microserv exceeded IBM's timeliness standards and found the parts and logistics business to be more profitable than IBM had.

Parts and logistics has turned out to be a more profitable business for Microserv than repair work requiring on-site labor. Since the beginning of 1998, on-site repair work has declined from 90 percent to 50 percent of revenues; parts and logistics has increased from 10 percent to 50 percent. The company provides parts management, warehousing, transportation, repair, and procurement. Unlike a parts distributor, however, it also knows how to fix equipment. These combined capabilities allow Microserv to provide same-day service for most personal computers.

For one large contract, Microserv partners with IBM's Technology Service Solutions (TSS) subsidiary. Microserv provides parts and logistics and TSS provides most of the on-site labor. In this way, each partner uses the core competency in which it has a competitive advantage. TSS had not been able to provide same-day service because its internal logistics—particularly its ability to warehouse and distribute non-IBM parts—were not up to the task and its related internal overhead costs were unacceptably high. Ryles believes one of Microserv's competitive advantages is the ability to use its parts and logistics capabilities to help large service providers such as IBM, Wang, and Unisys offer customers same-day service. To supply such a service effectively, Microserv will have connect to the larger service providers' information systems. Today Boeing sends service requests to IBM electronically; IBM then switches the requests to Microserv.

A staff member developed a pricing model that helps Microserv achieve a competitive advantage in providing logistic support services. Based on the type of equipment and the number of devices, the model can determine the number of employees, the field office and warehouse space, and the initial dollar investment required to fulfill a proposed service contract. Among the model's variables are the failure rate and estimated usage of each part for each type of equipment. This allows the company to base its contract pricing more on analysis and less on guesswork. Microserv's pricing model and specialty in logistics enable it to run this business more profitably than its larger competitors can.

Strategic Choices
As the information technology services market evolves, Microserv continually evaluates each segment to determine where it has a competitive advantage and where it can earn a profit. For example, the hardware support business is shrinking at about 3 percent per year, and profit margins are being squeezed as product life cycles shorten and hardware becomes more reliable. Microserv must minimize costs through leveraging large-customer relationships and achieving economies of scale. Microserv management is making similar evaluations of the asset-tracking and data-recovery service markets.

Management: Investment in the Future

In early 1997, all of Microserv's operating staff reported to either Ryles or the vice president and CFO. Ryles was a nontechnical manager who had to concentrate on running the business. He needed a manager to improve the company's pricing policies and supervise the technical staff. He hired a vice president of sales and marketing to take responsibility for delivery of Microserv's full line of services, which includes the repair depots, field-service technicians, the telephone call center, and parts and logistics. Ryles knew this employee needed to grow but thought he was the best the company could afford at the time. As the company moved from $8 million to $15 million in sales, the new vice president was not up to the job. Ryles learned he would have done better by hiring more capability than he needed in anticipation of business growth.

Ryles recognized at that point that, with the help of a sharp financial person, he could sustain the business at about $15 million in sales and increase his salary. But he preferred to invest in future growth, which required hiring "ahead of the curve." He hired an executive vice president (EVP) of business development and an EVP of finance and MIS with the talent to run a $60–80 million corporation. Ryles described the EVP of business development as an "experienced rainmaker." He had substantial sales and management experience with other corporations. The EVP of finance and MIS, in effect both the CFO and the CIO, had experience in cutting costs and in system conversions. They work as partners with Ryles, treating the company as a start-up. They have invested in the business and will be compensated partly with stock options.

CFO's Role

Ryles believes a CFO cannot be just "by the numbers" but must understand the business. The previous CFO lacked vision. His financial forecasts included no sensitivity analysis; they were mechanical and did not reflect sufficient thinking about where the business was going. He hired weak people, including a controller he did not give Ryles the opportunity to interview. Before being prodded by Ryles, the CFO had not recognized that Microserv's improved creditworthiness would help it negotiate new lines of credit with its banks to support further expansion. Since then, those lines have been tripled. The new CFO works closely with his marketing counterpart, estimating the cost of each new service contract and deciding how it should be priced. He compares the profitability of on-site technical support and parts support, recognizing that they are two different businesses. Board members find his presentations easier to understand than those of his predecessors.

Exit Strategy

Microserv's options over the next several years include raising more equity capital, buying a smaller company, or being acquired by a larger company. Ryles believes buying another company of the same size would be more administrative trouble than it is worth. After a recent informal, exploratory discussion, Ryles decided not to sell Microserv to a $30 million subsidiary of a $500 million company. The parent appeared incapable of making an all-cash acquisition, and its stock was not performing well enough to be of interest. Furthermore, Ryles did not believe the managers of this subsidiary could run a combined $50 million business.

Key Findings

- In all the companies with which he has worked, Ryles has learned that operating cash flow determines a company's survival. The income statement, balance sheet, and statement of cash flows in an annual report are the result of accounting, but the bills are paid from operating cash flow. If a company is not consistently generating enough cash to be healthy, the CEO must either fix the business or get into another business.

- Each stage of a company's growth requires different leadership and management skills. Many entrepreneurs are not capable of managing their companies when they grow.

- A CFO cannot work just by the numbers but must understand the business. The CFO must appreciate costs to manage margins. In Microserv's business, understanding costs is the foundation for profitable pricing proposals.

- A CEO must watch details and manage, manage, manage.

APPENDIX A

Annotated Bibliography

Alderson, Michael J., and Brian L. Betker. "Liquidation Costs and Capital Structure." *Journal of Financial Economics* 39 (1995):45–69.

Altman, Edward I. "A Further Empirical Investigation of the Bankruptcy Cost Question." *Journal of Finance* (September 1984):1067–1089.

Presents empirical evidence on direct and indirect costs of bankruptcy.

_____. *Distressed Securities: Analyzing and Evaluating Market Potential and Investment Risk.* Washington, DC: Beard Books (1999).

_____. *The High Yield Debt Market: Investment Performance and Economic Impact.* Washington, DC: Beard Books (1998).

Andrade, Gregor, and Steven N. Kaplan. "How Costly Is Financial (not Economic) Distress? Evidence from Highly Leveraged Transactions that Became Distressed." Chicago, IL: Graduate School of Business, University of Chicago and National Bureau of Economic Research (1997).

Aran, Andrew M. "Caveat Creditor." *Institutional Investor* (April 1989):47–48.

Asquith, Paul, Robert Gertner, and David Scharfstein. "Anatomy of Financial Distress: An Examination of Junk-Bond Issuers." *Quarterly Journal of Economics* (August 1994):625–658.

The authors examined different ways in which financially distressed companies try to avoid bankruptcy, including public and private debt restructurings, asset sales, mergers, and capital-structure reductions. Their study was based on a sample of 102 companies that issued high-yield "junk" bonds during the 1970s and 1980s and subsequently got into financial trouble. Poor firm-specific performance was the primary cause of distress for 69 firms; poor industry performance was the primary cause for 69 firms; and leverage was the primary cause for nine firms. Thus, the authors concluded that junk-bond issuers suffer primarily from economic distress and relatively few encounter financial distress for purely financial reasons. One of the main conclusions was that there is an important link between the structure of a company's liabilities and the way financial distress is resolved. When there are many debt issues outstanding, restructuring of claims is more difficult, and therefore firms are more prone to file for Chapter 11. When there are many public creditors, each has an incentive to "free ride" and not offer debt relief. This limits the extent to which banks are willing to make concessions. The authors find that the sale of assets, including the sale of the whole firm, is a frequent way to avoid Chapter 11, particularly for firms with many debt issues outstanding. However, industry factors can limit a company's ability to sell assets. Firms in highly leveraged or distressed industries often have trouble selling assets.

Bahr, C. Charles. *Attention to Seven Warning Signs Can Keep Companies Out of Trouble.* Dallas, TX: Bahr International, Inc. (1988).

The author believes that companies don't have to get into trouble in the first place. The key is to recognize the warning signs that inevitably signal real trouble. Bahr's seven warning signs are discussed in Chapter 4, Comparison of Financial Turnarounds.

_____. "How Not to Go Bankrupt in the First Place." Dallas, TX: Bahr International, Inc. (1993).

Bahr's guidelines fall into 19 categories: (1) Business success is scored with numbers, and management must be able to understand and communicate what they mean. (2) A successful commercial business gives its customers the most value per unit cost available in the marketplace while retaining an appropriate profit. There is no substitute for quality, honest value, superb service, and reliable excellence in a product or service vendor. The customer's need must dominate the vendor. The art is matching a market opportunity with a provider capability and focusing on the issues that count. (3) People want to be part of something lasting and great, but also to be recognized by others for their accomplishments and to have self-esteem. (4) In a successful enterprise, the management team has a common purpose, uses similar methods, appreciates each other's styles, and resolves conflict easily. (5) A company needs an adequate presence of physical, mental, spiritual, and emotional health. The tone is set at the top. A strong, independent board of directors can detect when the CEO is failing to exercise proper leadership. (6) While a positive attitude is desirable, unrealistic optimism and failure to pay attention to problems and warning signs are dangerous. (7) Emphasizing strengths and minimizing weaknesses can be carried too far not just by salespeople, but by production, finance and other people in the organization, creating a distorted view of reality. (8) Expensive perquisites and other facades of success at the corporate and personal level may be well deserved but may mask poor performance or may become ends in themselves to the detriment of good performance. (9) Managers who are lazy, ignorant, stupid, asleep, or lacking in guts can sometimes correct deficiencies brought to their attention, but usually must be replaced. (10) An excessive CEO ego or a culture of greed, including chiseling customers, vendors, employees, and the government, can start a company on a gradual process of sickness and decline and also create an environment for employee theft. Greed in the form of excessive expansion, uncontrolled growth, unjustified fixed-asset expansion to reduce costs, bulk purchases or speculation in inventory, or accepting marginal credit orders to increase sales may work out or may attract competitors, cause antitrust action by the government, or backfire in a recession. (11) While considered, reasoned, managed nepotism occasionally may be condoned, competent performance is still a requirement for a management job. The absence of a clear decision maker in a family-controlled company can result in family squabbles and fracture a company. (12) Growth is necessary, but it must be managed. Growth beyond a certain rate absorbs disproportionate resources and can cause a business to spin out of control. (13) Well-managed companies have a process of setting and following priorities that helps them manage scarce resources such as cash and key-management time and remain profitable. (14) Companies and individuals need clarity concerning where they are going. A company needs a mission, goals, objectives, plans, and paths. Paths are commonly agreed processes for achieving desired goals. (15) Lack of candor with commercial lenders can compromise a source of support. (16) Regulatory, political, and legal constraints, whether helpful or harmful to the business, cannot be ignored. (17) A company is vulnerable to critical relationships such as a single dominant customer, a key employee with difficult-to-replace skills, a dominant vendor or raw material source, or a single lender. This is difficult to avoid for a start-up business. A company also is vulnerable to a stupid competitor who prices at a suicidal level, produces a bad product, or alienates industry constituencies. (18) A company is a feedback control system. Objectives are set, action taken, results or progress measured against objectives, and appropriate corrective action applied. Good managements identify key factors in their businesses and measure them frequently. Absence of prompt, accurate internal and external financial reports is a red flag. The art of priorities applies to control. (19) Running out of cash is a single, ultimate, and immediate moment of truth. Regardless of the excuse, the real reason this happens is that company affairs are not planned and executed with the number one goal of protecting positive cash. Corporate cash follows Murphy's law in being easier to deteriorate than replenish. One protective measure is to borrow only to preset levels that are less than available levels, which encourages lender willingness to advance more when it is needed on favorable terms. Control for profit and control for cash are equally important, but more divergent than the smaller the company.

Baker, George P., and Karen H. Wruck. "Organizational Changes and Value Creation in Leveraged Buyouts: The Case of O.M. Scott & Sons Company." *Journal of Financial Economics,* 25 (1989):163–190.

A case study of a successful management buyout.

Barclay, Michael J., and Clifford G. Holderness. "Control of Corporations by Active Block Investors." *Journal of Applied Corporate Finance* (Fall 1991): 68–77.

Bernstein, Aaron. Grounded: Frank Lorenzo and the Destruction of Eastern Airlines. Washington, DC: Beard Books, 1999.

Bernstein, H. Bruce. "An Update: Leveraged Buyouts and Fraudulent Conveyances." *The Secured Lender* (November/December 1994): 70–77, 153–157.

Betker, Brian. "The Security Price Effects of Public Debt Defaults." *The Journal of Financial Research* (Spring 1998):17–35.

The author compares the costs of bankruptcy and out-of-court workouts by examining security returns around a sample of public debt defaults. He concludes that bankruptcy is more costly than a workout but that the cost differential is reduced for companies with large net-operating-loss carryforwards. He finds this evidence consistent with the argument that equity has greater option value in a workout relative to bankruptcy.

Bi, Keqian, and Haim Levy. "Market Reaction to Bond Downgradings Followed by Chapter 11 Filings." *Financial Management* (Autumn 1993):156–162.

Bibeault, Donald B. *Corporate Turnaround: How Managers Turn Losers Into Winners!* Washington, DC: Beard Books (1999).

Bower, Joseph L., and Clayton M. Christensen. "Disruptive Technologies: Catching the Wave." *Harvard Business Review* (January–February 1995):43–53.

The authors note that one of the most consistent and ironic patterns in business is the failure of leading companies to stay at the top of their industries when technologies or markets change. By gearing themselves to serve the needs of their mainstream customers, these companies often ignore disruptive new technologies that initially do not meet the needs of those customers and appeal only to small or emerging markets. Managers tend to back low-risk projects where the market seems assured. To manage strategically important, disruptive technologies, the authors recommended the establishment of independent, entrepreneurial business units where fast, low-cost forays into ill-defined markets are possible and where overhead is low enough to permit profit even in emerging markets.

Branch, Ben, and Hugh Ray. *Bankruptcy Investing: How to Profit From Distressed Companies.* Washington, DC: Beard Books (1999).

Bruner, Robert F., and Kenneth M. Eades. "The Crash of the Revco Leveraged Buyout: The Hypothesis of Inadequate Capital." *Financial Management* (Spring 1992):35–49.

The authors found that the Revco Drug Stores LBO was inadequately capitalized and had a low probability of generating sufficient cash to meet its debt obligations.

Chaterjee, Sris, Upinder S. Dhillon, and Gabriel Ramirez. "Resolution of Financial Distress: Debt Restructurings via Chapter 11, Prepackaged Bankruptcies, and Workouts." *Financial Management* (Spring 1996):5–18.

Chen, Yehning, J. Fred Weston, and Edward Altman. "Financial Distress and Restructuring Models." *Financial Management* (Summer 1995):57–75.

Christensen, Clayton M. "Why Great Companies Lose Their Way." *Across the Board* (October 1998):36–41.

Chura, Hillary. "Ben Franklin Seeks Bankruptcy Court Protection, Cites Competition." Associated Press, July 29, 1996.

Ben Franklin Stores, where the late Sam Walton honed his merchandising skills, filed for Chapter 11 protection in July 1996. It was the latest victim of competition from superstores such as Wal-Mart, which offer wide variety and low prices. Other recent retail bankruptcies included Caldor Corporation, the nation's fourth largest discount store chain, and Bradlees Inc., a northeastern discount operator. Ben Franklin had shifted eight years ago from a five-and-dime format to specialize in arts and crafts supplies. It had 930 stores in 49 states. The company planned to attempt to sell its 33 company-owned stores and close those it was unable to sell.

Cooper, Stephen F., Michael E. France, Leonard J. Lobiondo, and Norman A. Lavin. "When to Hold and When to Fold." *Financial Executive* (November/December 1994):40–45.

The authors suggest five steps to take in evaluating the viability of a business unit:

(1) Understand the characteristics of the industry in which your business unit resides.

(2) Critically analyze and challenge your business unit's position within its market.

(3) Thoroughly dissect the economic model of how your business unit generates profits.

(4) Evaluate your business unit's capital structure.

(5) Most important, assess the business unit's management and the related management processes.

Cressy, Robert C. "Debt Rescheduling versus Bankruptcy: The Creditor's Decision Problem." *Journal of Business Finance & Accounting* (October 1996):1141–1156.

Darden Graduate Business School, University of Virginia. "Corporate Bankruptcy: An Overview for the Uninitiated and Untainted." Charlottesville, VA (1991).

Datta, Sudip, and Mai E. Iskander-Datta. "Reorganization and Financial Distress: An Empirical Investigation." *Journal of Financial Research* (Spring 1995):15–32.

For a sample of 135 firms that filed Chapter 11 petitions between January 1980 and December 1989, the authors tracked restructuring activities from two years before bankruptcy until their emergence from bankruptcy. They examined four forms of restructuring: financial, asset, governance, and labor. They found that the success or failure of financial restructuring before bankruptcy is a function of the security status of private lenders. Private financial restructuring attempts fail more often when lenders are secured. This suggests that secured lenders consider themselves better off when the firm is in bankruptcy. The authors also noted that attempts to restructure financially may fail because of information asymmetry between management and creditors or holdout problems. They found little evidence that bankruptcy is used to break labor contracts unilaterally. They showed that Chapter 11 is soft on management of firms in bankruptcy. Finally, they showed that more restructurings are undertaken by companies with higher leverage.

Daughen, Joseph R., and Peter Binzen. *The Wreck of the Penn Central.* Washington, DC: Beard Books (1999).

DeAngelo, H., and L. DeAngelo. "Dividend Policy and Financial Distress, An Empirical Investigation of Troubles NYSE Firms." *Journal of Finance* 45 (1990):1415–1431.

Deloitte & Touche LLP. *Understanding the Restructuring Process.* Toronto, Canada (1999).

APPENDIX A

Denis, David J., and Diane K. Denis. "Causes of Financial Distress Following Leveraged Recapitalizations." *Journal of Financial Economics* 37 (1995):129–157.

> The authors discuss possible reasons for the failures that befell nearly a third of the leveraged recapitalizations completed between 1985 and 1988.

Denis, David J., Diane K. Denis, and Atulya Sarin. "Agency Problems, Equity Ownership, and Corporate Diversification." *The Journal of Finance* (March 1997):135–160.

Donaldson, Gordon. "Voluntary Restructuring: The Case of General Mills." *Journal of Applied Corporate Finance* (Fall 1991):6–19.

Easterbook, Frank H. "Is Corporate Bankruptcy Efficient?" *Journal of Financial Economics* 27 (1990):411–417.

Eberhart, Allan C., and Lemma W. Senbet. "Absolute Priority Rule Violations and Risk Incentives for Financially Distressed Firms." *Financial Management* (Autumn 1993):101–116.

Fridson, Martin S. "What Went Wrong with the Highly Leveraged Deals (Or All Variety of Agency Costs)?" *Journal of Applied Corporate Finance.* (Fall 1991):57–67.

Gilson, Stuart. "Management Turnover and Financial Distress." *Journal of Financial Economics* 25 (1989):241–262.

_____. "Transaction Costs and Capital Structure Choice: Evidence from Financially Distressed Firms." *Journal of Finance* (March 1997):161–196.

Gilson, Stuart, Kose John, and Larry Lang. "Troubled Debt Restructurings: An Empirical Study of Private Reorganization of Firms in Default." *Journal of Financial Economics* 27 (1990):315–353.

> The authors showed that companies with more public debt relative to bank debt are more prone to file for Chapter 11 and less prone to restructure out of court.

Grace, H. Stephen, and John E. Haupert. "The Case of the Missing Management Model." *Financial Executive* (January/February 1996): 44–48.

The authors convened 10 financial executives to examine various management tools that had been popular in the past two decades to determine why many of those concepts had proved to be ineffective and whether there is a common framework or management model in which they should be used to make them more useful going forward.

Hansen, Thomas. "An Introduction to Practical Workouts and Bankruptcy." *The Practical Accountant* (December 1997):17–40.

Hanson, Randall K., and James K. Smith. "A New Chapter in Bankruptcy Reform." *Journal of Accountancy* (February 1999):47–51.

Hendel, Igal. "Competition Under Financial Distress." *The Journal of Industrial Economics* (September 1996):309–324.

Hickey, Denis. "Look Beyond the Balance Sheet: Behavioral Warnings of Troubled Businesses." *Commercial Lending Review* (Fall 1991):54.

Troubled companies often begin their decline before their financial statements reveal problems. Among the behavioral indicators bankers can use to forecast trouble are: lack of balance because of emphasis on one functional area such as sales; high lifestyles; follower attitudes, where there is not enough creativity to command high margins; lack of strategic plans and product profitability reporting; lack of values, such as a get-rich-quick rather than a long-term-building philosophy; harmful relationships such as bad hiring decisions, acquisitions, or mergers; and old age, with entrenched management lacking the energy and creativity to face new challenges.

Holthausen, Robert W., and David F. Larcker. "The Financial Performance of Reverse Leveraged Buyouts." *Journal of Financial Economics* 42 (1996):293–332.

Huffman, Stephen P., and David J. Ward. "The Prediction of Default for High-Yield Bond Issues." *Review of Financial Economics.* 5(1) (1996):75–89.

Hunn, Paul H. "The Uses of Adversity: The Rewards and Risks of Financial Restructurings Within the U.S. Market." *Professional Investor* (March 1995):51–58.

The author noted in 1993 that the restructuring market for distressed corporations' securities was merely simmering, but that a renewed pace of initial public offerings and high-yield debt offerings might bring some new "product" to the market before long. Industry experts estimate that investors in the distressed securities of companies such as Toys 'R Us, Revere Copper and Brass, Show-Biz Pizza, Wheeling-Pittsburgh Steel, and G. Heileman have realized returns in the 25 to 30 percent range. But riding the risk curve left investors with financial scars in the cases of Crazie Eddie, Phar Mor, and Leslie Fay, all of which involved fraud. A number of well-known companies such as Continental Airlines, Telex, Western Union, Addressograph-Multigraph, and Sharon Steel have filed for bankruptcy twice in the past 15 years. While several companies fell victim to unique event risk, Hunn believes that the *leitmotif* of the late 1980s and early 1990s was the aggressive pushing of the envelope of financial engineering through relaxed credit standards. Many of the bankruptcies resulted at least partly from excess gearing of unsuitable LBO candidates with high-yield securities. Often those securities were either zero-coupon bonds or payment-in-kind (PIK) bonds, and often they were subordinated. Starting in the 1970s, distressed-securities investors such as Michael Price, Michael Steinhardt, and Martin Whitman found niches where securities were valued strictly on cash flow but had the potential to be revalued on earnings per share. The new guard of the 1990s reflects both financial muscle and an appetite for confrontation. Leon Black, formerly of Drexel and financed by Credit Lyonnais, acquired the huge Executive Life portfolio of distressed securities, which gave him major positions in large workouts that he was able to enlarge to gain equity control. Black's technique has been emulated by senior investors who have bought junior securities to enhance their influence in restructuring plans. The legal vehicle used in distressed-securities investing is typically the limited partnership of fewer than 99 sophisticated investors. The increased depth and liquidity of the distressed-securities market is largely a result of a change in the stature of large commercial banks. Rather than protecting their capital with workouts, they have preferred to cleanse their books of cited loans to look better in the eyes of the rating agencies—an important consideration as they rely more on purchased funds and move more toward investment banking. Even insurance companies, the ultimate long-term lenders, are selling some of their claims. This has made restructuring more difficult and reduced the chances of many companies to regain long-term viability. In the opinion of Mike Neilson, managing director of Hellmond Associates, there could never be another out-of-court restructuring such as International Harvester in the current environment.

_____. "The Evolution of Leveraged Buyout Financing." *Commercial Lending Review* (Fall 1986):37–46.

Jensen, Michael C. "Eclipse of the Public Corporation." *Harvard Business Review* (September–October 1989):61–74.

Jog, Vijay M., Igor Kotlyar, and Donald G. Tate. "Stakeholder Losses in Corporate Restructuring: Evidence from Four Cases in the North American Steel Industry." *Financial Management* (Autumn 1993): 185–201.

This article analyzes four major cases of restructuring in the steel industry: Algoma Steel in Canada, LTV Steel, Wierton Steel, and Wheeling Pittsburgh Steel. It investigates the impact of restructurings or announcements of bankruptcy not only on the wealth of shareholders and bond holders but also on other stakeholders, including other creditors, suppliers, labor, and government agencies.

John, Kose. "Managing Financial Distress and Valuing Distressed Securities: A Survey and a Research Agenda." *Financial Management* (Autumn 1993):60–78.

John, Kose, Larry H. P. Lang, and Joseph Netter. "The Voluntary Restructuring of Large Firms in Response to Performance Decline." *Journal of Finance* (July 1992):891–917.

John, Teresa A. "Accounting Measures of Corporate Liquidity, Leverage, and Costs of Financial Distress." *Financial Management* (Autumn 1993):91–100.

Kale, Jayant R., Thomas H. Noe, and Gabriel G. Ramirez. "The Effect of Business Risk on Corporate Capital Structure: Theory and Evidence." *Journal of Finance* (December 1991):1693–1715.

Kaplan, Steven N. "Campeau's Acquisition of Federated: Post-Bankruptcy Results." *Journal of Financial Economics* 25 (1994):123–136.

The author shows that a highly leveraged transaction can increase value even though a company is unable to meets its debt payments. He also shows that the net costs of financial distress, and even bankruptcy, need not be large.

Kaplan, Steven N., and Jeremy C. Stein. "The Pricing and Financial Structure of Management Buyouts in the 1980s." University of Chicago Working Paper, January 25, 1981.

The authors presented evidence to support the hypothesis that the market for highly leveraged transactions became overheated in the late 1980s, resulting in deals that were overpriced and poorly structured and thus should not have been undertaken.

Khanna, Naveen, and Annette B. Poulsen. "Managers of Financially Distressed Firms: Villains or Scapegoats?" *The Journal of Finance* (July 1995):919–940.

In a sample of 128 companies filing for Chapter 11, the authors explored the extent to which failure is caused by managers' actions or other factors. They compared the Chapter 11 sample with a control sample of firms with better performance. They compared public announcements of several categories of management actions, including downsizings (such as plant closings, asset sales, and layoffs) and changes in financing arrangements (such as loan extensions, renegotiation of credit agreements, and debt-for-equity swaps). They found that managers of firms in the two samples tend to make similar decisions and that neither set of managers was perceived by the market to be taking value-reducing actions. The authors found that when managers are replaced in firms that eventually file for Chapter 11 protection, the market does not respond positively, whether replacement comes from inside or outside the firm. These findings suggest that financial distress more often than not is caused by factors outside management's control. Courts and legislatures have tended to permit existing managers to continue making decisions even after a firm has declared bankruptcy. This suggests that lawmakers do not believe that existing managers in failed firms are incompetent or prone to self-serving behavior.

Labich, Kenneth. "Why Companies Fail." *Fortune* (November 14, 1994):52–68.

Every corporate disaster has its own awful story, says Labich, but most debacles are the result of managers making one or more of six big mistakes: (1) Identity crisis—Managers don't understand the fundamentals of their business. They neglect to address central issues such as their core expertise, reasonable short- and long-term goals, and key drivers of profitability. With such a lack of understanding, they may diversify into fields far from their core expertise, often through unwise mergers or acquisitions. (2) Failure of vision—Management fails to foresee changes that will affect its business, such as new technologies, new regulations, and changing customer preferences. (3) High leverage—Although a heavy debt load reduces the cost of capital and disciplines management, it also reduces a company's ability to weather market downturns and respond to competitive challenges. (4) Reliance on past strategies— Management has trouble rejecting a technique or strategy that has worked well in the past. (5) Not listening to the customer—Management fails to question customers who no longer want the company's product or service, does not consider the needs of customers all along the value chain, or does not train its sales force properly. (6) Enemies within—Management does not care for its workers or create reward systems consistent with the behavior it is trying to encourage.

Lai, Jim, and Sudi Sudarsanam. *Agency Monitoring and Turnaround of Financially Distressed Firms.* London: City University Business School, 1998.

The authors examined the influence of lenders and outside shareholders on 201 UK firms that experienced financial distress during 1985 to 1993.

May, Don O. "Do Managerial Motives Affect Firm Risk Reduction Strategies?" *Journal of Finance* (September 1995):1291–1308.

Mella-Barral, Pierre, and William Perraudin. "Strategic Debt Service." *The Journal of Finance* (June 1997):531–556.

Miller, Harvey, and Paul M. Basta. "Creditors Are Not Shareholders: Who Is Entitled to Control the Reorganization Process?" Unpublished presentation handout (June 1998).

Miller, Merton H. "Tax Obstacles to Voluntary Corporate Restructuring." *Journal of Applied Corporate Finance* (Fall 1991):20–23.

Minor, Raleigh C. "Recognizing Management's Destructive Behavior." *The Secured Lender* (March–April 1992):6–8.

Minor believes that only 10 to 20 percent of company failures are caused by the economy; the rest are caused by management mistakes. The personality traits of those holding key management positions must be recognized by close associates such as lawyers and bankers and by the managers themselves. The author describes how the behavioral traits of an example of an owner/manager can evolve as a company runs into trouble. The owner or senior manager of a smaller company may be reluctant to acknowledge problems because doing so seems like an admission of failure and the company is an extension of the person's ego. Some managers thrive on challenge and crisis, assimilate large amounts of data, and make decisions quickly. Others fear making mistakes and keep collecting and analyzing more information before making decisions. Often a company CEO does not have the skills required to turn a company around. The sooner a company's downward spiral is halted, the better the chances of a successful turnaround. Company managers and even lenders sometimes take too long to act. There are two types of professionals who can help turn around a company. Turnaround planners can act as counselors, identifying problems and helping management establish controls and run the business more effectively. Crisis managers take control of companies for whatever length of time is required to bring them around. Minor emphasizes the importance of creating an environment of trust within the company and mending relationships with customers, suppliers, and lenders. A lender has a long-term vested interest in a company and can be helpful to a turnaround manager.

Monks, Robert, and Neil Minow. "The Director's New Clothes (Or the Myth of Corporate Accountability)." *Journal of Applied Corporate Finance* (Fall 1991):78–84.

Monroe, Ann. "My Banker, My Boss." *CFO* (January 1992):22–30.

Writing during the credit crunch that followed the 1990–91 recession, the author described intense lender scrutiny, high interest rates, collateral requirements, interest-coverage ratios, usage limits, and other evidence of tightened lending terms and conditions that seemed onerous to middle-market borrowers but would seem perfectly reasonable to a seasoned banker—especially after painful lessons banks relearned at the end of the 1980s. She also described the turnaround of a frozen food company in Maine in which the lender showed patience, recommended and worked with a turnaround specialist, and forced the borrower into a course of turnaround management.

Moore, Terence F., and Earl A. Simendinger. *Hospital Turnarounds: Lessons in Leadership.* Washington, DC: Beard Books (1999).

Muczyk, Jan P., and Robert P. Steel. "Leadership Style and the Turnaround Executive." *Business Horizons* (March–April 1998):39–46.

Unqualified support for democratic leadership and individual autonomy has been the cultural norm of U.S. society since World War II. The philosophy of participative leadership has been attached to management approaches such as management by objectives, quality control circles, total quality management, and self-managed work teams. But many organizations, including those in need of a turnaround, are not ready for participative leadership. To be effective, management's leadership should exhibit, at the very least, three dimensions: consideration for people, concern for production, and incentive performance. Beyond that foundation, whether participative or more directive management is more appropriate depends on the situation. When an organization's survival is threatened, members look to the leader, and autocratic and directive leadership may be more acceptable than under normal circumstances. But sound employer-employee relationships are still possible during a turnaround. The turnaround leader must have not only a viable strategy or vision for reversing the fortunes of the organization but also a cadre of key people to buy into that vision. According to George M. C. Fisher, CEO of Kodak, a CEO must not only have a vision but also articulate goals, a strategy for accomplishing those goals, and a plan to measure success along the way. At the same time, the CEO must be socially responsible by striving to reduce workplace anxiety.

Mueller, P. Henry. "Bank Liquidity, Short Memories, and Inescapable Basics." Lecture at the Darden Graduate Business School, University of Virginia, February 11, 1998.

Mueller, P. Henry. *Perspective on Credit Risk.* Philadelphia: Robert Morris Associates, 1988.

Muller, John M. "Workout Investing for Fun and Profit." *The Secured Lender* (March–April 1997):8–18.

Ofek, Eli. "Capital Structure and Firm Response to Poor Performance: An Empirical Analysis" *Journal of Financial Economics* 34 (1993): 3–30.

Opler, Tim C. "Controlling Financial Distress Costs in Leveraged Buyouts With Financial Innovations." *Financial Management* (Autumn 1993):79–90.

Opler, Tim C., and Sheridan Titman. "Financial Distress and Corporate Performance." *Journal of Finance* (July 1994):1015–1040.

The authors found that highly leveraged companies lose substantial market share to their more conservatively financed competitors in industry downturns.

_____. "The Determinants of Leveraged Buyout Activity: Free Cash Flow vs. Financial Distress Costs." *Journal of Finance* (December 1993):1985–1999.

Perlmuth, Lynn. "The Blessing of Bankruptcy." *Institutional Investor* (June 1997):28–30.

The author summarizes a recent study by Stuart Gilson of the Harvard Business School that suggests that companies that restructure in bankruptcy fare better than those that restructure out of the courts. He cites three reasons: (1) Outside Chapter 11, it is hard to get all creditors on board. (2) Banks and insurance companies play hardball outside bankruptcy. (3) The tax liability resulting from debt reduction is less for a company that goes through a Chapter 11 reorganization.

Platt, Harlan D. *Why Companies Fail: Strategies for Detecting, Avoiding, and Profiting from Bankruptcy.* Washington, DC: Beard Books, 1999.

Pressman, Aaron. "Can Chapter 11 Be Put Back Together?" *Investment Dealers Digest* (April 27, 1992):16–20.

Seth, Anju, and John Easterwood. "Strategic Direction in Large Management Buyouts." *Strategic Management Journal* (May 1993):251–274.

This article examines the nature of the post-transition restructuring activities of 32 large U.S. corporations that underwent management buyouts between 1983 and 1989. It investigates whether buyouts are primarily mechanisms for breaking up the pieces of public corporations and selling the pieces to related acquirers. Evidence indicates that restoring strategic focus is an essential function of the buyout.

Shleifer, Andrei, and Robert W. Vishny. "Liquidation Values and Debt Capacity: A Market Equilibrium Approach." *Journal of Finance* (47):1343–1366.

_____. "The Takeover Wave of the 1980s." *Journal of Applied Corporate Finance* (Fall 1991):49–56.

Simpson, Thatcher & Bartlett. "Recent Interpretation Regarding Highly Leveraged Transactions." April 5, 1991.

Stiglitz, Joseph E. "Some Aspects of the Pure Theory of Corporate Finance: Bankruptcies and Take-overs." *Bell Journal of Economics and Managerial Science* (Autumn 1972):458–482.

This is an early attempt to show that the unsymmetrical incidence of bankruptcy costs can create the conditions for a capital structure that will maximize value.

Sull, Donald N. "Why Good Companies Go Bad." *Harvard Business Review* (July–August 1999):42–52.

Umbreit, W. Terry. "Fairmont Hotels' Turnaround Strategy." *Cornell Hotel & Restaurant Administration Quarterly* (August 1996):50–57.

Weil, Gotschal & Manges. "Solving the Insoluble: A Legal Guide to Insolvency Regulations Around the World." *International Financial Law Review* (June 1990):2–62.

Weiss, Lawrence A. "Bankruptcy Resolution: Direct Costs and Violation of Priority of Claims." *Journal of Financial Economics* 27 (1990):285–314.

Whitney, John. O. *Taking Charge: Management Guide to Troubled Companies and Turnarounds.* Washington, DC: Beard Books, 1999.

_____." Turnaround Management Every Day." *Harvard Business Review* (September–October 1987):49–55.

The author contends that the leader's best insurance for continued leadership is to employ methods from the successful turnaround: a finely tuned sensitivity to opportunities and problems in the business environment, comprehensive surveillance of the competition, daily attention to cash and operational details, and a streamlined operation in close contact with its workforce, suppliers, and customers. The CEO should hold regular staff reviews of the company's cash forecast to emphasize the importance of each activity furnishing accurate, timely information. In a turnaround situation, the CEO should talk directly to customers, bankers, and employees at all levels to get reality checks on information filtered up through the hierarchy. A flattened organizational structure can create or preserve the vitality of turnaround management and also prevent the chaos of excessive jumping of the chain of command.

Wruck, Karen Hopper. "Financial Distress, Reorganization, and Organizational Efficiency." *Journal of Financial Economics* 27 (1990):419–444.

The author explained that financial distress is often accompanied by changes in management, governance, and organizational structure.

_____. "What Really Went Wrong at Revco." *Continental Bank Journal of Applied Corporate Finance* (Summer 1991):79–92.

The author highlighted key factors behind the Revco failure. She noted the need for LBOs to have strong, predictable cash flows, and of equal importance, to have a strong management team, a proven business strategy, and an effective sponsor organization.

Glossary

Absolute Priority Rule. A rule under Chapter 11 that all senior claimants must be satisfied completely before more junior claimants receive anything.

Anticipation Payments. The practice of offering customers discounts for immediate payment.

Bankruptcy. A situation in which an individual or institution becomes insolvent and can no longer pay debts owed. Under U.S. law, there is involuntary and voluntary bankruptcy. In an involuntary bankruptcy, the court is petitioned by one or more creditors to have a debtor deemed insolvent. In a voluntary bankruptcy, the debtor petitions the court.

Chapter 11. An integrated business reorganization statute enacted under the Bankruptcy Reform Act of 1978 that grants to the debtor and creditors the flexibility to work out a plan of reorganization that will meet the interests of all parties.

Cram Down. A court can cram down a reorganization plan over the opposition of some creditor or shareholder classes if it considers the plan fair and equitable to all impaired classes.

Cross Default Provision. A provision in a credit agreement that defines as an event of default a default under another credit agreement.

Debt Overhang Problem. Difficulty in raising capital when at least some of the proceeds will be used to pay off existing creditors.

Debtor-in-Possession Financing. Lending to companies that already have filed for Chapter 11 protection.

Drop Shipment. The delivery of merchandise directly to a retailer rather than through a distributor.

Dutch Auction. An auction system in which the price of the item auctioned is gradually reduced until it elicits a responsive bid. In the case of a financial instrument, the organization conducting the auction would distribute stock to all bidders at the highest successful bid price.

Financial Distress. A situation in which cash flow is insufficient to cover current obligations.

Fraudulent Conveyance. A transfer of assets that works to the detriment of creditors.

Free Rider Problem. *See* Holdout Problem.

Funds from Operations. The most widely used real estate industry cash flow measure. It is calculated as net income from operating activities before the impact of depreciation and amortization of assets unique to real estate. Assets unique to real estate exclude items such as office equipment and cars.

Holdout Problem (also known as Free Rider Problem). Small debt holders have no incentive to exchange their debentures or other debt securities for more junior claims such as equity or other debt securities with lower principal or deferred payments. They have no effect on whether or not the exchange offer succeeds. If the offer does succeed, small debt holders retain their original claim while others bear the cost of the exchange offer.

Impairment. A class of creditors is impaired if its claims are not satisfied in full.

Insolvency. Often used as a synonym for financial distress. There are two types of insolvency: A firm with a flow-based insolvency is unable to meet current obligations. A firm with a stock-based insolvency has a negative economic net worth; the present value of its cash flows is less than its total obligations.

Key Performance Indicators (KPIs). The most important financial and nonfinancial indicators of a company's performance.

Liquidation. Converting some or all of a company's assets to cash and distributing the cash to claimants.

Over-Advance. A credit extension beyond the maximum borrowing base defined by the lender's inventory- and receivables-based formula.

Pari Passu. Refers to credit claims that have equal financial footing.

Prepackaged Bankruptcy. A bankruptcy proceeding in which a reorganization plan has been negotiated in advance of the filing and agreed to by all or enough creditors that, if necessary, those classes not agreeing with the plan can be forced to accept it. Prepackaged bankruptcies are also used to eliminate the tax consequences of debt forgiveness. Except under bankruptcy, forgiveness of debt is treated as income for tax purposes. Under bankruptcy, however, forgiveness of debt results in a reduction of any tax-loss carryforwards.

Private Financial Restructuring. Negotiation of possible restructuring with debt holders prior to filing for Chapter 11 protection.

Reorganization Plan. A plan for settlement of claims under a Chapter 11 proceeding that is subject to the approval of all parties.

Strip Financing. The practice of investors holding more than one class of security, often including both debt and equity. Strip financing can help in negotiation among equity and debt holders in the event of financial distress.

Workout. A resolution of financial distress without resorting to the bankruptcy courts.

Turnaround Specialists Interviewed

Stephen F. Cooper
Managing Principal
Zolfo Cooper LLC
New York, NY

Robert N. Dangremond
Principal
Jay Alix & Associates
New York, NY

Stanley B. Frieze
Managing Partner
Carl Marks Consulting Group LLC
New York, NY

Thomas M. Gaa
Attorney
Murray & Murray
Palo Alto, CA

Abraham Getzler
CEO
Getzler & Co.
New York, NY

Jeff Goodman
President,
Best Practices, Inc.
Sarasota, FL

H. Stephen Grace, Jr., Ph.D.
President
H.S. Grace & Company Inc.
Houston, TX and New York, NY

Paul H. Hunn
Independent Consultant
New York, NY

Matthew Kahn
President
GB Equity Partners (a member
    of Gordon Brothers Group)
Boston, MA

Deborah Hicks Midanek
Principal
Jay Alix & Associates
New York, NY

Richard A. Peterson
First Vice President
Bank One
Chicago, IL

John Podkowsky
Managing Director
Citicorp, Structured Finance Division
New York, NY

David R. A. Steadman
President
Atlantic Management Associates, Inc.
Bedford, NH

W. A. Treleaven
Partner
Deloitte & Touche LLP
Toronto, Ontario

A P P E N D I X   D

Epilogue

As the case studies demonstrate, turnarounds are not permanent and circumstances can change quickly. Since this book first was published by the FEI Research Foundation in early 2001, three significant company changes have occurred:

Ames Department Stores, Inc. filed for Chapter 11 protection and announced a decision to close 47 of its 452 stores on August 16, 2001. After performing relatively well in 1999, Ames faced a difficult retailing environment in 2000 and 2001. The problem was compounded by the additional debt the company took on in 1999 to acquire Hills Stores. On its website, www.amesstores.com, management makes the following statement: "Ames' base of more than 400 stores will remain open while we reorganize. Through those locations, Ames will continue to serve its customers, pay its Associates, and reimburse suppliers on normal terms for merchandise delivered and services provided after the filing. We will also continue to make the needed investments in our operations in order to ensure our competitive position moving forward."

GenRad Inc. recorded a significant loss in the first half of 2001, primarily because of falling demand for testing equipment for printed circuit board assembly. The company agreed in August 2001, subject to a favorable shareholder vote in October 2001, to be acquired by Teradyne Inc., the world's largest supplier of automated test equipment and a leading supplier of high performance interconnection systems. In November 2001, Robert M. Dutkowsky, who had succeeded James F. Lyons as CEO of GenRad in April 2000, was named President of Teradyne's Assembly Test Division. GenRad's operations are being integrated with that division.

USG Corp. filed for bankruptcy on June 25, 2001 to protect itself against asbestos litigation. More than 40 companies so far, and 8 in the past 18 months, had sought similar protection from asbestos-related personal injury claims. At that time, the company had $76.3 million in insurance funds and more than $1.1 billion in anticipated lawsuit settlement claims. Between 1930 and 1972, USG used a minor amount of asbestos in some of its plaster and joint compounds. Historically, USG had faced only small asbestos liability compared to companies such as Owens Corning that made asbestos insulation. However, after other defendants such as Armstrong World Industries, Inc., Babcock & Wilcox Co., Owens Corning, and W.R. Grace Co. filed for bankruptcy, plaintiffs' lawyers raised settlement claims against financially healthy companies such as USG.

Henry A. Davis is a consultant and writer specializing in corporate finance and banking. He is managing editor of the *Journal of Project Finance* and *Strategic Investor Relations,* both quarterlies published by Institutional Investor Journals, and a contributor to *International Treasurer, Latin Finance,* and *Risk* magazines. Mr. Davis is former vice president of research and consulting at Ferguson & Co., director of research and treasurer at the Globecon Group, vice president at Bank of Boston, and assistant vice president at Bankers Trust Company. He is the author or co-author of seven previous studies published by the Financial Executives Research Foundation, including *Building Value with Capital-Structure Strategies* (in 1998 with William W. Sihler) and *Cash Flow and Performance Measurement: Managing for Value* (1996). In addition, he is the author of *Project Finance in Latin America: Practical Case Studies* (Euromoney Books, 2000) and *Project Finance: Practical Case Studies* (Euromoney Books, 1996), and co-author of the *Lender's Guide to the Knowledge-Based Economy* (Amacom Books, 1996). Mr. Davis holds a bachelor's degree from Princeton University and an MBA from the Darden Graduate School of Business Administration, University of Virginia.

William W. Sihler currently holds the Ronald Edward Trzcinski Professorship in Business Administration at the Darden Graduate School, University of Virginia. He began his teaching career at the Harvard Business School in 1964, resigning in 1967 to accept an appointment as associate professor at the Darden School. From 1977 to 1991, he also held the position of executive director of the Center for International Banking Studies, which was located at the Darden School under the auspices of the Bankers' Association for Foreign Trade. Dr. Sihler co-authored *The Troubled Money Business* (HarperBusiness, 1991), *Financial Management: Text and Cases* (Allyn and Bacon, 1991), and *Financial Service Organizations: Cases in Strategic Management* (HarperCollinsCollege, 1993), and he has authored many anthologized cases and a number of articles. He is president of Southeastern Consultants Group, Ltd., which provides educational and problem-solving consulting, and also serves on the board of the Curtiss-Wright Corporation. Dr. Sihler received his AB, MBA, and DBA from Harvard University.

ACKNOWLEDGMENTS

A research project of this nature is not completed without the help of many people. The authors thank the entire Research Foundation staff; Jim Lewis, former executive vice president, for his overall guidance; Gracie Hemphill, director – research, for her help in managing every phase of the project; and Rhona Ferling and Carol Lippert Gray for editorial support. We appreciate the hard work, frequent communication, and expert advice provided by the Advisory Committee, including Paul Smith, chair, and David Steadman, Stephen Grace, and Bob Sartor. We also thank the turn-around specialists and executives at each of the case-study companies who took the time to be interviewed, shared their valuable insights, and reviewed the case studies in detail. Finally, we thank Libby Eshbach for her background research on case-study candidates and other technical aspects of the project.

INDEX

INDEX

The *Financial Times* delivers a world of business news.

Use the Risk-Free Trial Voucher below!

To stay ahead in today's business world you need to be well-informed on a daily basis. And not just on the national level. You need a news source that closely monitors the entire world of business, and then delivers it in a concise, quick-read format.

With the *Financial Times* you get the major stories from every region of the world. Reports found nowhere else. You get business, management, politics, economics, technology and more.

Now you can try the *Financial Times* for 4 weeks, absolutely risk free. And better yet, if you wish to continue receiving the *Financial Times* you'll get great savings off the regular subscription rate. Just use the voucher below.

8 reasons why you should read the Financial Times for 4 weeks RISK-FREE!

To help you stay current with significant
developments in the world economy ...
and to assist you to make informed business
decisions — the Financial Times brings you:

❶ Fast, meaningful overviews of international affairs ... plus daily briefings on major world news.

❷ Perceptive coverage of economic, business, financial and political developments with special focus on emerging markets.

❸ More international business news than any other publication.

❹ Sophisticated financial analysis and commentary on world market activity plus stock quotes from over 30 countries.

❺ Reports on international companies and a section on global investing.

❻ Specialized pages on management, marketing, advertising and technological innovations from all parts of the world.

❼ Highly valued single-topic special reports (over 200 annually) on countries, industries, investment opportunities, technology and more.

❽ The Saturday Weekend FT section — a globetrotter's guide to leisure-time activities around the world: the arts, fine dining, travel, sports and more.

For Special Offer See Over

FT FINANCIAL TIMES
World business newspaper